MICHAELA'S

Miracle

A. D. Stowers

ISBN 979-8-88644-433-9 (Paperback)
ISBN 979-8-88644-435-3 (Hardcover)
ISBN 979-8-88644-434-6 (Digital)

Covenant Books
11661 Hwy 707
Murrells Inlet, SC 29576
www.covenantbooks.com

This book is dedicated to my loving family, especially Mom; Dad; and my children, Shawn, Jonathan, and Sophia Grace. In addition, thank you to all my friends and an extra special thank-you to Sarah P., Kaylis B., and Sara J. To all of them, I have nothing but infinite gratitude.

Gratitude is not only the greatest of virtues,
but the parent of all others.

—Cicero (106–43 BCE)

Contents

Foreword

This is a true story of an amazing love and her miracle. It details how what one learns in their childhood and early relationships transforms them as they journey through life. Most names were changed as Michaela was a very private person and anonymity was extremely important to her. But rest assured that all events occurred just as described and quite frankly words do not fully articulate how powerfully heart-wrenching it all was in real time!

Prologue

$\mathcal{M}$oving forward after a loss of one so *loved* and *cherished* is difficult! Michaela said it was a *miracle*, but Alex was not having any part of it. It had been two weeks since she had gone to heaven and to say that he was heartbroken would be the greatest understatement. To make matters worse, a handwritten letter from Michaela arrived in the mail a couple of days after she passed. It would be another week or so before Alex could muster up the courage to read the letter. Michaela and Alex were together for about ten months, but they were the most incredible months of his life! She had passed away fighting both metastatic breast cancer and ovarian cancer. Having either would be detrimental at that time, but having both together was in and of itself rare and obviously deadly.

A few weeks after Michaela and Alex met, she filled him in completely about her cancer diagnoses. She and her doctors were very upbeat and feeling positive about her prognosis. She was over four years progression free survival (PFS) for the breast cancer and right at three and a half years PFS for the ovarian cancer. She was adherent to her medications, all her ongoing tests were showing positive results, and she was edging closer to attaining their goal of five-years progression free survival.

All was going so well, then...

The cancer came back about five months after they met; it was disheartening to say the least. Alex stood there in the hallway outside of her hospital room as the doctor explained the test results. He started by saying that all her tests from the previous month were normal, but now four weeks later is a different story. He went on to say that the cancer has spread all over her body and is extremely aggressive!

Having a medical background, Alex fully understood what this meant. He knew that surgery would be out of the question but did ask about chemotherapy or radiation. The doctor looked at Alex with sad eyes and said with a whisper, "No!"

After a moment of silence and disbelief, Alex collected himself enough to ask, "How long?" The doctor quietly looked at him, paused, and said in a soft voice, "I'm sorry, but I don't think she'll see Christmas."

As tears began to fill his eyes, Alex asked softly, "You mean, this coming up Christmas?"

The doctor said, "Yes, I estimate she only has about four weeks left."

The nurse standing beside him placed her hand on his shoulder and whispered, "I am so sorry."

Alex did everything in his power to keep it together as tears filled his eyes. Now they had to go into the room and tell Michaela! Alex's toughest conversation ever. How does one tell the person they not only love but waited their entire life to meet that they only have a month to live!

After her passing, Alex sat in his apartment one morning, wondering if God had abandoned them as they had prayed every single day for her cancer to be healed. His *faith* was being shaken to the core when suddenly something was telling him in his heart to read her letter. So Alex did!

Her letter began with "My dearest Alex," and the tears flowed. Every word was griping and heartfelt. Afterward Alex sat there and cried, simply unable to control his grief. Alex's heartfelt pain was more hurt than he had ever encountered. He now understood her *miracle* but was painfully brokenhearted. Alex prayed for help!

Sitting there crying, he kept having this inward feeling or voice saying Psalm 34:18.

Alex paid no attention, but the voice repeated Psalm 34:18.

Finally, Alex said out loud, "Psalm 34:18, what is Psalm 34:18?"

He opened his Bible to Psalm 34:18 and read, "The Lord is close to the brokenhearted and saves those who are crushed in spirit."[1]

Although he had always had the innate ability to focus, he was struggling. Over the next few weeks, Alex began to slowly get back into the swing of his everyday life. A friend of his was a clinical psychologist, so discussions with him were invaluable. He stressed that with all love as strongly connected as theirs, it will never fade nor be forgotten. Well, his friend was correct; here, it is some twenty years later, and the love Alex felt for her is still as powerful today as it was at that time.

His friend noted, "The best thing that Alex could do to honor Michaela was to not try to understand the *why* but simply to jump back into life full bore. That is what she would want and that is how you honor her!" When he said that, it reminded Alex of a proverb that was drilled into him growing up by his family and church. They said whatever happens in your life, always remember Proverbs 3:5–6. The verse states, "Trust in the Lord with all your heart and lean not on your own understanding; in all your ways submit to him, and he will make your paths straight."[2]

Alex's life was returning to normal, and he became busier than ever. His pain was still there, and quite frankly, Alex still bears grief all these years later. He could always wipe the tears in his eyes, but he could *not* wipe the pain in his heart. Her letter so eloquently described her *miracle*, but she also laid out for Alex his own path forward.

She ended the letter by saying, "I will be waiting for You in heaven where we will once again be able to view all of His stars. It will be many, many, many years for you, but only a moment for me. Alex, I love you!"

1

Life's Journey Is Never Easy

Alex was a regular guy who had gone through extraordinary circumstances. He was a year removed from having to make the toughest decision of his life. Alex's wife suffered from multiple mental illness issues for several years. She was diagnosed a few years prior and if she was compliant with her medication therapy, she remained somewhat stable. However, with continued non-compliance to therapy, her decline began to accelerate. It became exceedingly more difficult for Alex to get her to stick with her prescription regimen. Cynthia's illness reached a point where Alex had to place her into a mental health facility for a twenty-eight-day stay. Then a couple of months later, there was another twenty-eight-day stay in the facility.

This cycle continued to repeat itself where Alex would have to place Cynthia into a facility, she would get discharged and seem to be doing better, and then the cycle would begin again with another admission. At first it was twice over the year, then three times the next year, then five times the next year. Even with medications Cynthia deteriorated to the point where Alex had to commit his wife to a mental health facility full-time. It was agonizing for Alex to watch his wife go downhill year after year. Even worse, it was a heart-wrenching decision to have her placed into a mental health facility.

*****

Alex and Cynthia met early in his air force career while he was stationed at Hurlburt Field in Ft. Walton Beach, Florida. Alex met Cynthia quite by accident.

Alex had stopped by the grocery store one day after work. When he pulled into the parking lot, one of those late afternoon gulf coast thunderstorms was ripping through the area. He sat in his vehicle, waiting for the monsoon downpour to pass when he noticed a young woman trying to scamper to her car. She had no umbrella, not that it would have done any good with the wind whipping the rain horizontally. She was striving to reach her car, wearing heels she was half-running when one of her grocery bags split open. Oh my, her canned goods went rolling away from her. It was a sight to see for sure. Drenched in the downpour, bending down trying to corral her groceries, she looked up at the sky, all disgusted, looking worse than a wet mop. For a moment, Alex couldn't help but laugh then thought, *Well, I guess I'll go help her out.*

Alex sprang from his vehicle and ran over to assist. He was in uniform and got soaked just as quick. He gathered up her groceries, and they ran for her car. She piled in while Alex put all that he was carrying into the back seat. Cynthia was very grateful for the help and quickly said thank you and began to drive off. Alex ran back to his vehicle then he looked back. She had stopped halfway out of the parking lot. Alex drove over to where she was stopped. He lowered his window and asked, "Is something wrong?"

She said, "Something isn't right on the right side of my car."

Alex walked around the car in the pouring rain, and sure enough, she had a flat tire.

He looked at Cynthia and kind of laughed and said, "This really isn't your day! You have a flat tire."

Alex, standing there, all soaked in his uniform, looked at Cynthia and replied, "Tell you what, get in my vehicle, and I'll get all your groceries and take you home. Then I will come back and change your tire for you."

All Cynthia could think was *Where did this angel come from?* as she said, "Yes, I'll go for that, thank you!"

Alex took Cynthia home and took the groceries in for her. For some reason, she trusted Alex and gave him her car keys. Alex returned to the parking lot. By this time, the heavy rain had subsided to a light shower. He changed her tire and then drove her car to a nearby gas station that fixed flats. He waited there as they fixed her flat tire and returned it to its front right location. Alex then drove her car back to Cynthia's place. When he arrived, Cynthia had dried out and had time to get cleaned up. When she opened the door, Alex thought he was looking at a vision! He was standing there all wet, and it took him a moment for him to catch his breath. Finally, he handed Cynthia her keys and said with a sly grin, "Your chariot is ready to drive again, my lady."

This made Cynthia laugh as she asked, "How can I ever repay you for your help?"

Alex, with a slight smile, simply said, "Maybe give me a ride back to my vehicle, please?"

With a big smile, she was like, "Of course!"

On the drive back to the parking lot, they talked for a few minutes. As they arrived at his vehicle, Cynthia said again, "Thank you so very much." Alex merely shrugged his shoulders as if to say "No big deal." Then he stepped out, his clothes were still wet. As he walked toward his vehicle, the sun began to peek out from behind the clouds. Alex looked up at the sun and turned back toward Cynthia and said, "Now it decides to come out." This got another laugh out of Cynthia.

Cynthia was feeling so grateful to Alex, and she really didn't know what she would have done if he hadn't come along. Just as he opened his vehicle door, Cynthia said, "I want to thank you again. I feel like I owe you something."

Alex smiled and replied, "No, you don't owe me a thing." Alex paused while looking at Cynthia and finally said, "However, you could have dinner with me tomorrow night?"

Cynthia stared at Alex for a moment then with a smile, and with her little laugh, she replied, "Yes, I would like that, and anyway, I'm kind of a softy for a man in uniform."

Alex said, "Does six thirty work for you?"

"Yes, it does!"

"Then I'll see you tomorrow night."

They had dinner and hit it off from the beginning. More dinners led to more time spent together until one day he asked her to marry him. And that is how Alex and Cynthia met. It all started off by him taking care of her, and now several years later, he is still taking care of her.

Cynthia was from the Pensacola area with all her family living in the region between Pensacola, Gulf Breeze, Ft. Walton Beach, and Destin. They had the privilege to be married at the Officers' Club on Pensacola Naval Air Station. Over the next ten years, Alex had four more assignments. During this time, he had been deployed in Middle East operations to sites in Europe and Asia, on special operations missions, on multiple humanitarian missions in Africa, Central and South America. Plus, served as an executive officer to two different general officers, traveled extensively with them, and been to places like Thailand, Indonesia, India, South Africa, Australia, Diego Garcia, Greenland, Japan, and many more. Alex was well traveled and at this time had visited just over one hundred countries around the world. While his active-duty career was progressing very nicely, unfortunately his wife Cynthia's mental status kept declining. With this further decline, Alex made a decision that he thought was best for her, which was resigning from Air Force active duty, although reluctantly.

Alex was honored when a couple of Air Force general officers came to him and insisted he stay on in the Air Force Reserve, which he did. Alex loved serving his country, but maybe even more than that, he cherished the people he had the honor to serve with.

Once transitioning from active duty to the reserves, Alex was quickly hired into an excellent highly compensated corporate position and moved to the Birmingham, Alabama area. His employer was very military service friendly. So for the next few years Alex worked his primary job, served an average of two to three months annually in the reserves, and took care of Cynthia.

However, with each passing year, Cynthia was spending more and more time admitted into a mental health facility. Then finally, her physicians recommended she be admitted to a facility full-time. Alex could not make this decision alone nor did he take it lightly. He engaged into discussions with his mother-in-law, Elizabeth, his father-in-law, Charles, and sister-in-law, Kim. After input from the physicians and thorough conversation among all family members everyone felt that it was in her best interest to be placed into a proper facility to provide around the clock care. Yes, it was a most difficult decision for all involved. Since there were no acceptable facilities within the state of Alabama, and since all her family lived in the Florida panhandle, a facility was chosen in that area.

*****

In the months that followed, Alex struggled without having her around each day. He loved her so and she helped him to keep his bearing, focus, and purpose. She was in a facility which was four hours away, so going back and forth was challenging.

Alex jumped back into his primary job full throttle to ease his loneliness.

He continued to perform his Air Force Reserve duties, all of which kept him busy and his mind somewhat off Cynthia. But Alex always had this feeling of guilt about having to place his wife into a facility. He always wondered if he could have done more. Alex was an extremely quiet person and liked to keep his private life to himself. Yet in his business and air force responsibilities he was very engaging and managed relationships with great expertise.

*****

Alex would visit his wife on the weekends and would always stay overnight with his in-laws. On one such weekend visit, about five months after her commitment, the family gathered and sat down with Alex to discuss Cynthia.

Elizabeth and Charles, her mom and dad, started the discussion by stating, "Cynthia was unfortunately never going to be able to leave the facility." They continued, "Alex, you have been a terrific husband

5

and that no man could have taken better care of our daughter. Honestly, you'll never know how much we all appreciate and love you for all that you've done for her."

Kim was there as well and began crying while simply saying that she more than agreed with what her parents were saying.

Elizabeth continued with, "Alex, really there is nothing more you can do for Cynthia, so we all feel that it's time to let her go."

She went on to say, "Please don't take this wrong, but hear us out, we propose and are asking that you divorce our daughter so that you can move on with your life as that is what you deserve."

This took Alex by surprise, and he was rendered speechless; he didn't know what to say.

Charles walked over behind Alex and placed his hand on Alex's shoulder and quietly whispered, "We understand that it may feel like this is coming out of the blue, and we apologize for bringing this topic up in such a way. We know that this will be an agonizing decision, but we don't want you to feel as if you are abandoning her as you will always be a member of this family."

Charles continued, "Give it some thought son and get back to us."

Alex's mind was simply racing and wondering, *What do I do?*

This family request certainly took Alex by surprise. He was contemplating their request, but also tried to adjudicate the request with his own values around oaths, vows, and promises. Alex took oaths very seriously, such as the one he swore to defend this country and believed that they were not to be broken.

He also took his wedding vows with all sincerity. Particularly, the vows that applied in this case which said, "Through sickness and in health," as well as the last part that says, "Till death do us part." Alex grappled with this decision as it went against his basic instincts and values. He needed more counsel as Alex was a man of great faith and sense of duty.

He reached out to three individuals with whom he was very close. He met with his pastor on several occasions who concluded that he had done all that he could, and that Cynthia's life forward was now in the hands of God.

Alex had a friend who was an Air Force clinical psychologist. They talked at length, and he told Alex that he was a good man who had gone above and beyond with Cynthia. He pointed out that the simple fact that her family had come to him with this recommendation shows how much respect they have for you.

Lastly, Alex sat down with a close friend and workmate James. James was taken aback as he had no clue that Alex was going through all of this in his life. Alex simply told James that he has always been a very private person and able to keep secrets which afforded him well in his military career. After taking some time to absorb all the information, James said to his friend, "My wife and I think the world of Cynthia, and honestly, we feel that you have stuck by her this whole time without even registering one complaint to anyone we know. That, in and of itself, is remarkable."

James went to say, "My wife and I think you have done all that you can, and it is time to move on with your life." James continued by saying, "We will help you, Alex, in any way we can. That's what friends do!"

An extremely painful decision!

After further conversations with both Elizabeth and Charles, Alex had decided to move forward with the divorce with their blessing. Elizabeth had arranged to get Cynthia placed on her medical insurance as a disabled beneficiary through her employer. Plus, Alex had recently sold their home, so he took all the accrued equity which was around $200,000 and placed it into a trust account for Cynthia, naming Elizabeth as the account custodian.

Over the last few years, Cynthia amassed considerable medical debt in the six-figure range, so Alex began the task of paying off all those bills. Alex sold most of the furniture and a few other items in the home and gave all the proceeds to Elizabeth. Cynthia had some very nice jewelry and watches, which Alex also gave to Elizabeth to do with as she saw fit. Most of her other items Alex simply donated to local charities. After the sale of their home, Alex moved into a gated apartment complex. He then did what he could to move forward with his life.

2

Moving Forward

Alex was discovering that the reality of moving forward was a painstaking process. It took a couple of months after the divorce before he could muster up the courage to even take off his wedding ring. He always had the innate ability to truly focus when he needed. So that is exactly what he tried to do.

During this time, Alex concentrated on both his primary job as a medical and clinical lead and on his Air Force Reserve responsibilities. He never really talked about nor was he very willing to discuss his marriage, but he didn't try to hide anything either. That was just him…he was a private person. Alex liked his privacy.

As time progressed, the word of Alex's story began to circulate among his work friends, peers, and colleagues. Experiences like this usually invoke feelings of sympathy from people, and this was no different. Alex received a tremendous number of offerings of sympathy, well-wishes, and simply what can we do for you. True to himself, Alex just modestly told them thank you and that by them reaching out to him means more than they'll ever know.

Alex was a person of great faith, but also had an impressive talent for understanding reality. He would often say, "Many times during the course of our lives, things will occur in which we would have absolutely no control over."

Many a person have heard him provide this advice, "We can only focus on those things in life that we can control, but we must have faith that other things out of our control will work out."

*****

James and Alex worked closely together as they were a tag-team for the company throughout the gulf coast states. Alex was the clinical and medical lead and consequently had access into customers where others in the company did not. It was well known within the company that Alex was top shelf when it came to developing customer relationships, executing strategies, and getting results. He was very instinctive into understanding the needs of the customer and placing their requirements above his own. His awareness and customer understanding propelled him into a level of trust between him and his customers that is rarely seen. Customers trusted Alex because they could easily see that he was a person of sound character and integrity.

James negotiated contracts with health care plans and organized medical customers. James and Alex were such a great team that they would be honored nearly every year for their continued high performance. Being a high performer had its perks as they were presented with award trips to very nice locations.

A couple months after the divorce was finalized, Alex found out that he was selected once again as a multiple award winner. The nice thing about these award trips is that the winner was always able to bring a plus one. Of course, most brought their wives or husbands, others might bring another family member because they were amazing trips as a thank-you for your high performance.

Since Alex wasn't dating anyone, he decided not to bring a plus one to either of these trips. The first trip was to The Greenbrier Hotel and Resort in West Virginia. It was truly a gorgeous place and Alex enjoyed spending time with a few other colleagues from across the country. Plus, he was delighted to play golf for three straight days on some terrific courses on someone else's dollar! These few days immersed in total relaxation was just what the doctor ordered. It did wonders to help his psyche.

The second trip was to the JW Marriott Desert Springs Resort and Spa in Palm Springs, California. Again, he chose to go by himself. While there he once again enjoyed playing golf on multiple courses. First, on the Desert Springs Golf Course there at the JW Marriott, then at the Shadow Ridge Golf Club, and finally at the PGA West Mountain Course. Three terrific courses and it certainly did help to reinvigorate Alex upon his return home.

*****

In this time, Alex joined a small group at his church. Alex had always had great faith in his beliefs. By joining a small group, it allowed him an outlet to stay engaged and continue to serve others while widening his sphere of acquaintances all at the same time.

He continued to talk with his psychologist friend as he had discovered those counseling sessions were very worthwhile. Some years back after returning from a most difficult air force deployment, Alex realized that having a counseling session or two with one of the base psychologists helped to alleviate any negative effects from the deployment. He learned that speaking with a counselor had great value both during difficult times or simply the value it afforded one through life's daily ups and downs. Alex became an advocate and felt that everyone needs a counselor or someone that they can speak with who is unbiased and listens.

James and a couple of other friends along with their wives had attempted to set Alex up on some dates but he was not yet interested. Oh, he appreciated what they were trying to do but as he told James's wife, Dee, he simply wasn't ready.

Dee was always joking with Alex that he was far too picky.

He would tease right back at her and say, "Well, of course, isn't it best to be selective!"

Dee would tell Alex, "You are such a wonderful, trustworthy, and caring man that you deserve someone very special."

In usual Alex fashion, he just chuckled and would say, "Okay, knock it off… I'm no better than anyone else."

Dee would reply, "That sentiment is exactly what makes you so desirable and a great catch for any woman."

Alex would just say, "Oh, you're biased," and let it go.

In reality, Alex was not looking for another relationship and quite frankly he still carried some guilt from having to commit Cynthia. He would tell Dee and others that he was humbled by the fact that they were trying to set him up with some very nice ladies, but he was simply not ready yet. He told her that he had faith that when the time was right someone would walk into his life.

He would tell Dee, "You know the good Lord has a plan for all of us. The problem is, we don't know His plan. But we need to be ready in our heart and mind when He does present us with His opportunity."

*****

Alex would perform Air Force Reserve duty monthly. He was assigned at this time as a squadron commander and held the rank of lieutenant colonel. As a reservist, he would backfill our active-duty forces when needed. Besides his primary responsibilities, he was frequently asked to engage in other duties in which he had expertise. One such undertaking that he thoroughly enjoyed was teaching the topic of leadership to officers and senior enlisted personnel. Personnel attending his educational lectures loved the way he broke down Leadership into easy-to-understand principles.

Attendees would always remember his opening remarks when he would say, "Rule #1 of leadership was…always take care of your people!"

Then he would note, "Rule #2 is…refer to rule #1."

He made sure participants understood that if they thought leading was about themselves then they were absolutely wrong. He would remind everyone that it wasn't about yourself, but about the people you serve.

*****

It was Memorial Day, and Alex had just walked off the golf course after playing with some friends when his phone rang. It was his Air Force boss, a general officer, who said he had been tasked to perform some operational reviews at a few overseas installations and wanted him to join his team. The general went on to say that he already had two others—a colonel and his command chief—but needed one more very experienced officer. He stated, "I want you on my team."

The general noted, "We will be gone about three weeks, can you get away?"

Alex thought what a terrific opportunity and replied, "Count me in!"

He made arrangements with the company to perform active service. The team had a primary itinerary that included stops across several countries. Yet the team had a little flex time worked into the schedule for any other extracurricular activities.

For their first stop they flew to Ramstein Air Base, which is in the Kaiserslautern area of western Germany. This stop was great for Alex as he had been to this part of Germany many times earlier in his air force career and even prior. The time spent at Ramstein allowed him the opportunity to look up some old friends whom he hadn't seen in quite some time. In addition, during their downtimes Alex was able to reacquaint himself with his favorite wine. It's well known that the Moselle River valley region of Germany has the best Riesling wines on the planet.

It was the general's first time in Germany, so he thoroughly enjoyed the fact that Alex knew his way around the area. While the team was at Ramstein they also made their way up to both Bitburg and Spangdahlem Air Bases which were about 120 km north. These stops were not on their original itinerary, but since they were so close they went ahead and included them.

From Ramstein the team flew to Incirlik Air Base in southern Turkey. They performed the operational assessment then moved on to the next base on their itinerary. From Incirlik they flew down to Al Udeid Air Base in Qatar. It was June so yeah, it was hot! Everyone enjoyed seeing several friendly faces in Qatar.

On the way back to the states from Qatar they stopped at Aviano Air Base which is northeast of Venice, Italy. The group spent a few days there in northern Italy and amongst other things enjoyed some terrific cuisine. After leaving Aviano, they stopped over at Lajes Field on the Azores.

It was a good work trip but extremely busy, assessing multiple operations and discussing strategies to improve results with local commanders. On the final leg from the Azores, the general, with Alex's assistance, wrote the final report that outlined the recommendations for each base evaluated. The general submitted his final report prior to landing. The general then thanked and commended the team for all their efforts and expertise during this mission. After being gone for three weeks, it was now back to work for Alex at his primary job.

*****

Alex returned home from his mission and had a lot of work to catch up. He received several FedEx packages a week, which were always dropped off at the apartment complex office. Over the past few months, he had the opportunity to get to know the apartment manager, Sheryl, well. Since Alex traveled, she was good about holding his packages until he returned. Sheryl was a nice person, very personable, and she and Alex were becoming friends. Alex didn't know anyone else who lived in the apartment complex, so he would stop by the office and have a cup of coffee and chat with Sheryl at times. Alex traveled overnight occasionally, but when he was home, he had his office in his apartment.

During one of their chats, Sheryl had asked Alex about his previous marriage. After filling her in about what had transpired with Cynthia, Sheryl was amazed, and the story crystallized her thoughts about Alex, which were simple…he was a man of great character!

Sheryl had asked Alex if he was interested in beginning to date. Alex laughed and told Sheryl, "You know my friends have been trying to set me up for the past few months."

Alex said, "I appreciate it, but I have faith that the right person will one day appear. I don't know who, or when it may happen, but my heart tells me to have faith that the Lord has a plan! I have a belief that what is meant to be will always find a way!"

He continued, "Sheryl, you are the only person that I have shared that with, but that is what my faith is telling me. He has a plan, but we just don't know what that plan is...at least right now."

Alex told Sheryl, "The way I see it when you find that special someone whom you think is the right one, what you do is love them with all your heart and soul, always serve them, show them gratitude, love them unconditionally, and you can only hope that they reciprocate the same. If they do, then that is the potion for a lifetime of happiness." He continued, "You know I have learned from my experiences that loving relationships are not about getting things, but about giving. We shouldn't fall in love to necessarily make ourselves happy, but we fall in love to make the person we fall in love with happy."

Sheryl didn't say a word! After she heard that touching explanation from Alex, she was astounded and privately thought to herself that this is a remarkable man that deserves nothing but the best.

This made Sheryl think; there was a woman who had moved into the complex in the past couple of weeks who seemed like a very nice person, plus she was incredibly beautiful! Sheryl thought, this new lady named Michaela who had moved here from the Atlanta area was interesting. Her thoughts went further as she thought that Michaela and Alex might be a good match for each other. But Sheryl knew she needed to move slowly and first get to know Michaela better before she could begin to play cupid. Sheryl thought women of her natural and stunning beauty are rare and so she wondered, what was her story?

3

Someone Special Appears

Sheryl had been strategizing over the past few days how to get Michaela and Alex together. She had reached out to Michaela a couple days ago and invited her to lunch. They each enjoyed lunch. Sheryl had the opportunity to get to know her a lot better and discovered that she was a charming person.

Furthermore, she found out that Michaela had a tough childhood and was married while living in Atlanta, but that fell apart. Sheryl was impressed with Michaela; she thought she was charming and wondered what kind of man could screw up being married to her. Lunch was nice, and Michaela thanked her for asking her to join. Sheryl thought Michaela was very genuine.

Sheryl asked her, "Why Birmingham?"

Michaela said, "I needed to get out of Atlanta, so I asked my boss if he had an opening. Birmingham was the opening, so I took a lateral move."

She went on, "I've been focusing on getting to know my customers, which has kept me busy."

They agreed to hang out again soon.

It had been a couple of days since they had lunch, so Sheryl thought she would invite Michaela over to her place for dinner. Sheryl believed this would allow them more time to get to know each other or more specifically more time for Sheryl to get to know Michaela. Sheryl lived in the complex, so having dinner on a Friday night was easy. Michaela was thankful for having something to do to relax after a difficult week at work. Sheryl made a nice dinner, and they settled into the evening with some wine.

Talking for several hours that evening, Sheryl learned a great deal about Michaela. Besides the fact she was over five feet, eight inches tall, statuesque with long dark brown hair, the prettiest smile, the bluest eyes, and skin that most women would die for, barring all that she was simply stunning. Even more she discovered that she was genuine, quiet, seemed very honest, and a private person.

Sheryl told her sincerely, "You are so beautiful inside and out!"

Michaela quietly whispered, "Thank you, but so often I wish I could just be invisible."

"Why?"

"Well, people tend to guess who I am all wrong."

"What do you mean?"

"They take one look at me and formulate their own ideas of who I am."

Michaela continued with, "The worst part is guys hit on me, and candidly, they're always the very guys you don't want to get to know!"

Sheryl snickered, "Isn't that the truth!"

They both laughed so hard!

Sheryl and Michaela spent some more time together over the next several days. They were really getting to know each other and were becoming good friends. Sheryl had found out so much about Michaela, and now she was sure that she and Alex would make a terrific couple! But she now had to figure out a plan to get them together without it seeming like she was playing cupid.

*****

Michaela had indeed had a difficult childhood. Her childhood was quite normal until she was ten years old. That was when her father, mother, and little brother were killed in a car wreck on the highway north of Chattanooga, Tennessee. Michaela would generally be a ward of the court to the nearest relative, but she had none.

All four of her grandparents had passed-away. Her mother was an only child so no relatives on that side of the family. Her father had a brother; however, he had died of cancer a couple years prior having never married. Michaela's father had told her that Uncle Jim suffered from issues resulting from the time he spent in Vietnam…today we call it post-traumatic stress disorder (PTSD). That is where he probably picked up his cancer as well. Thus, with no blood relatives, Michaela became a ward of the state.

Michaela was initially sent to a temporary foster care family for a few months until she was placed with another family. She was with this family for about two years until circumstances forced them to have to move to Virginia. Michaela was then sent to a third foster family. This third family was the first family where she felt like she was part of the family. However, once again this family had to move away. The father got a promotion, so they moved to the Tampa Bay area. Michaela was heartbroken as she really liked this family. She was then placed into her fourth foster care family at the age of sixteen. This family never seemed to be very caring to Michaela. She always felt like all they were interested in was getting the money from the state. They had a total of eight foster care children, and she shared a bedroom with another girl who was fourteen.

Her high school years were difficult, but she always remembered what her mom told her, which was that an education is more powerful than anything else you could do so always strive to learn. Remembering that from her mom helped to keep her motivated during high school.

In addition, they lived a couple of houses down from a church, so she attended services nearly every Sunday. Her foster family did not attend church, but they did not try and restrict Michaela from attending especially since it was only a couple hundred feet away. Attending church really helped her to keep her faith, and she was able to get counsel from one of the associate pastors. This pastoral relationship would end up helping her greatly after she graduated from high school.

Once Michaela graduated from high school, she was out! Her foster care family were no longer receiving their monthly stipend from the state of Tennessee, so they basically kicked her out. She was now on her own...what to do?

She had always kept her grades up as she was a national honor society honoree and finished very high in her graduating class. Fortunately, she had a good mentor in the associate pastor who assisted her with getting her own apartment and a job. She went to work as a waitress at a very nice and busy restaurant, which allowed her to make enough to make ends meet.

She wanted to go to college, so she applied and was accepted. She was able to get some grant funding, plus an academic scholarship, which ended up paying for about 80 percent of her college costs. The remainder she reluctantly had to take out a student loan. Michaela went to class and worked nearly every shift she could get and managed to graduate in five years.

By attending career day, she met with several potential employers. In the end, Michaela accepted an offer from a hospital services and supplies company and promptly moved to a north Atlanta suburb. She really enjoyed her job and quickly adapted to her position. She was well liked by both her employer and even more importantly by her customers. Michaela was a true introvert and being around a lot of people made her uncomfortable. She operated very well in small groups and especially in one-on-one relations with her customers. Thus, Michaela always said she was kind of boring...she was not the normal twentysomething. She didn't enjoy going out to bars and comparable places that many of her peers seemed to love.

During her career day at college, she also met a woman with a modeling agency out of Atlanta who immediately wanted to sign Michaela as one of her models. Michaela really wasn't interested in becoming a model, but after she got settled in the Atlanta area, she contacted the agency. The woman remembered her and hired her on the spot. She told Michaela she had that rare beauty and was very photogenic so she could go as far as she wanted to in modeling. Michaela was not really interested in becoming a top model. All she wanted was to do some local gigs and maybe print ad modeling. She simply wanted to make some extra money to pay off her student loans and then begin to save money for a home down payment.

Hence, Michaela did some modeling on the side while working for the hospital services company. She modeled for about five years and was able to pay off her student loans plus save up enough money to put down over 40 percent on a new home.

During this time, she had met a guy that she dated for about eighteen months when he proposed. She said yes, and they were married about four months later. He was a mortgage specialist at a local bank. Michaela had come a long way from foster care to working her way through college to working two jobs to be able to get ahead, and now she was married to a man who she thought would be with her for life. Just when life seemed to be going so well…

4

Life Falls Apart for Michaela

Michaela's work was going well as she had developed some excellent customer relationships at many of her accounts across north Georgia. She had recently stopped modeling as she really didn't care to model but used it to earn the extra money to meet her needs. That extra income came in handy for a home down payment and to build an emergency savings nest egg. She and her husband had recently been discussing having a child within the next year. Michaela felt contentment as they had been married going on three years. Yet of late, there was something gnawing at her about her husband, something seemed a little out of sorts, but she couldn't put her finger on it. She simply blew it off to each having busy lives.

One Saturday, Michaela was having lunch with three of her closest friends. She asked her friends if any of them had ever had a breast exam. They asked why. "I think I found a couple of lumps in each of my breasts."

Looking shocked, her friends agreed as they all were quick to say, "You need to get that checked out immediately."

Michaela informed them, "Yeah, thanks, I already scheduled a mammogram for this coming week."

They all wished her the best of luck and tried to assure her that everything would be okay.

*****

Michaela had her doctor's appointment and mammogram as scheduled. The results were not what she was hoping for as her doctor found several lumps in each breast. The mammogram then confirmed her suspicions. She was immediately scheduled for a biopsy and consultation to an oncologist.

More bad news when the biopsy results determined that she had cancer in each breast and that it had entered her lymph nodes as well. It was further ascertained that it was an extremely aggressive form of breast cancer, one with a high mortality rate. She was scheduled almost immediately for surgery where they performed a radical total mastectomy.

Michaela started her chemotherapy and had radiation therapy as well. As most do, she started losing her hair around her fourth chemotherapy treatment and ended up shaving her head and wearing a cancer head turban. The treatments were particularly rough on Michaela, and she was nauseated most of the time. She continued to perform at her job as best she could but having to cut some days short because she felt sick or just too tired. Yet she was staying positive with great hope for the future.

Ever since the diagnosis and start of treatment, her husband seemed to be more and more disengaged and withdrawn. She wasn't sure if he was in a state of denial, a state of shock, or just unwilling to accept the reality. Plus, he was getting ever increasingly distant and so difficult to talk with. She thought just give him some space as it takes some people longer to get their head around tough situations in their lives.

It was one of those days when she was feeling poorly that she decided to go home early and arrived just after noon. When she arrived home, she saw that her husband's vehicle was there, which surprised her. She didn't know he was going to be home that day.

She walked into the house and called his name…no answer. She went into their bedroom and discovered him in bed with another woman. Michaela just stood there horrified and shocked! They saw her as well, and it was as if time simply stood still. All three of them were frozen.

Finally, Michaela turned to walk away then stopped and said, "I'll be back in one hour and I want you and your friend gone!"

She left and drove around for a couple of hours in disbelief and attempting to get her head straight then finally went back home. When she arrived, no one was there. Needless to say, she tossed and turned all night.

The next morning, she called an attorney to begin divorce proceedings.

She took the time to call a couple of her girlfriends to let them know what she had walked in on at home. It was all so surreal to her and simply unimaginable. All that she was going through, and he hadn't really been showing much support, but this egregious disrespect for their marriage was simply despicable.

Unfortunately, for the most part she was dealing with this confluence of events all by herself. She had no family and no one else very close. Michaela was a survivor and had the *faith* that the good Lord wouldn't heap more upon her than she was ultimately able to deal with. But right now in the moment, she felt so alone.

She would often pray, "Lord, I trust you to help me lift my burdens."

It took a few days, but Michaela's attorney served her husband with divorce papers, and the wheels turned to get the proceedings going as soon as possible. Her husband didn't put up any fight with the divorce.

About the only thing he truly said was, "I don't want to be married to half a woman!"

That was so hurtful to Michaela! But it also showed his character or should we say his lack of character.

People in general are always diverse with different allegiances in situations like this. Most of Michaela's friends and acquaintances thought her husband was an "a" number one scumbag and that God was holding a special spot in hell for him.

However, there were a couple of her friends who thought that he shouldn't have to be married to half a woman. It's incredible that someone would think like that, but a couple did!

A few days later, Michaela had lunch with three close friends. In addition, by this time the word had gotten out about what her husband had been doing on the side. Her friends hadn't seen Michaela for a couple of weeks. So when Michaela sat down at the table running a few minutes late, her friends were almost shocked to see the way she looked! Here was once a statuesque, tall, lean, beautiful woman with long, dark-brown hair, and now she's hairless with a head turban and no eyebrows. She had even lost some weight, so she was beginning to look a little gaunt.

They tried to keep their composure, but they were stunned! Almost immediately, a couple of them showed almost no empathy for everything Michaela was going through and those two basically started treating her like a pariah or outsider.

Michaela was taken aback! She asked, "Hey, what's going on here?"

What was really going on was that those two friends were afraid to even be around Michaela. For whatever reason, they were scared, not so much for Michaela but for themselves. Seeing how Michaela looked now versus how gorgeous she was previously made them think that what if it happened to them, and they just couldn't handle the whole situation. Fear had essentially overtaken them!

Michaela tried to tell them that her cancer wasn't contagious. But they just couldn't handle it! She felt almost betrayed by her so-called friends. Here she was expecting maybe some support, yet she got almost the opposite. Michaela was privately thinking how interesting it was that fear could overwhelm some people.

Those friends finished their lunch and quickly came up with an excuse to leave without saying much more. Michaela never saw them again!

Conversely, the other friend strived to try and make Michaela feel bad for divorcing her husband.

Michaela was like, *What?*

She was dumbfounded and asked, "Could you please explain that to me because it makes no sense."

Her friend said, "You're not considering the feelings of your husband."

"What? Unbelievable!"

Her friend went on to say, "Look, you are going through significant chemotherapy and your appearance is quite a bit different now, so can you blame your husband for hooking up with someone else?"

Michaela was simply perplexed by her friend's exclamations.

Her friend went on to say, "You should think about forgiving him for his transgressions because, after all, they weren't really that bad."

Michaela was astonished: she fundamentally couldn't believe what she was hearing from her friend of all people. She thought that it was essential to learn to forgive others that was true, but he also trashed our wedding vows, and he needed to be held accountable for his actions.

Michaela asked her friend, "Do you think it's okay to commit adultery?"

Her friend quickly replied, "He didn't commit adultery!"

"Oh, so what do you think adultery is? He slept with someone outside of our marriage…that's adultery!"

Michaela's friend was like, "Yeah, but what do you expect him to do with you in your condition? Have you looked at yourself in the mirror of late?"

Michaela retorted, "Are you kidding me? I expect him to honor our wedding vows, to show commitment, support, loyalty, and to not sleep around. Good Lord, is that not too much to ask of your husband?"

She went on to tell her friend, "I can't believe you!"

Michaela left lunch that day bewildered as she thought what kind of friends I have! It was a shame as that was the last time, she ever was with any of those three friends, or now ex-friends.

*****

Over the next several months, Michaela's life went from difficult to downright discouraging. She had gone through this whole ordeal pretty much alone, except for some occasional assistance from work colleagues and her boss's wife. They were all so helpful and kind. But for the most part, they had their own families to deal with. Michaela was coming up on her final chemotherapy treatment and all was looking good. She was happy to still be alive even though life had been so strenuous of late.

A short time had passed, Michaela had completed all her treatments and was taking her medications. She had begun to gain some weight back and was feeling so much better. She had returned to work full-time and learning to take care of herself first. She had been through a challenging ordeal, and she was beginning to feel much better. Michaela had been doing some yoga and light workouts for a few weeks. She was starting to feel stronger with more energy when one morning, she noticed pains in her lower abdominal area. At first, she thought it was some soreness from the workouts, but they persisted. When the intermittent pain continued for a couple of weeks, she felt it was time to mention them to her physician.

Her physician examined her and sent her for some more tests.

The tests and radiological evidence showed that further examination was needed. She ended up having a biopsy performed on her left ovary. The biopsy results were not good! Michaela was now diagnosed with ovarian cancer. This was surprising as it was noted that this was not metastatic breast cancer; this was a different cancer.

Of all the luck, Michaela could only think what else could go wrong. She prayed and tried to have *faith* that this too would work out. Surgery was scheduled.

Her surgery went well; the surgeon removed her ovaries, fallopian tubes, uterus, and some surrounding abdominal tissues. Having finished her chemotherapy for her breast cancer a few months back, now she was embarking on another round of chemotherapy for the ovarian cancer.

Michaela asked her doctor, "Please give it to me straight!"

Her physician said okay. "Here it is: the five-year average survival rate for all women diagnosed with ovarian cancer is just less than 50 percent. She continued, life expectancy rates in cancer are determined by looking at the five-year survival rates of patients diagnosed with a certain stage of cancer. Cancer as you may recall from your previous treatments are categorized in stages I to IV, with IV being the worst. For stage IV ovarian cancer the five-year survival rate is 15–20 percent. However, we've put your ovarian cancer in the stage II–III category. Plus, we are confident that we got all the cancer during the surgery. For treatment, we will put you through a course of chemotherapy with radiation therapy."

The oncologist added, "Yes, the chemotherapy and radiation will be rough, but the goal here is to ultimately get you to the five-year point."

All Michaela could think about was, *Oh great!*

To say this was a difficult time for Michaela is an understatement. Fortunately, even after being abandoned by her closest friends, she had some work colleagues who stepped up for her and showed their mettle! They were empathetic sure but even more than that several were there to assist her in so many ways. That's what true friends do!

Michaela went through her round of treatments, and she was a shell of her previous self as one may expect. But her *faith* guided her even when times looked bleak. It was now thirty months since her initial diagnosis for breast cancer and her oncologists determined that she was cancer-free. That was a glorious day for Michaela but also sad that she didn't have anyone to share her joy!

Her doctors started her on the post-treatment medications. They stressed to her to be compliant with these medications. The goal was to get to five years or what they called the progression free survival point. They stressed if she could get to five years progression free survival then she would have an outstanding chance of licking these cancers for good. Those who remain disease-free at five years have excellent long-term survival rates. So that became Michaela's goal. She had ongoing appointments with her doctors to check her bloodwork and overall assessment.

*****

Michaela began to get back into her job, and people were ecstatic to see her back and feeling better. At one time, she had looked so gaunt and had lost so much weight it was scary. She was once again gaining her weight back, which was great. It had taken a few months, but she was looking like her old self. At a shade over five feet eight inches tall, she had gained 30 pounds back and was back up to her old weight of 120–125 pounds. She was both looking good and feeling good.

Michaela had gained her strength back along with the weight, so she was looking like herself again. But now, it was time for another surgery.

Her initial breast cancer diagnosis had forced the surgeon to perform a radical mastectomy. The surgeon had taken several pictures of her breasts so Michaela would be able to have breast reconstruction with implants, which would be as near as possible to her original size. Her original size was a 34 B-cup, which she thought were perfect for her height. Moreover, on one presurgical appointment the surgeon presented her with the idea to increase her breast size. She quickly squashed that thought. She was adamant in her belief that her original breast size was what the good Lord had blessed her with, so she felt blessed and comfortable with her original size. That is what she wanted—nothing more, nothing less. The breast implant surgery went smoothly, and she felt like they looked as good as new. Getting the breast implants helped Michaela to feel better about herself.

*****

It had been about a month since her breast reconstruction and implant surgery, and she was feeling stronger and stronger every day. She was back at her job full-time, and she felt she was getting back into the swing of things. By this time, it was coming up on three years since she was first diagnosed with breast cancer. Yes, three years, which at times felt like a lifetime!

It had been nearly two years since Michaela had gone back to work full-time. Her customer relationships were solid, and people were so happy to see her back and feeling better. Michaela loved working with her customers.

On the other hand, she was a quiet and an extremely guarded person, she liked her anonymity, basically an introvert. She loved talking with people but only within a small group setting as large groups in close quarters made her uncomfortable.

She had an excellent year and her boss honored her for outstanding performance with an award trip to Amelia Island, Florida. The trip was for two, but Michaela went alone and used the time to get away for a few days and relax.

While she was there, she got to thinking that maybe she needed a change. Over the previous two to three months, she had accidentally bumped into a couple of her old lunch friends and her ex-husband. This made her very uncomfortable. It made her remember how the people closest to her who should have been there to support and comfort her in her greatest time of need simply bailed on her. Seeing them periodically gave her feelings of angst and disgust. She needed a change. She needed to move.

Michaela had a quarterly performance review, and her boss told her she was doing well again. She took the opportunity to ask him if there were any openings or new positions available. She informed him that she needed a change and gave him the reason why.

He had a great deal of respect for Michaela for a couple of reasons; one was obviously she was a high performer, the second was for how she handled all her illnesses with such grace and dignity even through such turbulent times. He told her that he did have an opening, and it was in Birmingham, Alabama. He told her to think about it and let him know if interested. Her boss went on to say that the position was hers if she wanted, and he would simply perform a lateral transfer.

At first, she wasn't sure if she wanted to live in the Birmingham area, so Michaela prayed for guidance.

"What do I do, oh Lord?"

She continued to pray but it wasn't long until she felt in her heart that something was telling her to take the position and move to Birmingham. She continued to pray about it and the feeling to move became stronger and stronger, so she succumbed to her feelings and told herself to have *faith*. She let her boss know that she would take the lateral move.

Michaela had recently reached four years progression free survival from her breast cancer treatment. Moreover, she just surpassed her three-year survival point from the ovarian cancer treatment. She is feeling like her old self again for the first time in years! Michaela was now on her way to Birmingham. She was excited for the chance at a fresh start.

5

They Meet

It was Sunday afternoon with the long fourth of July holiday coming up. Alex stopped by the apartment complex office for a cup of coffee and to have a chat with Sheryl. Sheryl was glad to see Alex especially since she had been spending time with Michaela over the past couple of weeks.

She asked, "Alex, are you going to be around this week and through the holiday?"

He replied, "And what else would I be doing?"

Alex continued, "I stopped in to let you know that I'll be gone tonight."

As usual, he asked, "Could you hold my FedEx packages?"

Sheryl laughed. "Of course I will!"

"Where are you headed to this time?"

Alex let her know, "I've got to make a run down to Mobile."

He said, "I'll be home late Monday night. Then out again early Tuesday morning."

Sheryl asked, "So where are you going so early on Tuesday?"

"I'm speaking to a group of students at Auburn University as an air force officer, so I'll be in my service dress uniform." He continued, "I'll stop by upon my return to retrieve any packages that may have arrived."

Sheryl replied, "Oh, please do!"

"Why?"

"You know I've never seen you in uniform."

Alex smiled. With a little blush, he quietly said, "It's no big thing, but sure, I'll stop in."

He continued with a wry smile, "I need to get my FedEx packages anyway."

Sheryl asked, "Are you going to be around for the long holiday weekend?"

Alex replied, "Yes, I am." He went on to say, "Some friends are having me over for dinner and then we're going to watch the fireworks. The next day some friends and I are hitting the golf course."

"Of course, church Sunday morning, then I'll be in my office all afternoon catching up on paperwork and reports." He chuckled, "That's never-ending!" With a grin, he said, "That's my itinerary, you know same ol' boring stuff!"

Sheryl laughed! She was working the weekend so she said, "You know, Alex, I'll be in the office Sunday afternoon…you should stop by."

He said, "I will. Heck, I'll be needing a break by midafternoon anyway."

He went on to say, "Hey, thanks for the coffee, but I need to hit the road."

Agreeing Sheryl said, "Drive safely!"

"Thanks," he said.

As Alex walked away, Sheryl was trying to imagine what he looked like in uniform. Watching him walk away all straight and tall with purpose she could visualize him in uniform. In her mind, she was becoming ever more convinced that Michaela and Alex would make a great couple. As she plotted on how to get them together, she pondered on how to do it without it looking obvious. She needed to work it so that it seemed like they got together on their own. Sheryl was deviously working this problem!

By coincidence, as Alex was leaving out the front office doors, Michaela walked into the office through the back doors. Sheryl was standing in the middle of the lobby watching Alex leave when Michaela walked up behind her, taking her completely by surprise. Michaela placed her hand on Sheryl's shoulder which startled her from her trance and thoughts. Sheryl immediately thought, *That was close, they almost met.*

She greeted Michaela, "Hey there, you scared me!"

Michaela replied, "Sorry about that."

Michaela asked, "Who was that?" referring to Alex.

Sheryl replied, "He's a friend and resident."

Michaela didn't ask anything else about Alex. She and Sheryl spoke for a few minutes while she also sipped on a bottle of water.

Sheryl asked, "Are you going to be around this holiday?"

Michaela chuckled. "Of course, where else would I go!"

She continued, "I've been needing to get a little sun, so I thought I'd work on my suntan by the pool."

Sheryl was privately thinking, *This is perfect, they'll each be around for sure on Sunday, and she'll be out back here by the pool sunbathing.* The wheels in Sheryl's brain were really churning out a plan now!

Michaela added, "I need this upcoming holiday bad as I've been going full force, learning customers in my area of responsibility."

She was like, "I really need a breather to recharge. But for now, I need to get out of here, so I'll see you later."

"Yes, have a good day and we'll talk later," Sheryl replied.

Michaela left, but now, Sheryl had her plan, and she was going to execute her strategy next Sunday afternoon. Sheryl was smiling ear to ear as Michaela left the lobby.

*****

Alex had plenty of windshield time to think between Birmingham to Mobile before returning home. He continued to think often about Cynthia but began to think that his friends were correct that it was time to move forward. He asked himself and wondered if it was the right thing to do. In the end, the only thing he could do was pray. He needed some help and guidance. His heart still hurt for Cynthia and her circumstance.

He had just left Mobile headed north when Alex began to pray. He said, *Lord, you know I have great memories, and I remember every moment with Cynthia, but I need your help. Is it right for me to move on?*

Lord, I am asking for forgiveness for any missteps I made with Cynthia. At times, I feel like a broken man for not being able to do more for her. I feel like I let her down. I pray, and I am asking you, Lord, to help me to simply pick up the pieces of my life one piece at a time and rebuild it under your guidance. I need your help. I need to know in my heart that it's okay to move on with my life as I simply do not know. Please help me, oh Lord, and thanks for listening! Amen.

Alex had no idea whether his prayers were heard, but he did feel like a heavy weight had been lifted from his heart. He didn't know what it meant or what might happen, but suddenly, he was feeling better about his future. It wasn't clear what he was feeling in his heart; it did, however, make his drive home much easier, and time passed quickly. In fact, for the first time, his heart felt like it was ready to move forward.

*****

The presentation and discussion at Auburn University had gone well. Alex was driving back home, thinking he was looking forward to a long holiday weekend. He thought this had been a long couple of weeks and was looking forward to some extra days to relax.

Alex arrived home and took his computer bag into his apartment. He checked his mailbox. Then he recalled that he had promised Sheryl to stop by while still in uniform. So he walked up to the office. As he strolled into the lobby, Sheryl spotted him coming through the doors. She walked over to him wide-eyed, trying to soak him in from head to toe. As he came closer, she thought he did look very handsome in his uniform. She walked over and gave him a little hug and said with a smile, "Look at you!" She continued, "Anybody ever tell you that you are very handsome in uniform."

Alex, with a little blush, simply said, "Thank you, but I think you're biased."

They each laughed.

"Here's your FedEx, only a couple of letter envelopes, no boxes," as she handed them to him.

"Thanks again."

"I can't get over how good you look in that uniform."

With a little laugh he said, "Thank you again."

There was a long silence, and finally Alex interjected, "You know I'm really tired. I want to get out of this uniform and just relax. It's been a fast-paced couple of days so if you'll excuse me."

Sheryl was like, "Okay…you'll still be around this weekend?"

"Yes, I'll stop by Sunday afternoon, how's that?"

"Sounds good."

Alex walked out carrying his FedEx envelopes. As he passed out the second set of doors, he slipped his air force cap onto his head and was gracefully walking down the sidewalk all straight and tall. As Sheryl stood there watching him walk away, she was in a slight daze. She wasn't even aware that Michaela had come into the lobby from the other doors. Michaela walked over to Sheryl who was oblivious to her presence and interrupted her train of thought by saying, "Who are you watching?"

Her question startled Sheryl from her moment of silence as she turned and said, "Hello, I didn't even notice you come in."

Michaela continued, "Not surprising, you were focused on something else, or should I say someone else."

Sheryl not wanting to give anything away, simply said, "Oh, it's nothing, I was just thinking," while she ambled towards her office.

Michaela thought her reaction interesting as she stood there watching Alex walk away herself. She felt something drawing her to watch him until he was out of sight. She couldn't explain it, but something was pulling her to take notice! In addition, there was a quiet gentleness in her heart, which made her feel at ease. Then it hit Michaela, wasn't that the same guy that was leaving the other day when she had walked in…she thought, *Hmmm!* She walked over to Sheryl's desk who was trying to look busy.

Michaela asked, "Is that the same guy who was leaving the other day when I walked in?"

Sheryl, trying to be coy, said, "Possibly, many of our residents walk through here during the day."

Michaela said, "You know I could only see him from the back." She continued, "He's in the military?"

34

Sheryl replied, "Yes, an air force officer, lieutenant colonel I believe!"

Michaela replied, "An officer?"

Sheryl quickly added, "And a gentleman!"

Michaela with a slight smile says, "He looks like someone who would be interesting to talk to."

With a small smirk, Sheryl said, "Well, tell you what, next time he's around, I'll be glad to introduce you, sound good? Oh, and by the way, you are right. He is more than interesting. He is a very nice person!"

"Yeah, I'm up to meeting some new people," Michaela said.

"Okay then, I'll see what I can do," as Sheryl had a little grin on her face. She was thinking this might be working out great, but she needed to stick to her plan. Alex would be a little busy over the next couple of days, but he said he would stop by the office on Sunday afternoon. She thought, *I just need to make sure Michaela is around at that same time.*

*****

The weekend had great weather…warm and sunny! Alex played golf a couple of days while Michaela primarily worked on her suntan at the complex pool. After church just as Alex had planned, he crawled into his office chair and began banging away at some reports, data analysis, and other general items. He had been working at it for about three hours when the phone rang. It was Sheryl.

"Hey, Alex, watcha doing?"

He chuckled. "Paperwork…a never-ending pile of paperwork!"

"Well, it sounds like you need a break," Sheryl replied.

"Absolutely, I was just thinking about that…you going to be there?"

"I'm not going anywhere, come on down."

Alex said, "You'll see me in five."

As Sheryl hung up the phone, she rose quickly from her desk and scurried across the lobby to look out the side doors to the pool area. She was looking to see if Michaela was still there, which she was.

Sheryl walked over to speak with her. Sheryl let Michaela know that her tan was coming along fine.

Michaela said, "Thank you, but I think I'm about done for today as I don't want to get too dark."

Sheryl replied, "Okay, but before you go stop by my office."

"I will."

Sheryl turned and headed back inside, smiling to herself as she thought her plan was coming together.

A few minutes later, Alex came into the lobby. He and Sheryl started talking while Sheryl offered Alex a bottle of water. They were engaging in some small talk when some loud noises interrupted their discussion. The noises were coming from the pool area so they each went to the side doors leading out onto the pool decking. They began peering out the doors when Sheryl suddenly said, "Oh, great not those guys again!"

Alex asked, "What do you mean?"

She continued, "Those two guys share an apartment, I've had numerous noise complaints against them, plus they like to come to the pool and drink. Then sometimes they start bothering some of our other residents. I've warned them a couple of times, but they seem to be what my dad called knuckleheads!"

Alex laughed. "Yeah, that's what I call them too!"

They watched them for a moment then Alex's eyes caught a movement over to the right, and it was a woman sunbathing off by herself. Alex began focusing solely on her, or one could say he was staring. It was a moment later that Sheryl realized that Alex was staring at someone else. She looked around and noticed that he was staring directly at Michaela as she laid on the lounger. She watched him stare for a moment then she broke the silence with, "Who are you staring at?"

Startled at being caught staring, Alex quickly asked, "Who is that laying over there on the lounger?"

Sheryl was trying to suppress her smile of joy and said, "You mean the woman over there in the black bikini?"

"Yes."

"Well, her name is Michaela and she moved in about a month ago."

Alex asked, "Is she single?"

"I'm pretty sure she is, why?" Sheryl kept up her act of intrigue yet all the while smiling profusely on the inside.

Alex again replied, "She is striking, but there's something else about her... I can't quite put my finger on it."

Sheryl said, "What do you mean?"

"I don't know as it's more of a feeling I get just looking at her that she is someone with what I would characterize as having substance!"

Sheryl thought that was an interesting observation by Alex and although she didn't reply to his thoughts she agreed with his assessment.

Sheryl asked, "Would you like to meet her?" as she kept working her plan.

A quick reply, "Oh, absolutely, can you arrange it?" said Alex.

She nonchalantly said, "Yeah, I can do that."

She started to say something else when she noticed one of the knuckleheads, the one named Matt was making a beeline toward where Michaela was laying.

Sheryl quickly said, "Oh, crap, I think Matt is going over to bother Michaela."

Alex heard that from Sheryl and noted, so her name is Michaela. They watched and Alex cracked the door open so that they could each hear the conversation.

Sheryl was like, "I hope I don't have to go out there again to warn them."

Alex jumped in and said, "If so, I'll go out with you, and be your backup if you would like."

"Thanks, I might need you," as they continued to watch and listen.

They eavesdropped as Matt walked up to Michaela and said, "Hey, darlin', I'm Matt, me and my friend have a bunch of beer. Why don't you come on over and join us?"

Michaela with a quick retort, "No, thank you, I was just leaving."

As she swung her legs off the lounger facing the opposite way with her back to Matt as if to say take a hike. But Matt wasn't going to give up that easy as he stepped around the lounger and grabbed Michaela by the upper arm. Michaela quickly brushed his hand from her arm and stood up. When she stood up, it became clear that she was a couple of inches taller than he, which appeared to take Matt by surprise.

Michaela then glared at him and said in a very terse voice, "Do not ever grab me again, and please go away!"

Matt, flustered and kind of pissed off, turned and walked away. As he did you could hear him say very loudly, "What a bitch!"

Alex watching and hearing this was thinking, *Way to go, lady, you put him in his place!* Sheryl heard the encounter as well but was also watching the look on Alex's face.

Michaela put on her bikini coverup, gathered her stuff and headed for the lobby. Sheryl and Alex, seeing Michaela gathering her stuff, had already walked back into the middle of the lobby area. They were standing there, talking, when Michaela came through the doors and walked over to Sheryl and Alex. As she came toward them, Alex was thinking, *Oh my gosh, the word* beautiful *doesn't do her justice!* As she came closer, Alex kept telling himself to be cool and smile, but in reality, his insides were doing backward handstands! Michaela walked right up to them and had the prettiest smile with these unbelievable crystal blue eyes that sparkled. She said hello, and Alex returned the greeting in kind.

Sheryl very quickly said, "Michaela, this is Alex. He's a friend of mine."

Michaela reached out with her hand, which Alex took and said with a little shake in his voice, "Very nice to meet you!"

Sheryl broke the moment by asking Michaela, "I hope Matt didn't bother you too much!"

Michaela quickly said, "Who?"

"That guy out there," Sheryl said. She continued, "He's been a problem ever since they've moved in about three months ago."

Michaela replied, "Nothing I couldn't handle."

The three of them continued to chitchat about nothing really important. All the while Alex was gazing in admiration at Michaela when she was addressing Sheryl and Alex felt her eyes on him when he was facing more toward Sheryl.

Then suddenly, Michaela realized something, and she asked, "I think I saw you the other day."

Alex recoiled a little and said, "Really...when?"

She continued, "Weren't you in a military uniform the other day? I only saw the back of you as you walked down the sidewalk."

Alex, with a quick smile, turned his back to Michaela and said, "Does that help?"

Everyone got a good laugh out of that one. Then Alex said, "Maybe you did, I'm in the Air Force Reserve and did a presentation last week, and I did stop into the office to pick up some items that Sheryl was holding for me."

Michaela replied, "So that was you because it was on Tuesday."

There was a silence among the three of them, but Michaela was thinking he seems like a very nice person!

All this time, Sheryl was observing each of them closely, their body language, their smiles, their slight blushes, their laughs, and all she could think was this was working out perfectly.

Sheryl broke the silence by asking Alex, "Didn't you tell me that you were going to go out to eat somewhere in a little while?"

Alex underwent a moment of hesitation then took the hint and said, "Yes, that's correct, I am."

Sheryl looked at Michaela squarely in the eyes and said, "You should join him for dinner so you guys could talk some more!" Sheryl continued to stare at Michaela with a slight nod of the head as if to say "Go, go, go!"

Michaela began to say, "That would be nice," but Alex interrupted. He said with a smile, "Sheryl, look, if I'm going to invite someone to have dinner with me, I can do it myself."

Sheryl nodded. "Got it."

Alex turned to face Michaela directly, and looking her square in the eyes, he asked her, "Michaela, would you join me for dinner tonight?"

Sheryl was in the background thinking, *Okay, Michaela, you better say yes, so don't screw this up!*

Michaela, with a pause that kept them waiting for a moment, smiled. "Yes, I would like that!"

Alex said, "Great, then it's a date!"

Michaela said, "A date?"

Alex replied, "Yes, a date!"

Michaela, with a big smile, said, "Yes, a date!"

Sheryl was over on the sidelines with the biggest smile on the outside, yet on the inside, she was cheering and doing handstands and giving herself high-fives.

Alex asked, "Does six o'clock work for you?"

"Why, yes, it does…that's actually perfect."

He said, "So what's your apartment number?"

She replied, "It's 2207."

Sheryl was smiling from ear to ear as she knew they only lived five doors apart. Yes, they lived in the same building on the second floor only five apartments between them.

Alex was quietly astonished and stated, "I'm in 2212, just down the breezeway from you."

They gazed at each other for a moment before Alex finally said the obvious, "I can't believe we haven't run into one another before now."

There was a moment of silence between all of them.

Then Alex broke the silence. "I need to run for now," and then he turned to Sheryl and said, "Great to see you as always," then turning back to Michaela he said, "Great to meet you, and I'll pick you up at six!" Alex scurried out, just beaming!

Sheryl and Michaela watched as he left and walked down the sidewalk. Once out of sight, Sheryl turned to Michaela and stated in a quiet humble voice, "He's the finest man I've ever known!" It came out with such a matter-of-fact whisper that Michaela's mind began to drift. She had come to trust Sheryl in such a short period of time, and she thinks Alex is a terrific guy. She thought, *I need to pay close attention, maybe he is a good man.*

Sheryl continued by saying, "I could tell you so much more, but I want you to find it out on your own!"

Michaela turned back to face Sheryl and started to say something but hesitated for a moment then finally said, "Yes, he does seem like a fine person."

*****

Alex got back to his apartment and suddenly it hit him. "I have a date!" He then realized, "Oh my gosh, I have a date and it's in two hours. What am I going to do?" Alex was in a slight bit of panic as his brain was firing on all cylinders wondering what to do. He immediately called Sheryl, and as she picked up the phone, he blurted out, "I have a date!"

Sheryl, smiling, said, "You sure do."

He responded, "Not just a date but a date with the most beautiful woman on the planet! What am I going to do?"

Sheryl, still smiling, "First calm down, take a deep breath! Alex you're a good guy, well-rounded so just be *you*! And by the way, yes, Michaela is simply gorgeous but do not make a big deal about that okay. She doesn't like it! Just get to know her! Keep it simple, be different but be you, got it?"

Alex, after taking a few deep breaths, closed his eyes for a moment and told Sheryl, "I got it, thank you!"

He gave it some thought for a few minutes and formulated a plan. He thought back to the short interaction that he had with Michaela and tried to think about what was so nice about her besides the obvious outward beauty. It came to him; her laugh was enchanting, and the tone of her voice was soothing and made him just want to listen. Alex thought to himself just relax it's going to be all good. He needed to get something for the date, so he quickly rushed to the store.

It was time, Alex slipped into a sport coat and strolled down the breezeway. He hesitated for a moment, took a deep breath, and whispered to himself, "Here we go," as he lightly knocked.

As Michaela opened the door Alex went momentarily wide-eyed and silently under his breath said, "Wow!" There she was in this three-quarter length bluish summer dress and heels. Her eyes sparkled and her smile was intoxicating as Alex asked, "You ready?" He blurted out, "You look very nice!"

Michaela replied, "Oh, thank you, and you look nice too."

He responded, "Thank you." He continued, "By the way, I brought you these flowers."

Michaela, with a surprised look, said, "Thank you that is so nice, oh, these are lovely." Alex had gotten her three orange roses.

She said, "I'm going to leave these here, it's too hot out still, I'll put them into some water now and arrange them in a vase later. Orange roses, those are very pretty, thank you again."

Walking down the breezeway, she momentarily paused at the stairway and took hold of the railing. Alex noticing this and knowing that she was wearing heels took her free hand and arm and helped to balance her going down the stairs. He then opened the car door for her, plus before closing it, made sure her dress was completely in as well. As they were pulling out of the parking lot, Michaela asked, "So where are we going?"

Alex replied, "Copeland's."

"That's perfect, I've been wanting to go there," she replied.

They walked into the restaurant and over to the seating desk. It was Sunday evening early, so they were not busy whatsoever. Alex said to the young lady at the desk, "Reservations for two at six fifteen for Alex."

Michaela was standing, noticing every detail. She thought, *Here it is.* Sunday evening, and he knew that the restaurant would not be busy, but he still called and made reservations. It made her smile and think that he had enough respect for this date that he thought it important enough to make a reservation, even though it wasn't necessary. That simple act of making a reservation touched her and made her feel respected.

After being seated, they started with some regular date chitchat when Alex stopped and said, "Okay, here's the deal. We are not going to talk about everyday regular first meeting or first date conversation.

I'm going to assume you have a job or career and I do as well, so why take up time talking about something that will come to light in the future anyway if we get that far. So let's talk about other stuff."

Michaela was thinking, *This guy is a take-charge guy... I kind of like that.*

She said, "So what should we talk about?"

"Well, let's order first."

"Okay, sounds good."

Alex asked, "Red or white wine?"

"White wine for sure," she replied.

"So Chardonnay, Sauvignon Blanc, Pinot Gris, Riesling?"

She said, "I don't care for Chardonnay, but the rest are fine."

As the waitress came back Alex said, "Bring us a bottle of Prosecco."

After toasting each other Michaela asked, "So what do we talk about?"

Alex thought, *Let me see what would be different?* He was thinking it over when he said, "I've got it." Alex started off by saying, "This might sound strange, but it's different. The question is what are your two favorite sandwiches?"

Michaela replied, "That's different." Michaela was thinking and started to say something when Alex interrupted her with, "Hold that thought!"

He stopped the waitress and asked, "Do you have a piece of paper and pencil or pen?"

She said, "Sure, here you go."

Alex noted, "I'll write down my favorite two sandwiches first," which he did and folded his note.

Michaela then said, "Well, you're probably going to think this is weird, but my favorite sandwich is tuna salad, with egg salad a close second."

Alex sat there with an astonished look on his face, thinking, *Did she just say what I thought she said?* He didn't say anything for a moment when Michaela finally broke the silence and said, "What did you write?"

43

Alex slid his note to her. She opened it up and read, "Tuna salad and egg salad." Michaela was briefly stunned. "That's amazing, I can't believe we like the exact same sandwiches. What are the odds?" Michaela's mind was racing wondering what just happened.

This really broke the ice, and they began to effortlessly engage in conversation. It was like they were just so at ease with one another. Amazing what liking the same two sandwiches started. They talked about different things they each liked to do and discovered neither liked to be around large crowds. Michaela loved to stargaze, watch movies, go have appetizers and wine early, and a few other things. She liked a nice dinner sometimes but more often she liked to keep things simple. She giggled when she said, "You know sometimes you just have to have a good burger!"

This made Alex laugh and say, "I agree."

Alex told her he liked to play golf or simply go to the driving range. Sometimes he liked to go to the library and just sit and read with a cup of coffee or better hot chocolate. He, too, enjoyed watching movies and some conversational quiet time with a glass of wine.

Their conversation was so easy; they were each laughing and having a great time as they polished off their bottle of wine. Michaela was thinking to herself that she hadn't felt this at ease with anyone in a long, long time. She was looking Alex over very closely as he was speaking. Michaela thought, Sheryl was right, he is a fine man. She told herself, *Just be patient and let's see how things pan out.*

It was then that Alex asked, "Here's one for you. What are your favorite movies?"

Michaela quipped, "That's a good one, let me think a moment." She thought about the question for a few seconds then exclaimed, "I've got it!" She continued, "I like the movie *Ghost*. The music is beautiful and that scene at the pottery wheel is so romantic."

Alex said, "That's a good one, and you must like the song 'Unchained Melody.'"

Michaela queried, "'Unchained Melody'?"

"Yes, that's the song that plays three or four times during the movie. It's by the Righteous Brothers, but actually Bobby Hatfield sang it solo."

"I didn't know that, but I love that song. It's the most beautiful love song ever!"

Michaela continued, "Another couple of movies I like are *Pretty Woman* and *Dirty Dancing*. Oh, and one more is an older movie with Audrey Hepburn in Rome where she is a princess."

Alex added, "You mean *Roman Holiday?*"

"Yes, that's it."

She said, "Well, those are probably my favorites, so what are yours?"

Alex quickly said, "My all-time favorite movie is *The Sound of Music*. It has everything, love story between a military man and beautiful woman, great music, children, an unbelievable location setting around Salzburg, Austria, and finally they get the best of the Nazis. Who could want anymore!"

Michaela replied, "You know I've never watched that movie all the way through, I've seen only bits and pieces."

"Well, we may have to change that!"

Michaela smiled. "Maybe so."

Alex continued with, "I also think *Casablanca* is one of the all-time best movies as well. But my third one many have never heard of but trust me it's a great movie and that is *Goodbye Mr. Chips* from 1939."

Michaela agreed, "You're right I've never heard of that movie but if you say it's good, I'm sure it is."

Alex quipped, "You'll be pleasantly surprised, trust me."

"My fourth is another movie which you may not have seen, that is *An Affair to Remember* with Cary Grant and Deborah Kerr. It's one that touches my heart!"

After a pause, Michaela surprised Alex by saying, "We should have some movie nights."

Alex looked at Michaela with a little grin and eyes beaming, "You know you're right…what a great idea!"

They laughed and continued to talk while sipping on their last bit of wine. Michaela asked, "What does your week look like?"

Alex responded with, "I'm in my home office all day tomorrow working on reports and such…fun, fun! And you?"

"Pretty much the same stuff going by to see customers, but I'll be in the area tomorrow.

Things were going well. There was a little pause when Alex spoke up.

"Michaela, there's something I have to tell you," Alex said, sounding all serious.

She said, "Yeah, what's that?"

He continued, "I have to tell you now that I don't kiss on the first date!"

Michaela, with a little smile, replied, "I see."

Alex went on with, "No, don't try and change my mind because you are not getting to first base with me tonight." They both broke out laughing as Michaela thought it was charming. The comment was also disarming and made her feel even more comfortable. Michaela couldn't resist as she playfully asked, "So when is it okay to kiss?"

He responded, "Well, let's see how our date on Wednesday night goes."

Michaela looked at him and softly said, "So we have a date Wednesday night?"

"Yep, does that work for you?"

She replied with a shy smile, "Yes, I'd like that."

"Great, let's make it early again, say six? You know it's a school night!"

Michaela thought that was adorable and actually thoughtful. They left the restaurant and Alex walked her to her apartment door and shyly said, "Michaela, I had a very nice time tonight…thank you for joining me!"

She responded, "I, too, had a great time, I needed to laugh and have some good conversation, thank you for asking me."

"My pleasure," as Alex leaned in and gave her a quick hug. He continued, "Hope you have a good night, see you soon."

After Michaela went inside and locked the door, she leaned with her back against the door and took a deep breath. Her mind was racing. She thought she just had the best evening with a terrific guy, and there was no pressure. She was thinking he was just so genuine, easy to talk with, he actually listened! She thought he was someone she could trust…he seemed like a good man. Her thoughts continued, *He seems like such a great guy, but is it right to get involved while I'm still recovering from cancer.* She wondered but was so looking forward to seeing Alex again.

*****

Sheryl couldn't help herself, she had to call Michaela to find out how the date went and what she thought of Alex. Michaela had no more than taken off her shoes when the phone rang. It was Sheryl. Michaela answered, "Hello, Sheryl."

Sheryl jumped right to the point, "So how did your date go with Alex?"

Michaela couldn't help smiling over the phone as she replied, "It was great, he's a true gentleman and he makes me feel so at ease. He's got a charming side to him, and I believe there's a lot to him and that he's so much smarter than he would ever let on."

Sheryl with a deep sigh of joy, "Well, it appears you two really hit if off!"

"It was only one date," Michaela said, "but we are going out again on Wednesday."

"Wednesday, really?"

"Yep, that's right, but you know, Sheryl, I hope I see him before then."

"Well, Michaela, you realize he only lives five doors down!"

"Yeah, I know. But, Sheryl, there is something else that is bothering me."

Sheryl says, "Oh, what's that?"

"Should I tell him that I am still trying to recover from cancer? Is it right for me to enter into a potential relationship yet? I just don't know."

Sheryl was quick to react as she said, "Wait, wait, wait…slow down and let things play out. I think you'll know when it's the right time to tell him more. Plus, I'm not going to give anything away about him, but you're going to find out that he'll be very understanding as he's been through a lot as well. And that's all I'm saying."

47

Michaela replied, "Maybe you're right!"

Sheryl was like, "Trust me on this. Alex is going to be more than you ever expected."

Sheryl's words had a calming influence on Michaela. She said, "Sheryl, thank you for your words and guidance. Your friendship is precious to me! Let me say, I know it has only been one date, but Alex has touched my heart like no one ever has… I simply can't explain it."

This made Sheryl very happy, and now she couldn't wait to speak with Alex to see what he thought.

6

An Enchanting Week

That night, Alex tossed and turned most of the night, thinking about her. He kept thinking that she was truly someone very special, yet he kept telling himself it was just one date.

One thing was for sure this Monday morning: Alex was looking forward to his next date with Michaela. He started early this morning working on a couple of customer data sets and pulling it together into a report. He was gathering and analyzing the data into a potential journal publication for a customer.

Sheryl waited as long as she could the next morning. She finally had to phone Alex. He was in his office working away when she called. Alex answered, "Good morning, Sheryl, I'm surprised you waited this long."

She quickly replied, "Funny!"

Alex continued, "I'll bet I know why you're calling?"

She goes, "Okay, smarty-pants, give it to me straight." Then with a wry smile she gently says, "So how did you like Michaela?"

Alex paused for a moment then finally whispered, "She was exquisite!" Sheryl was smiling as Alex continued, "She is adorable, and I felt so relaxed with her." He continued, "Yes, she is utterly gorgeous, but you know Sheryl she is a much more stunning person on the inside, simply elegant!" Sheryl was speechless on the other end of the phone as he said, "I can't wait to get to know her better."

Sheryl, playing coy, said, "So you going to see her again?"

Alex replied, "Like you don't already know, yes, we have a date on Wednesday." This all made Sheryl very happy.

*****

Alex was working away at his desk. When at home he generally starts his workday prior to 7:00 a.m. and many days he worked past midnight. Alex is one of those rare individuals who never required much sleep. Between the reports, doing a little research, a couple of conference calls he had been going full throttle when there was a knock at his door.

As he heard the knock, he yelled out, "Just a second, I'll be right there!" He finished typing his thought then went to the door. As he opened the door, he was startled, "Michaela, hey, come in, what's up?"

Michaela smiled and said, "I knew you were working in your home office today so I thought I would bring you some lunch."

"That is so thoughtful," as Alex was smiling from ear to ear. He continued, "That is so funny, I was just thinking about lunch. Hey, come on back." As they entered his office, he said, "Have a seat." Alex had a settee couch in his office where they each sat.

Michaela opened her bag, saying, "I stopped down here at this deli, and I had them make up one tuna salad and one egg salad sandwich on wheat."

He stared at her for a moment. "That is awesome. While you're getting it set up, what would you like to drink?"

"Oh, water is fine."

"I'll be right back," as he went and grabbed a couple bottles of water.

They sat there eating their sandwiches as they shared half of each one. They were so comfortable sitting there, talking.

Alex looked at Michaela and said sincerely, "Thank you so much for bringing lunch. You really surprised me!"

She smiled. "My pleasure." They were sitting there quietly looking each other in the eyes, not saying a word but actually saying a lot when the phone rang.

Alex walked around his desk hit the speaker and said hello.

"Hey, Alex, it's Amanda."

"Hello there, by the way, I have you on speaker and I have a friend sitting in my office as we are having some lunch. Michaela, this is Amanda."

"Hello, Amanda."

Amanda replied, "Hello to you back, nice to meet you, kind of!" They all laughed.

Alex says, "What's up? And oh, by the way, I was working on the manuscript this morning and performed some more statistical analyses. The additional data I built into another table and expanded on the results. I have a little more to do this afternoon, and I will forward you the latest draft later today."

Amanda says, "That sounds great, but that's not why I was calling."

"Okay."

Amanda continued, "I wanted to let you know that everyone loved your presentation here at Auburn the other day! Several students came up to me later and asked how we could have him back more often. They were taken by your knowledge and experiences and the way you conveyed those into great stories. So just wanted you to know that it went extremely well. Also, I think the dean of the school is going to call, so heads up."

"What for?"

"To say thank you and who knows what else."

A little flummoxed, Alex said, "Well, thank you, I didn't expect that."

Amanda went on, "I need to run, have a class starting shortly, but we'll definitely want you to come back and speak to some of our other students. Oh, I'll be looking forward to the updated version. Thanks, and talk soon."

"Yep, talk to you later."

Michaela was listening to the conversation and what particularly stuck out was how it was so obvious that others thought Alex was terrific as well. She remained quiet as Alex hung up the phone. Then she quickly jumped up and said, "Look at the time. I need to run as

I've got some more things to do today. I will see you on Wednesday for sure."

As she was leaving, Alex walked her to the door and said, "Thank you so much again for the lunch. That was so sweet."

Smiling, she said, "My pleasure, and by the way, I like your apartment."

Alex leaned in and gave her a big hug and said, "See you soon, and by the way, you need to wear either shorts or jeans on Wednesday."

As she left, Michaela was thinking, *Shorts or jeans? Hmmm, I wonder what he's got up his sleeve.* She was smiling inwardly as she thought, *I can't wait until Wednesday.*

*****

Wednesday evening rolled around, and it was date night. Alex and Michaela were leaving the complex when she leaned over and sweetly said, "So what are we doing tonight?"

Alex smiled. "Give it a few minutes and you'll see." A few minutes later, Alex pulled into the parking lot of a bowling alley.

Michaela looked at him with a big smile. "Bowling! All right, I love to bowl, let's go!" She was excited!

They bowled several games, laughed so hard at times, congratulated each other for good results, and teased one another on misses. If one didn't know it, you would think that they've been together for a long time. They simply felt at ease with each other. Between games, they ordered a couple of cheeseburgers and fries with a Coke. They talked and talked, relaxed, and just had fun! As he was walking Michaela back to her apartment, she said, "Alex, I had a blast tonight. That was so much fun!"

Alex could only smile and say, "I'm glad." After a pause, they reached her door and he said, "So Friday night?"

Michaela with a wink let him know, "I would like that."

As Alex leaned in and gave Michaela a hug and this time a little peck on the cheek, he said, "It's a date, and it will be formal, so I'll be in a coat and tie. I'll see you later!" He turned and walked away as Michaela closed her door, and he listened for her to lock it.

Michaela's curiosity was running rampant as she got herself ready for bed. She thought, *I just had a marvelous time tonight.* She reflected for a moment at how going bowling was a stroke of genius as she told herself, "I had such a good time."

Now she was curious, she wondered, *Where are we going Friday so dressed up?* The anticipation was more than intriguing to her.

Sheryl called Michaela the next day right on que to ask how the date went and Michaela said, "We went bowling and I loved it!"

Sheryl was like, "Bowling? Really?"

"Yes, and I had the best time!"

This plainly made Sheryl smile and filled her heart with joy. Sheryl wanted to press her for more info, but it was clear that they had a great time together. She also observed that whether they had figured it out or not they had natural chemistry.

*****

It was now Friday and Michaela was almost giddy with anticipation. To her, the wait for the last forty-eight hours had been almost cruel, but it was now time for her date. She was excited while she was getting ready. Finally, the time came and Alex as usual was right on time.

Michaela opened the door, and there was Alex looking all GQ in a great suit. She whispered, "You look very handsome!"

Alex was slow to reply as he was in awe, simply speechless, but he finally managed to squeak out a "Thank you."

Alex, still awestruck upon seeing Michaela, was searching his brain for the right words when he suddenly blurted out, "Michaela, you are beautiful!"

With a little blush, Michaela said, "Thank you...you are too kind!"

After a moment, Alex managed to collect himself enough to ask, "Are you ready?"

"Yes, I am."

As they were driving, Michaela leaned over and placed her hand on Alex's shoulder and asked with a smile, "Where are we going, or is it a surprise?"

Alex, with a grin, said, "No, no surprise tonight. We have reservations at the Hot and Hot Fish Club."

Michaela said, "I've heard of that place. I hear it's one of the best restaurants around."

Alex continued, "Well, that's where we're going as I've always loved the cuisine and dishes that Chris Hastings creates. He's the master chef, and I think the owner as well. Anyway, I thought you would enjoy eating there."

On the drive, Michaela was smiling as she thought how Alex always had a plan for their evenings, they were never predictable. This made her feel like she was important and respected. She reflected on how guys previously, which included her ex-husband, would take her out trying to impress her. She felt like she didn't need to be impressed because she thought if she said yes to go on a date with someone, then trying to further impress her wasn't needed. By her thinking, if someone was going out of their way to impress her, then they weren't being genuine. And really all she wanted was to be treated with respect and like a real person, and most of all, she wanted to know that who she was out with was being honest and genuine. Working to impress her from her perspective was not being either honest or genuine. Yet with Alex, she felt he wasn't trying to impress her, he was simply being himself, being genuine. She could see in him that he was like, "This is who I am, take it or leave it." But what she noticed most about Alex were the little things. He respected people, and in turn, people respected him. As they neared the restaurant, Alex found a parking space about a block away. Michaela felt this is going to be a very nice evening with Alex as she had a smile on her heart!

Once again, they were right on time for the reservation. It was an early reservation, six thirty, but the restaurant was packed. Partly because of his training, it made Alex fully aware of what was going on around him. He took notice as they walked through the restaurant to their table at how people would stop talking to stare at this statuesque woman who was quite literally stunning! Alex held Michaela's chair as she sat down. Even after they were seated, he felt many sets of eyes watching them. It didn't bother Alex, but he was fully aware. He wasn't sure if Michaela was aware or not, but he was not going to bring it up as he wanted her to feel comfortable.

Michaela, reviewing the menu, leaned over the table and asked, "So what's good here?"

Alex whispered kind of jokingly, "Everything! Chris Hastings is one of the best chefs around, so you can't go wrong. I was thinking about one of the fish dishes."

Michaela said, "That is what I was thinking."

Alex asked, "Would you like to share a dessert?"

"Yes, that sounds good. Which one?"

"May I suggest the white chocolate and raspberry bread pudding."

She responded, "Oh, that sounds delicious."

The waitress came to the table and asked, "Are you ready to order?"

Alex replied, "Yes, we will have a bottle of sauvignon blanc. The lady will have the hearts of escarole and arugula salad, the grilled black grouper, and I will have a cup of gumbo along with the roasted red snapper."

The waitress said, "Excellent choices!"

Alex continued, "For dessert, we will share the white chocolate and raspberry bread pudding with some decaf coffee."

Dinner was beyond delicious as it always is at the Hot and Hot. They talked and laughed all during dinner as if they had been close friends for years. While they were enjoying dessert, Chris Hastings stopped by their table to say hello and ask how their meals were.

"Excellent as always," Alex replied.

Chris said, smiling, "So glad you all came out tonight and that was a good wine selection with your fish dishes." Looking at Michaela, he asked, "How do you like the bread pudding?"

She said, "It's the first time that I've had it, and I love it!"

"Great!" he said. "Thank you and look forward to seeing you again!" This was Chris Hastings' way, as he routinely walked through the dining areas throughout the evening to greet and talk with guests.

They finished their bread pudding and talked for a little longer. As they were about to leave, Michaela looked at Alex and said, "Thank you for bringing me here, this place was really good!" This made Alex very happy. He paused for a moment then looked Michaela right in the eye and said with all the sincerity that his heart could muster, "Michaela, you look so elegant and simply gorgeous tonight!"

Michaela, surprised and with a little blush, said, "Thank you" as she placed her hand over her heart. She broke the moment by asking, "So what are we going to do now?"

Responding, Alex said, "We are going to watch a movie at my place, if that is okay with you?"

"That sounds fun…what movie?"

Alex said, "How about *The Sound of Music*?"

Michaela said, smiling, "That sounds perfect!"

"I have wine, coffee, and popcorn."

She says with a smile, "Well, what else do we need!"

They left the restaurant, and Michaela leaned into Alex and whispered, "We need to come back here sometime." This made Alex smile.

As they were walking to the car, Michaela reached over and gently clutched Alex's hand as they strolled down the sidewalk hand in hand. As they neared the car, Alex stopped and stepped in front of Michaela. He paused for a moment, looking deeply into her bright, crystal-blue eyes, not saying a word. With his left hand, he pushed her long brown hair behind her ear. Alex put his right arm around her waist and slowly moved close then leaned in and kissed her. As he did, Michaela wrapped both arms around Alex and kissed him back as passionately as she could. They were in a long embrace, which got the attention of a couple of passersby who honked. They didn't even notice. Finally, they separated; it nearly took their breath away, and they each had a slight blush and a big smile, thinking that was awesome. They went on to the car, and as they were driving home, Michaela placed her hand on Alex's arm. She laughed as she kiddingly said, "You know it took me three dates to get to first base with you." They each busted out laughing!

Arriving back home, Alex stopped at her door and said, "Why don't you get into something more comfortable to watch the movie?" She thought that was a good idea and said, "Okay."

As she entered her apartment, Alex said, "Let me say again you looked lovely tonight!"

She smiled and responded, "Thank you, give me about fifteen minutes."

"Okay, just come on in no need to knock."

While changing into some shorts and T-shirt, Michaela was still thinking about that kiss. She thought that kiss greatly surpassed her dreams, that it touched her heart! She felt as though she had "stayed kissed," it touched her so passionately.

She walked into his apartment, and he had already changed into some shorts and a T-shirt himself. Alex said, "Grab a spot on the couch I'm making some popcorn." After taking a seat, Michaela spoke up, "Hey, I like your couch it's very comfortable, wow!"

Alex chuckled. "Yeah, sometimes I think too comfortable as I've fallen asleep so many times right where you're sitting." He brought in the popcorn and drinks then placed the movie into the DVD player, turned it on, and said, "And away we go." As he sat down on the couch, Michaela proceeded to move close.

Michaela, who had never seen the movie, was really enjoying it. She commented on how beautiful the surroundings were in the movie. Alex informed her that much of the movie was shot in Salzburg, Austria, and that area. He let her know that whole valley and south of there was a beautiful area.

She noted, "It sounds like you've been there!"

Alex, with a short, quiet response, said, "Yes, I have." And let it go.

Michaela took note of his response and thought he's been to Europe. Her mind wandered from the movie for a moment as she wondered where else has he traveled.

The movie was nearing the end, and Michaela had cuddled up with Alex. Her head was laying against his shoulder as the movie ended. He started to say something and then noticed that Michaela was sound asleep. She looked so peaceful he didn't have the heart to wake her. He laid a pillow at the end of the couch and gently laid her head down on it while swinging her legs up onto the couch. The soft blanket he had laying across the back of the couch he pulled over her and covered her up. He just let her sleep.

Alex locked the door and cleaned up their mess as quietly as he could. Before he turned out the lights, he took one last look at her… his mind drifted as he believed she looked like an *angel*.

Alex is one to not need much sleep. Thus, the next morning, he was an early riser. He was quiet as he walked to the kitchen to make some coffee. Michaela was sound asleep and still looking like an *angel*. After fixing his coffee, he went into his office and started doing some work as it was still early. Alex had been working for a little more than an hour at his desk when this *angel* wrapped in a blanket poked her head around the corner.

Alex said, "Well, good morning."

Michaela, looking a little sleepy, said, "You were right, that couch is comfortable. I think it's more comfortable than my bed," as she chuckled. She continued, "When did I fall asleep?"

Alex replied, "I'm not exactly sure, but I think it was in the last fifteen to twenty minutes of the movie. In fact, I rewound the movie back to about that point so you could finish it this morning." He continued, "I have some coffee made and some breakfast for you."

"Oh, yeah, what do you have?"

"How about some yogurt, fresh strawberries, blueberries, and grapes with some orange juice."

She said, "That sounds great, I would like that!"

He said, "Just have a seat back on the couch and give me a minute."

Michaela sheepishly whispered, "I must look awful."

Alex quickly disagreed, "No, you don't, you look great!" This helped her feel relaxed.

He turned the movie back on and she watched the final fifteen minutes. Alex made her a cup of coffee. He knew just how she liked it because he had watched her preparing her coffee the evening prior. He got breakfast ready and sat down on the couch with her while they ate. They were chatting away when suddenly, there was a knock at the door. Alex looked bewildered as he said, "I wonder who that can be."

When Alex cracked the door open, there was Sheryl. He said, "Good morning, Sheryl."

She responded, "I'm sorry to bother you this early."

"Early? It's not early. It's about eight thirty, whatcha need?"

Sheryl continued, "I was looking for Michaela, but when I knocked on her door, she didn't answer, yet her car is here. Do you know where she could be?"

Alex playfully answered, "Maybe, what's it worth to you?"

Sheryl stared at him for a moment then Alex broke the silence with, "I do know where she is because she's sitting right here," as he opened the door further.

Michaela, with a little grin, said, "Come on in."

Sheryl with a big grin on her face said, "Okay what's going on here?"

Michaela, being coy, somberly said, "Breakfast."

Alex asked, "Would you like a cup of coffee?"

"Yes, that would be great," Sheryl answered with a smile.

When Alex went to the kitchen, Sheryl leaned over to Michaela and whispered, "Did you sleep here last night?"

Smiling, Michaela with a little tease in her voice, answered, "Why yes, I did!"

Sheryl, looking a little shocked, said, "Really?"

Michaela laughingly said, "Yes, I did right here on the couch."

Sheryl, looking a little perplexed, somewhere between relieved and disappointed replied, "For a minute, I…" That's all she got out when Michaela interrupted her and softly said, "No, I only got to first base." She laughed quietly.

"What?" Sheryl replied.

"Don't worry that's a joke between Alex and me," Michaela noted.

Sheryl drank her coffee and was dying to ask more questions, but she managed to suppress the urge to ask. The three of them talked for a few more minutes when Sheryl said, "I need to leave, so I guess I will see you guys later."

Sheryl had left, and Michaela was getting ready to leave as well when Alex told her, "This week, I will be performing Air Force Reserve duty on the gulf coast. I'm leaving out tomorrow and will be back next Sunday." He went on to say, "I was thinking that since I will be gone all week, that we might go out again tonight if you're not busy?"

Michaela, with a big smile, replied, "Yes, that would be nice."

"That's terrific, I'm still working out what to do even though I have an idea. So wear jeans, bring a sweatshirt, and I'll stop by at six thirty."

As Michaela was leaving, she stopped, turned, and gave Alex a big kiss and then stated with a huge smile, "I had an awesome time last night, see you later!"

As Alex closed the door, he had that feeling of a warm heart. A feeling that he hadn't experienced in a long, long time.

*****

To prepare for his date, Alex dug out an old astronomy book that he's had since his college days. He refreshed his memory of the cosmos and star clusters. During the afternoon, he bought several items for the date. Alex was looking forward to this date as he felt that things were developing nicely with Michaela. In addition, he was really liking this lady; she was something else! Something special! Finally, he was going to be gone for a week so he wondered if the separation would make him yearn for her company.

That evening, Alex and Michaela were leaving the complex when she asked, "So what are you going to surprise me with tonight?"

He smiled at Michaela and said, "As tempting as it is to keep you in suspense"—as he reached for her hand—"I'm not going to do that to you." He continued, "We are going on a picnic at Oak Mountain State Park and just enjoy ourselves until dark then we are going to do some stargazing." Continuing, "Also, because it's been a long time since my astronomy class in college, I brought my textbook to help us sort out the constellations."

Michaela kissed his hand as she said, "I love picnics, and it's a nice clear evening, plus I love to stargaze." She went on, "I'm glad you brought your astronomy book, but I know many of the constellations." Michaela noted, "Gazing at the stars provided some tranquil time, which assisted in getting me through some difficult times in the past." Alex thought that was interesting.

They found a great spot in the state park. It was by the lake where they spread out their picnic blanket. Alex cracked open a bottle of wine, and they dug into their meal. Afterward, they went for a walk around the lake as their conversation flowed so easily.

It was getting dark, and soon, it would be dark enough to see the stars. They were far enough outside the city that hopefully the ambient light would be diminished enough to see clearly. Michaela had slipped on her sweatshirt, and they were laying on the blanket quietly sipping their wine. They were holding hands when Michaela started thinking she felt so peaceful with Alex. She thought, *He's respectful, he's genuine, he makes me feel good about myself.* She could hardly believe that they only met a week ago, and yet it feels like she's known him forever. She glanced over at Alex and thought, *He seems to always be composed, nothing seems to ruffle him, he has a quiet strength, he truly cares, and he makes me feel safe.*

Michaela felt in her heart that this may be going someplace good with Alex. This got her to thinking, *Was it right to go much further without telling him what she's been going through for the past four years? He's such a good man and I don't want to hurt him just in case he couldn't handle the situation.* This was weighing heavily on her mind, but she also felt like she was beginning to fall for Alex.

Michaela looked at Alex and whispered, "Can I ask you something?"

Alex rolled over onto his side and replied, "Of course, you can ask me anything you want!"

She continued, "I don't want to go into any detail right now, but how do you deal with turmoil in your past?"

This perked Alex up, as he moved a little closer to Michaela rolling onto his stomach. She was laying on her back, and Alex held her hand. He gazed into her eyes for a moment of silence then said, "Michaela, listen to me, I don't know what your past is, and I figure you'll let me know when you feel the time is right. Just know that many people have deep roots and deep wounds. We have some wounds that have never healed, and we have lived with them for so long that we don't even know that they are still there. Pain generally has deep roots and the only way to dig it out is to forgive others, to forgive ourselves, and to have *faith*. Now, I don't know if that applies to you, but it sure applies to me!"

That admission took Michaela by surprise. She had been thinking, *Here is this great guy who always seems to have his life together, and he is admitting that he's been through tough times.* It made her curious, but this was not the time.

Alex continued, "Michaela, know this, there is nothing you could say that would change the feelings I have growing for you! We don't live in the past, we live in the present, and for the future. Let me say a couple more things, after which I'll shut up so we can look at the stars. You make me want to stand and smile every day! Plus, what I believe is, what is meant to be will always find a way. Just have *faith!*"

Michaela laid there, trying to fight back tears thinking Alex is a terrific person!

Seeing that she was getting a little teary-eyed, Alex leaned over and gave her a nice kiss. He then said, "Okay, enough about that for now, let's look at some stars."

Michaela replied, "Absolutely, I'm going to show you some good ones."

She paused for a moment longer as she thought it was sure nice lying here next to Alex. She spoke up, "You know this was one of my favorite things to do when I was a little girl."

Her silence was broken when Alex squeezed her hand and pointed over to the constellation of Orion. Alex had a decent knowledge of the stars, but this was one of Michaela's passions, so she began to point out other stars and constellations.

She pointed out stars like Sirius, Antares, and Altair. She continued, "You mentioned Orion, did you know that the upper left star of Orion is the red giant Betelgeuse and the star at the bottom right is Rigel? Also, the starry area under the belt is the Orion Nebula. I don't recall the names of the three stars on the belt, but I do remember that two of them begin with an A." She said, "See that bright star over there, that's Vega, it's in the constellation of Lyra."

Michaela continued to scan the sky when she pointed, "Right there above Orion is the Pleiades star cluster, and that bright area to the left is the Perseus star cluster or constellation."

Alex said, "Wow, that's impressive!"

Michaela then pointed and said, "See that fuzzy looking star right there?"

"Yes, what star is that?" Alex replied.

"It's not a star, it's a galaxy." Michaela continued, "That's the Andromeda Galaxy. Our galaxy is the Milky Way, which has between two hundred to four hundred billion stars. But Andromeda has over one trillion stars."

Alex was listening intently and keenly focused on Michaela's every word sometimes glancing over to stare at her in amazement.

After a pause, she went on to say, "God is so vast He goes on to infinity… I can't grasp or even imagine His enormity!" As she swept her hand across the sky, she says, "You know all of this is His canvas, and He creates all these trillions of stars like it's His painting."

There was a moment of silence then Michaela goes on, "Our glorious God, the God of trillions of stars and billions of galaxies… *He* knows my name!"

At this, Alex's eyes widened, he quickly turned his head and gazed at Michaela in sweet adoration.

Then Michaela repeats it, "The God of all of this knows my name! And he has a plan just for me, and I'm going to figure it out one day what that plan is!" She then takes a deep breath and sighs.

After a moment, she ended the silence as she says, "And that's how I see this whole thing we call life."

Alex hadn't uttered a sound, had listened carefully, and was literally in awe of this woman!

Michaela took another breath and peeked over at Alex and said, "What are you thinking?"

Alex turned his head and peered directly into her eyes and softly said, "I've never known anyone like you before."

Michaela, looking back skyward, nonchalantly replied, "Well, I'm simply a single star in an infinite universe."

Alex, pausing for a moment while looking skyward, softly replied, "Yes, but some stars are brighter than others!"

Michaela still peering toward the heavens had a big smile come over her face and her heart smiled even more.

They continued to stargaze a little longer as they snuggled closer as the summer night air turned a bit cooler. Not saying much, they simply enjoyed each other's company before finally calling it a night.

As they said good night, Michaela realized that she wasn't going to see Alex again for a week. This made her sad.

All the while, Alex was thinking the same thing. He wouldn't get to see her for a week. He told her that no matter how busy that he would find time to call her in the evenings. This made Michaela very happy.

7

Their Relationship Grows

Alex was all packed for his week of Reserve duty. He had loaded his car and was readying to leave but needed to make one stop. Alex walked down the breezeway and knocked on apartment 2207. It was a moment later, Michaela answered the door. When she saw Alex, a beaming smile came over her face as she said, "Hello."

Alex spoke up, "Well, I'm all packed, loaded, and ready to leave but wanted to say goodbye."

Michaela was standing there all solemn when she quietly said, "I'm going to miss you this week!" This made Alex's heart feel all warm inside as he reached out and grabbed her hands. He moved in a little closer and concurred.

"I'm going to miss you too!" Focusing his glance directly into her stunningly beautiful crystal blue eyes, he felt as if time was standing still. After a few moments of silence, Michaela leaned in and kissed Alex so tenderly. They held that embrace for several moments. Finally, Alex said, "I guess I better hit the road. I will definitely call you when I arrive."

Michaela whispered, "Thank you and please drive safely."

"I will," as Alex walked away.

She watched until he went around the corner and down the stairs. Her mind wandered, assessing all that had happened since last Sunday. She thought, *I've only known this man one whole week, so why does it feel as if I've known him for much, much longer?* She couldn't put her finger on it, but whatever it was, it made her heart smile and feel so warm!

*****

Sunday evening and Sheryl asked Michaela over for dinner. Afterward, they cracked open a bottle of wine. They began to talk when Sheryl with a giggle said, "So what's new this week!" They each busted up laughing.

Michaela was sipping on her wine while she examined her facial expression, then she asked, "You planned this, didn't you? I mean, you set us up, Alex and me."

"Who me?" Sheryl snickered with a guilty look all over her face. Then Sheryl came clean. She replied, "Okay, I'm busted, but you see I've known Alex for quite a while and I'm one of the very few people who knows a lot about him. You have probably figured out he's a private person as far as his personal life goes. I won't tell you anything further about his past as I feel it's his decision to inform you of his history when he's ready. Oh, don't worry, it's not bad, but once you find out more about his background, I think you'll respect him even further. That's all I'll say at this time. And yes, to answer your question, I will come clean. I did work to get you guys to meet each other. Like I said, I've known and respected him for quite a while, and then after I got to know you better, it became so obvious to me that you two could really hit it off!"

Michaela was thinking for a moment then said, "So did he ask you to introduce us?"

"Oh, not at all it was all me." Sheryl continued, "I'm pretty sure he had never seen you prior to the day you met. On that day, we were looking out the doors wondering about the noise around the pool. He spotted you laying there in your black bikini. He asked, who is that?"

So I asked him to stick around for a few minutes as I thought you would be coming in shortly, and you did just as I had planned! I hope you're not mad?"

Michaela, smiling, said, "No, I'm not mad at all. I should probably thank you!"

Sheryl said, "From what I've seen and heard, it appears that you guys have great chemistry."

Michaela replied, "I feel like we do. He's been a gentleman, respectful, seems honest, and not put on either, he is simply genuine! I've never met anyone quite like him. With him there's no charade, he's like, 'This is who I am as a person.' He's quiet, and I can tell when I'm talking, he is listening to me attentively. He makes me feel that I'm the most important person in the room."

"So how many dates have you guys been on?" Sheryl asked.

Replying, Michaela said, "We've been on four dates, and they have all been so very different, I've had a blast!" She continued, "Most guys always want to take you to dinner then go to a movie, you know the same old thing every time. So boring and never do they ask me what I like to do! But our dates have been so creative. Most importantly, the dates showed me that he was listening to me on our first date when we each discussed what we liked to do."

Sheryl was staring at Michaela over her wineglass; smiling, she said, "You're going to miss him this week, aren't you?"

Michaela with a blush admitted, "Yes, I'm missing him already, what is wrong with me."

"Well, I would say nothing is wrong...actually I would say everything is right!" Smiling, Sheryl continued, "You like him, don't you?"

"Yes, I do!" she said with a dreamy look on her face. Michaela went on, "You know what he told me on our first date?"

"No, what?"

"We had a nice meal, some wine, our conversation was so effortless, he made me feel relaxed. It was getting about time to leave while we were sipping on the last of the wine. He all of a sudden had this serious look on his face and said, 'I've got something that I need to tell you!' I didn't know what he was about to say! He went on, 'I need to let you know that I don't kiss on the first date!'

"I was taken aback, totally off guard, but it was so cute the way he said it and totally disarming. It took any stress I had left completely away, it made me feel respected. I started to say something, and you know what he said?"

Sheryl looked amazed. "No, what did he say?"

Michaela, still smiling, said, "When I started to say something, he held up his hand with a little laugh and said, 'No, don't try and change my mind. You're not getting to first base with me tonight!'"

"He did?"

"Yes, he did and then we each broke out laughing! He made me feel so comfortable, and I can't explain it, but I feel very safe with him as well."

Sheryl curiously said, "So did you kiss on the second date?"

"Nope!"

"Really, so have you two kissed yet?"

"On our third date! We got all dressed up and he took me to dinner at the Hot and Hot Fish Club, it was awesome! We were walking to the car after dinner when suddenly he stopped, stepped right in front of me, brushed my hair back, and gently kissed me. Oh, it was passionate, I had to hold onto him to keep from buckling! Let me tell you, I don't think I've ever been kissed like that before, ever!"

Sheryl, fanning herself, simply said, "Whew!"

Michaela says, "Exactly, also that kiss, our first kiss was like a promise of the love that was to come, I can't explain it but that's just how I feel."

Sheryl was like, "Wow, he really touched your heart! I am so happy for you!"

Michaela replied, "Thank you, but I also keep telling myself that it's only been a week."

Sheryl replied, "Okay, cut that out, yes, it has only been a week, but it is so obvious that you two have chemistry and a special connection! It's written all over each of you."

Michaela asked, "So have you talked with Alex?"

"Not really. I saw him in passing yesterday afternoon and I asked him how things were going."

"And?"

"He's not one to say much on personal matters. When I asked how things were going with you, he blushed and had a slight smile then only said, 'She is extremely special, I like her, a lot!' He didn't say much as that's not his way, but the *way* he said it, I could tell that he is more than smitten!"

Sheryl continued, "I told you that I wouldn't give you any more information, but there is one point I would like to make."

Michaela said, "Oh yeah, what's that?"

"You said for some reason you feel very safe when you are with him, right?"

"Yes, I did," Michaela responded. "I don't know what it is, but he makes me feel safe!"

Sheryl added, "Well, think about it like this, you should feel safe around him. He's one of those quiet people, he wouldn't say anything, nor flaunt his abilities. But know he is military-trained in combat fight; and prior to joining the military, he studied for a while, learning the Wing Chun style of kung fu, whatever that is. He showed me one time where a couple of pressure points were on the body. He said that if I ever got into trouble, I could aim for those and hurt someone enough to get away no matter how big they are. He showed me one spot, he squeezed this pressure point with his finger and firmly pressed. I immediately went 'Ouch, ouch,' and he had to hold me up because my knees buckled…it hurt! So yeah, you should feel very safe with him! He would never let anyone harm you in his presence!"

Michaela in a low whisper said, "I never thought about him like that, but he is in the military, isn't he?"

Sheryl added, "Yes, he is, but more than that he is a remarkable person! Just stay the course, you'll find out." Sheryl looking at Michaela saw that she was in deep thought. She finally interrupted her silence by asking, "What are you thinking about?"

Michaela added, "You know, being around Alex, one would never guess that he had that kind of expertise, especially since he is so quiet and calm."

Sheryl quickly said, "But he could flip the switch, so to speak, and protect someone in an instant!"

Michaela continued by asking, "Sheryl, when should I tell Alex that I'm still recovering from cancer? I'm a little fearful it would make a difference in the way he thinks about me?"

Sheryl was adamant, "Let me tell you right now, it will *not* make one bit of difference to Alex! He is *not* that kind of a guy! He does *not* cut and run from challenges."

"So when should I tell him about my cancer?"

"I don't know, I can't answer that question. All I can tell you is to have *faith*, have patience, you'll know in your heart when the time is right," Sheryl answered.

*****

While Alex was out of town performing his Air Force Reserve duty, it allowed Sheryl and Michaela some time to get together. Michaela stayed busy by working and taking care of some of her new customers. The two of them had dinner together several times and were able to engage in some quality conversation time. This was great for Sheryl as she was able to get to know Michaela even better. Yet it kept Michaela busy, so the week would go by faster because she was indeed missing Alex.

Alex arrived home from the coast in the afternoon on Sunday. As he pulled into the apartment complex, he stopped at the office. Alex was wearing his air force battle dress uniform (BDUs), camouflage, as he walked into the lobby. As luck would have it, there were Sheryl and Michaela standing there talking. He walked almost right up on them before Sheryl finally saw him as Michaela had her back to the door. Sheryl leaned over and touched Michaela on the arm and whispered, "I think you should turn around."

Michaela turned and saw Alex standing there in his BDUs, and she couldn't help herself. She jumped into his arms with a slight tear in her eye as she squealed, "Oh my god, I can't believe your back, I missed you!" Then she planted a big kiss of welcome back on Alex. They were hugging when Sheryl began to clear her throat and finally interrupted by saying, "Hey, you guys, I'm standing right here too!"

They all laughed as Alex said, "Sorry about that, Sheryl."

He and Michaela turned and faced Sheryl and Alex gave her a quick hug. The three of them were talking, catching up, and just generally laughing. They were oblivious to their surroundings and Michaela was standing just to Alex's right as they faced Sheryl.

The three of them were so engrossed in their conversation that they didn't even see Matt coming up behind them. Alex was glancing to his left as something caught his eye out the front windows. Then he heard this voice behind him say, "Hey, babe, why don't you come on out by the pool."

Alex quickly looked to his right just in time to see this guy place his hand on Michaela's left shoulder. It was the "knucklehead," Matt.

Alex began to glare at the guy just as he said to Alex, "Hey, General." That statement didn't set well with Alex either.

It was then that Michaela shouted out sternly, "Take your hand off me!"

When the knucklehead didn't do it and said, "Oh, don't be like that, come on out by the pool and have some fun."

This triggered something in Alex. This guy had his hand on Michaela, and she clearly didn't want anything to do with him. Alex quickly launched into combat fight mode as he saw this guy as a threat to Michaela. He reached over with his left hand and grabbed the knuckleheads right-hand fingers on Michaela's shoulder. He twisted them in such a way that really hurts. Alex stepped in front of him, twisting first his fingers then his arm. He reached up with his right hand and grabbed the guy under his right bicep and pressed the key pressure point on the inside of the bicep with his thumb. Alex did this all-in-one quick motion taking the knucklehead completely by surprise. The pressure Alex put on him took the guy to his knees as the knucklehead began to yell, "Ow, ow, ow, that hurts!"

Alex said sternly, "Yes, it's supposed to!" He continued in a very forceful voice, "I believe the lady has asked you multiple times to not touch her, SO DON'T DO IT AGAIN! DO YOU UNDERSTAND?" He merely nodded, so Alex twisted his fingers and arm a little more and applied even more pressure, then Alex asked again, "I said, DO YOU UNDERSTAND?"

"Yes, yes, yes, I do!"

Alex continued, "Also, Sheryl has asked you several times to keep the noise down, and to stop bothering the other residents! So you need to stop, and you need to apologize to both of these ladies… now!"

Alex put a little more pressure to his fingers and arm, and he came through with, "I'm sorry, I'm sorry, I'm sorry…it won't happen again! Oh, please let go!"

Finally, Alex said, "And by the way, I'm not a general, I'm paid in the rank of lieutenant colonel, so either get it right or say nothing! Got it!"

"Yes, sir!"

Alex let go of his grip then helped him up. As the knucklehead was shaking his arm, Alex reminded him, "Now remember what you just promised. And by the way, this lady right here is my girlfriend! Understand!"

"Yes, sir, I'm sorry I didn't know!"

Alex guided and walked him to the lobby doors. Alex was walking with him and talking to him in a tone just low enough that the girls couldn't hear. They paused at the door for a moment then the guy exited out still shaking his hand and arm. They could hear him mumbling, "Damn, that hurt!"

During this interaction, Sheryl and Michaela were standing there in awe and disbelief. They were amazed at how quickly and easily Alex took the knucklehead down. Alex had walked with him to the door to ensure he exited.

When Alex stepped away, Sheryl looked at Michaela and said with a deep breath, "Did you see that?" She received no response from Michaela as she was standing there staring at Alex. Sheryl noticed her silent stare and remained quiet.

Finally, Michaela looked at Sheryl and softly said, "He protected me!"

Sheryl agreed, "Yes, he did!"

Michaela said in a crackly voice, "Nobody has ever done that for me before." She continued, "And he called me his girlfriend." This made her feel warm and tingly all over as her heart smiled in joy.

Right then, Alex had walked back over and asked, "Are you guys, okay?"

Sheryl quickly blurted out, "Thank you for doing that."

Alex simply waved his hand and replied, "Oh, no problem. I don't think you'll have any more problems with the knucklehead!" Alex continued, "You know that's the first time that I've done anything like that in over fifteen years. Sorry about that!"

Sheryl asked, "You could have really hurt him bad, couldn't you?"

"Yeah, but that was never my intent. I simply wanted to get his attention!"

Sheryl continued, "So what were you telling him as you guys walked to the door? We couldn't hear."

Alex paused for a moment as he peered outside then returned his glance back to Sheryl and said, "I told him that what he did, putting his hands on someone like that was very disrespectful. I told him that he needs to treat women with respect, which doesn't mean that he can place his hands on them. I further told him that he was an adult now, so it was time to begin to act as one. That means you respect everyone! Finally, I told him to stop acting like a teenager and grow up."

Sheryl with a smile replied, "I wonder what he'll do, after all he is a knucklehead!" They all busted out laughing.

Alex said with a smirk, "Well, give him some time. I've seen young guys like him for years. He's just trying to find his way as a young adult. I think he'll learn but be patient."

Michaela, stepping in close to Alex, faintly said, "Thank you!" Then she wrapped her arms around his neck and planted a light kiss!

When she finally broke the embrace, Alex said, "My pleasure, if that's the reward then I'll do it more often, wow!" All three laughed.

After this incident, Michaela learned a couple of key traits about Alex. One was that he thought it was important for people to respect others and that he did not like people being disrespectful. The second key feature was that he could and would engage with anyone who may threaten her. This made her feel very safe and the thought comforted her. She knew he was protective of her not in a macho way but in a very calm and easygoing matter of fact way. This warmed Michaela's heart with great trust.

*****

Even though Alex and Michaela talked several times during the week they still missed each other. Upon his return, they immediately picked up right where they left off.

Over the next month, they went out or saw each other three to four times a week. With his job, Alex had a few out-of-town overnight stays, but most of the time, he was home. They did so many fun things as they began to plan their dates together. Michaela really liked how Alex would engage her in their decision-making, this made her feel respected and a true partner.

They discovered they each loved Mexican food, sushi, Thai cuisine, and going on picnics. Watching movies at home with a bucket of popcorn cuddled up on the couch was a favorite pastime. In the evenings, they loved to stargaze and would take walks hand in hand. When they went out to restaurants, sometimes they would occasionally split an entrée and every so often, Michaela would pick up the check. Alex liked that and it made Michaela feel like a real and faithful partner!

Another of their favorite past times was to go to a restaurant bar, only order appetizers and wine, then have easy conversation. They just felt so comfortable together. And there was no need to try to impress each other…they were just themselves.

Alex would take her to the driving range. She had never hit a golf ball in her entire life, but she enjoyed it. Under Alex's tutelage, he noticed she had a natural swing. Her ball striking was pretty darn good! She was learning to enjoy the game, having fun! Plus, Michaela liked wearing the cute golf outfits. Alex liked them too!

There were times when they would simply take a drive on a Saturday through rural Alabama. They enjoyed looking at the scenery, stopping at parks, take a few pictures, just have fun. They liked to stop at some random small-town café and enjoy a country meal. They quite literally enjoyed each other's company!

*****

Alex and Michaela had been dating for a little more than six weeks. They enjoyed being around one another as they had very similar likes and dislikes. Michaela was getting to know her new territory and customers with her job very well.

One Saturday afternoon, they were out on a picnic. Music was playing as they relaxed on their blanket. They had finished lunch and were talking about various things. Occasionally, they would have moments of silence, which was nice to take in the smells, the sounds, and the fresh air.

Michaela was feeling so warmhearted in being with Alex. She was thinking, *he makes me feel so good about myself.* Michaela continued her thoughts, *I absolutely trust him, he speaks from the heart, I can confide in him, and he puts me before himself.* It was then that she decided, *Okay, it's time to tell him about my cancer.*

She sat up and said in a matter-of-fact tone, "Alex, we have been getting along great and I really like you!"

"Well, I really like you too, a lot!" he replied.

She went on to say, "I know you do, but wait a minute, I need to tell you some things and all I need is for you to listen."

Alex nodded. "Okay, you have my undivided attention."

Michaela began by saying, "I am in the process of recovering from cancer."

Alex didn't react, he just listened as he wanted her to talk. But that declaration from Michaela didn't surprise Alex. He had never let on, but he had seen her prescription bottles in her apartment and knew what those medications were used for. He already knew that she was recovering from breast cancer. Alex felt that she would tell him when she was ready.

Michaela continued, explaining that she was over four years survival from her breast cancer and seemed to be doing well. She told him that she had a total mastectomy and then had to go through reconstructive surgery.

Alex held up his hand as if he wanted to ask a question and Michaela said, "You have a question?"

"Yes, I wanted to ask, are you of similar breast size now as you were prior?"

Michaela with a smile answered, "Yes, I am exactly the same size as before. The surgeon took pictures and measurements prior to my original surgery that he used for my reconstruction. You see, I felt my original cup size was what the good Lord gave me so that was what was meant to be!" She continued, "I am the same now as before with the exception of a couple of scars." Alex didn't say a word and just smiled as he thought what a remarkable woman she is. He thought so many women would have let their egos get in the way and take the opportunity to increase their cup size, but not Michaela.

Continuing, she let him know that several months after her breast cancer diagnosis and chemotherapy that she was then diagnosed with ovarian cancer. Now this Alex didn't know. She described the chemotherapy that she had to endure. Talked about how she lost all her hair then kidded, "At least I didn't have to shave my legs." This made them laugh! She told him how she wore a head cover all the time.

She continued by telling Alex that she was married when she was first diagnosed, but she caught her husband cheating on her. Michaela described to Alex how she was going through her treatments all alone. She had no family and now no husband. She discussed how she thought she had a couple of girlfriends, but for one reason or another, they abandoned her. This made Alex's heart very sad. He already knew that she had grown up in the foster care system since the age of ten resulting from the death of her parents. But to be all alone dealing with the multiple cancers and treatments was nothing short of unfathomable. Alex had a difficult time trying to imagine how bad life must have been for her, yet she endured. This made him feel very proud of her, and he just wanted to hold her tight.

When she was finished, she sat there in silence with her head bowed. She wasn't sure how Alex would react to her confessions.

Alex scooted over next to Michaela, gently lifted her chin, and kissed her forehead. He then laid her head against his chest, stroked her hair, and held her tightly in silence. He finally raised her head and looked at her squarely in the eyes; she had some tears flowing.

Alex said, "Don't cry." He went on, "Did you know that you are a remarkable woman!" He kissed her gently on the cheek and said, "It was difficult, but you endured. God doesn't heap anymore upon us than He knows we can handle. So God is with you! Don't worry, I'm here as well."

She finally mumbled, "I was scared, I didn't know how you would take the news."

Alex replied to her, "Scared? Don't be scared!" Continuing, he said, "Look, Michaela, I like you! Neither one of us can change what has occurred in the past. Rest assured, I'll always be here for *you* for as long as you still want me around! Got it?" After he said it, he lifted her head and could see tears flowing! No words were said, just silence as he held her close.

To Michaela, no words were needed. Simply being held by Alex made her feel loved…maybe truly for the first time in her life!

Alex held her tight in complete silence for several minutes. Finally, Alex leaned back and said, "Thank you for sharing that with me!"

After a few moments, Alex continued, "Michaela, since it's a day for confessions if you're up to it, I would like to fill you in on some things too!"

Michaela wiping the tears from her cheeks, smiled, and with a little laugh said, "I'd like that."

Alex began by telling Michaela that he, too, was married. He explained how he was on active duty and described to her his assignments and some of his deployments around the world. He then began to describe his wife's mental health problems and how she progressively went downhill over time. He told her how it got to the point to where he needed to resign from active duty and transferred into the reserves. Yet in the end with assistance from her family, he had to commit her to a facility full-time. Then after a few months, he described how her family came to him recommending divorce so that Alex could move on with his life.

Michaela could see in Alex's face that by telling that story he must have agonized over some of those decisions. She could hear the torment in his voice still as he was telling her. This time, it was Michaela's turn to comfort him, and she hugged and leaned against him in silence. They sat there for the next couple of hours, not saying much when they finally called it a day. Michaela, initially worried what Alex may think or do once he found out about her past, was now feeling completely at ease. She now felt that no matter what happens that Alex would be there to support her! Michaela thought to herself, *Sheryl was right, I had nothing to worry about.* This all warmed her heart.

*****

That evening after the picnic, they decided to order a pizza for dinner. Then they turned on some music, opened a bottle of wine, and talked well into the night. They swapped more details from their pasts.

After a bit, they began to talk about the future.

Alex asked Michaela, "What kind of home would be your dream?"

She pondered that question for a few moments then smiled and said, "You know it wouldn't have to be a big home, but I would like to have a small acreage with a babbling brook running through it close to the house."

Alex teased her a little, "A babbling brook? Is that like a running creek?"

Michaela retorted back, "Yes!" With a big smile. She continued, "I would love to have a grassy field, big trees, with the babbling brook running through and a nice home up on a high spot a short way from the brook."

Alex thinking replied, "That sounds very nice, I like it!" All the while, Alex filed that very important dream of Michaela's away.

After some further discussion, Michaela leaned closer to Alex and said, "You realize I can never have children."

Alex said, "I know that!"

"Are you good with that?" she asked.

He sighed then solemnly said, "Look, Michaela, you are my main concern, and yes, I know that we couldn't ever have children naturally. But if it's okay with you we could look into adoption if we each agreed that we wanted a child."

Michaela asked, "You would do that for me, for us?"

"Well, of course, I would!"

This made Michaela feel so good and after a moment of quiet she said, "Hold me, just hold me." So they cuddled and eventually fell asleep right there on the couch.

*****

The next day, they were talking and out of the blue, Alex asked Michaela if she had ever fired a weapon. Looking a little confused, she said, "A weapon?"

Alex said let me clarify, "Have you ever been to a firing range before?"

Michaela answered, "No, I've never fired a weapon in my life."

"So would you like to learn to fire a weapon or at least go to a range and try it?" Alex asked.

She thought about it a minute and said, "Yes, I think that would be fun. Who would be my teacher?"

Alex retorted, "Me of course!" He continued, "I'll make some reservations to get us some range time in the near future."

While Alex was on a roll he asked Michaela, "Have you ever been to New York City? Or to a Broadway show?"

Michaela, looking a little surprised, said, "No, never been to either."

"Would you like to go?" Alex asked.

"Yes, I would, when?"

"Can you take off a week from Friday?" he asked.

She said, "That would be no problem."

"Great, I'll make the arrangements," Alex said.

*****

During this time, Alex was exceptionally busy with his clinical/medical position. After the situation with Cynthia, Alex dove headfirst into his work in an attempt to soothe the hurt he was feeling. In doing so, he had engaged in a vast number of clinical evaluations and studies with many of his customers. The data collection and analyses for these evaluations had Alex working many nights past midnight. If trying to get all these projects evaluated wasn't enough, a couple of months prior he had partnered with some customers to submit abstracts for national meeting presentation. They had over a dozen abstracts accepted for poster presentations for one National Clinical Meeting upcoming in early December in New Orleans. Besides the posters, Alex and one customer were approved for a platform presentation as each would share presentation duties from the podium.

Consequently, the pressure was on to get all these projects completed and ready for presentation in December. Alex wanted to spend as much time as possible with Michaela, but when not with her, one could find him burning the midnight oil nearly every night! At three months out from the December meeting, Alex was having a catch up call with Tim, his team manager.

Tim asked him, "How are all your projects coming along for December presentation?"

Alex chuckled and said, "Honestly, I'm not sure if there is enough time over the next three months for me to get all these done!" He went on, "But I'm not going to let down any of my customers either, so somehow, I'll figure it out!"

Tim replied, "You know, most people nearly flip out when they have something like two or three posters at one meeting to get ready, but you have fourteen. You know, Alex, just saying the number fourteen is so unbelievable! It's almost incomprehensible that someone could have that many presentations at one meeting!"

Alex was quick to reply, "I know, what in the world was I thinking! I may have bit off more than I can chew this time!"

"Well, one thing is for sure if you pull this off it becomes legendary!" Tim said.

Alex quipped, "Yeah, they'll be calling it legendary as they're paying last respects at my graveside!"

They each busted out laughing! Then Tim asked, "How can I help?"

Alex replied, "Hmmm, right now I'm not sure, but thank you. I have reached out to one of our internal statisticians. I asked him if he would double check all of my statistical work and he agreed, so that's good. What I could use is a proofreader. As I get the projects completed and the poster presentations developed would you be willing to review them?"

"Of course," Tim said. "Be glad to."

"Thanks, that will help."

Now it was on Alex's shoulders to get all his projects completed and ready for presentation. The task at hand was nearly overwhelming but he was determined to not let any of his customers down! He told himself, failure was not an option, not on his watch!

*****

Alex had a meeting at the company's headquarters in New York City, which began on a Tuesday afternoon and ended on Friday at noon. He flew up on an early morning flight and went ahead and dropped off his luggage at the UN Plaza Millennium hotel before going to the meeting.

Alex had invited Michaela up to join him in New York City. He made her flight arrangements, and she arrived just prior to noon on that Friday. To take the stress away from landing in a new city, Alex arranged for a car service to pick her up at LaGuardia airport and take her to the UN Plaza. He had also left a room key for her at the front desk; thus, she could go ahead and get into their room and freshen up.

At meeting completion, he quickly returned to the hotel. Alex entered the room as Michaela was taking in the views from their thirty-sixth floor corner room facing Manhattan. After a brief embrace, Michaela said, "Look at this view."

Alex quickly added, "Wait until you see it at night! The Empire State Building over there will be lit up, it's pretty impressive."

Alex started changing out of his suit into some jeans when Michaela asked, "So, what are our plans for this afternoon?"

He smiled and said, "Well, first, we're going to get on the subway and run up to Bloomingdale's. Maybe we can find something new for you!"

"Wow, I can't argue with that! It'll be my first subway ride. Then what?"

"We'll have an early dinner and then come back here to get ready because tonight we're going to my favorite Broadway show."

Michaela asked, "So what show are we going to see?"

Smiling, he simply said, "You'll find out, but for now let's go see if we can find you some new clothes!"

Michaela, grinning, replied, "What girl can argue with that!"

While in Bloomingdale's, they went to the ladies' fashion floor plus ladies' shoes were on the same floor. Michaela tried on several dresses with assistance from the department fashion consultant, who was delightful. She had great taste and pulled over several pairs of shoes which all seemed to go perfectly with each dress! Each time Michaela came out to model a new item, she was simply striking! The consultant told Alex several times that she is nothing short of gorgeous! *All I could do is say thank you and smile because she was!*

The trip to Bloomingdale's was fruitful for Michaela as she walked out of there with three dresses, a pant suit for work, an evening wrap, four pairs of shoes, and of course we had to stop in the lingerie department as well. We took the subway back toward the hotel but got off about four blocks short. From there we found a nice Sushi place to have an early dinner then we made our way back to our room.

Alex had arranged for a car to take them over to the Theatre District. Upon arriving, Alex assisted her out of the car as she was looking very elegant indeed. She had worn one of her new dresses. Michaela had ahold of Alex's arm as they walked over to the Will Call window. That's when Michaela realized what show they were going to see. She leaned in and whispered into Alex's ear, "Phantom of the Opera, I've always wanted to see this play!"

Alex thoroughly enjoyed watching Michaela during the performance as he could tell that she was totally entranced with the play and music! As they left the theatre, Michaela kissed Alex on the cheek and hugged him saying, "Thank you for bringing me here, I'll always remember this!"

She went on, "So what now?"

"I thought we would walk through Times Square and down to Bryant Park. It's just a couple of blocks, you think your feet can handle it?"

"I believe so, let's do it!"

They walked down to Bryant Park and sat on a bench. It was a warm night, so they got some ice cream and talked, and talked, and talked. After a bit, Michaela spoke up and looked directly into Alex's eyes and said, "Alex, we've been seeing one another for a few weeks, but I feel like I've known you for years!"

Alex with a slight smile said, "That's funny, I feel the very same about you too!"

Michaela, looking down then tracking her eyes up to Alex's she said in a very tender tone, "Alex, I Love You!" With a big smile, she said it again, "I Love You! I do!"

There was a pause, then Alex said, "Michaela, I Love You too!" He continued, "I've known for some time that I Loved You and I was going to tell you sometime this weekend. I was looking for the right time, but you know anytime is the right time with You!"

Each smiling, they kissed, then kissed again, then kissed again as this went on for a while. Finally, Alex asked, "You ready to go back to the hotel?"

"Yes, I am."

He called the hotel for a car service to come pick them up. They were a little hungry, so he ordered some appetizers and a bottle of wine be sent up to the room. They ate their appetizers and drank their wine while taking in the night view of the city. The evening was marvelous, and the night was passionate!

The next day, they went to the Museum of Natural History and to the Hayden Planetarium. She loved them both but especially the planetarium as looking at the stars was one of Michaela's favorite things to do. Afterward, they walked around the city. He treated her to a slice of New York-style pizza. They made there way through Rockefeller Center on their way back to the hotel.

That evening, Alex took Michaela for a most glamorous dinner at the restaurant in the Waldorf Astoria on Park Avenue. They enjoyed a multicourse dinner with a great wine. Michaela wore one of her other new dresses and she looked magnificent! Even in a city like New York, her stunning beauty turned heads every place they went. After dinner, they found a corner in the Waldorf's bar area where they simply enjoyed each other's company. They had another fantastic night!

Prior to their departure, they ordered room service breakfast. Saying "I love you" to each other came so easily. Neither really wanted the weekend to end, but they had to fly home and resume their daily lives.

They had such a great time and the love that they had for each other just oozed out all day. All they had to do was to look at each other and they would get all giddy and giggling. If two people were ever meant to be together it was them. Sheryl was right; they do make an incredible couple!

*****

All was going great between Alex and Michaela as they were seeing each other nearly every day especially since they lived only a few feet apart. They would share dinner at each other's apartments. Going outside the city area was a fun pastime in the evening to look at the stars on clear nights. Watching movies curled up on the couch with some popcorn was a favorite leisure. They had gone bowling again, went roller skating, and loved their walks. They returned to the

Hot and Hot Fish Club, the place they called their special restaurant. They had done so many things in a few short weeks.

It was Alex's forty-sixth birthday in early September. Alex had never been a person to make a big deal about his birthday. It was always fine with him if his birthday passed without any fanfare. However, Michaela discovered the date of his birthday, so she had made a small chocolate cake and surprised him. It really did take Alex by surprise and really touched his heart.

While eating cake, Alex asked Michaela, "So how did you find out it was my birthday?"

She simply smiled and said, "I looked in your wallet one day, I hope that was okay."

Alex responded, "Yeah, that's fine, I don't have anything to hide." He continued, "Thank you for doing this, it wasn't necessary, but you did make my day and surprised me too!"

At this Michaela leaned in and gave Alex a nice chocolaty kiss. Then she said, "Happy birthday!"

*****

It was a normal Tuesday morning; Alex was sitting at his desk sipping on some coffee checking emails. Suddenly, there was a rapid knocking at his door, and he could hear Michaela yelling to come to the door. Alex leaped out of his chair and raced to the door to see what was wrong. Michaela burst in; breathing heavily, she blurted out, "Are you watching the news?"

Alex said, "No, why?"

She continued, "A plane hit the World Trade Center."

"What!" he retorted as he was turning on his TV.

They stood there in disbelief as they watched the smoke bellow from the North Tower. Michaela screeched, "What could have happened?"

Alex stood quiet for a moment, thinking, then finally spoke up, "That's a terrorist attack! They said a plane hit the building, well, if it was a small aircraft, it would not have done that much damage. That much damage could only have been created by a larger jet flying into the tower."

Michaela was like, "How could a large jet fly into a building?"

Alex looked at her and said, "Exactly, it couldn't unless it was crashing, or it was hijacked with a suicide bomber." Alex continued, "I think it's a suicidal hijacking."

They continued to watch the news as the reporters were all speculating back and forth. Then suddenly another aircraft came into the picture and hit the South Tower of the World Trade Center with a massive explosion.

Alex quickly said, "That is *not* a coincidence that is a targeted terrorist attack using hijacked commercial planes."

While Michaela was gasping in disbelief, Alex was thinking and said, "You know the next question is since this was a targeted plan how many more planes have been hijacked?"

Michaela said, "You think there might be some more?"

He responded, "It wouldn't surprise me."

She asked, "So how are they going to figure it out if there's more?"

Alex says, "Well, they need to do a few things immediately. First, and I bet they've already done this but scramble our alert fighters around the country. Next, they need to quickly identify any aircraft who are not on their designated flight path. Lastly, they need to ground all commercial and private aircraft immediately. That is get all planes on the ground now, land at the nearest airfield. Then they can better assess the situation for what is still flying." He continued, "Next thing would be a decision would have to be made on what to do if another hijacked aircraft is discovered."

Michaela asked, "What do you mean what to do?"

He said, "If another hijacked plane is discovered, the alert fighters can track it down pretty fast but then the president will need to give the order to shoot it down."

Michaela replied, "Shoot it down, but that would kill all the passengers on board."

"Yes, but better than it flies into the Capitol building, or the Sears Tower, or a nuclear power plant, or something similar. That's why only the president should make that most difficult decision!"

Michaela thought about that for a moment and simply said, "Oh my, that would be a tough decision."

He replied, "Morally yes, but the president has to look at the bigger picture."

They kept watching the atrocity as it was unfolding. Michaela was holding Alex's hand firmly when Alex's cell phone rang. He glanced at Michaela for a second then answered the call. It was his mother; she quickly asked, "Where are you?"

Alex said, "Rest easy, I'm at home. Don't worry, can I call you back later?"

His mom said, "Yes, please do, but I just wanted to make sure you were safe." She knew that Alex traveled quite a bit including up to New York City so she was naturally concerned.

It wasn't long until another aircraft crashed into the Pentagon. Alex continued to watch and stated in a pissed-off voice, "This is happening to us now, but somewhere in the world someone is going to feel the wrath of the US soon!"

As the news broadcast showed the smoke billowing from the Twin Towers, Alex said, "Look there. That's a couple of fighter jets flying air cover over New York." He continued, "I bet there's some over Washington, DC, too."

As they continued to watch the news the South Tower began to collapse and then in a few minutes the North Tower started coming down. Alex looked at Michaela and said, "Oh, someone is going to pay for this!"

Michaela, still holding onto Alex's hand, asked, "Can I hang out with you today?"

"Absolutely, but don't you have to work today?"

"Yes, I do, but I'm not working the rest of the day."

Alex said, "Stay here as long as you like. I'm going back to my desk as I have a lot of work to do! Plus, I have that little twenty-three-inch TV hanging in the office if you would like to come watch it in there."

"Okay, I will."

It wasn't long and the news began to report there was a plane crash in southern Pennsylvania. Michaela said, "There was another one, but it crashed."

Alex thought a moment then said, "You know that plane could have been a shoot down. Or it was hijacked and there was a fight for control of the plane which caused it to crash. I seriously doubt that it crashed on its own!"

Alex looked at Michaela and said, "Remember this day, September 11, 2001, and remember where you were when this happened. This is one of those rare days in history that will live in infamy! Just like Pearl Harbor."

Michaela was quiet while watching the news and Alex had jumped back into some of his data analysis. Michaela was thinking. After a bit, she spoke up, "Alex, a couple of weeks ago you asked if I had any interest in going to a gun range. Will you teach me how to shoot? I would like to learn!"

Alex replied, "Okay, I'll make the arrangements."

*****

A week after 9/11, Michaela and Alex were talking and decided to get away for a couple of days. Alex made reservations at the Sandestin Beach and Golf Resort. Alex had a couple of friends living in the Ft. Walton Beach area, so he thought since they were going to be at Sandestin why not arrange a visit with each. He asked Michaela if it would be okay to visit a couple of his friends and her response was, "Absolutely, I'd like to meet some of your friends."

They arrived late one evening. After breakfast, the next morning, they went to the beach for a couple of hours. Afterward, they got cleaned up and made a short stop at the Silver Sands Outlet Mall where they picked up a couple of items. Then Michaela asked, "Who are we going to see?"

Alex smiled. "We're going to see two different people. First, is Darla, she was a staff sergeant under my command when I was on active duty. One day, she asked if I would help her go bootstrap.

That's an opportunity for enlisted personnel to go to college on an air force scholarship. While in college, they are paid at their military rank. After they earn their degree, they come back on active duty to serve a minimum commitment. Well, Darla has earned her degree and is now stationed over here at Hurlburt Field. Hurlburt is the air force headquarters for Special Operations Command. She is serving as a protocol officer. You'll see why I recommended her, she's a fine person.

"Next, we're having dinner with Bill and Marilee, he was my last commander while I was still on active duty. He was terrific as they were there while I was dealing with my ex-wife, Cynthia. Those were some difficult times and I think the world of them! He's made dinner reservations for us at a nice place in Shalimar."

After listening, Michaela said, "They all sound like some very nice people!"

Michaela had never been on an air force base. Arriving at the Hurlburt Field main gate, Alex presented his military identification card. After which, Michaela couldn't help but notice the armed airman came to attention and saluted Alex smartly! Alex returned the salute. Michaela had never witnessed this kind of interaction and respect in person before, it made her think even that much more of Alex. They went directly to the headquarters building where they met up with Darla. She gave Alex a big hug and said, "I'm so glad you called and stopped by, I can't believe it."

Alex said, "Darla, I would like for you to meet Michaela." He continued looking at Michaela, "Darla is a second lieutenant and I'm very proud of her!"

Darla had brought in some snacks that day, so they simply sat and talked for nearly two hours. She introduced Alex to some of the office staff and other officers as they strolled through. Michaela was listening with glee as they told their old stories and experiences and were laughing. Michaela could see that Darla had the highest of respect for Alex. It made her feel good that others thought so much of him.

A little later, they met Bill and Marilee at the restaurant. Michaela could tell that Alex was very happy to see Bill and his wife.

During dinner, Alex briefly explained what had ultimately occurred with Cynthia. Michaela could tell that they were truly empathetic to what Alex went through with Cynthia. But Marilee made it clear that they were so happy to meet Michaela. They all talked and talked and laughed and laughed for nearly four hours. Michaela could tell that Bill and Marilee without question thought the world of Alex!

As they were all walking out to the parking lot, Marilee took Michaela by the arm and said, "I am so happy to meet you! I was watching you two at dinner and let me say…you two fit! You do, that's undeniable. Please be good to him, he is so good! I doubt if he's told you much about his ex-wife, so let me say that man endured nothing short of hell and still managed to keep it together! So be good to him, but let me also say he's fortunate to be with you as well. You seem like a terrific person! Here's my number, call me any time."

This was so endearing to Michaela; it made her feel very special and that she was now a permanent fixture into Alex's life!

Alex and Michaela spent the next couple of days at the resort. They went to the beach each day for a couple of hours. They hit the driving range and played a round of golf. Frankly, all they did was relax and enjoy themselves. They loved to talk about life, goals, dreams, and what the future may look like. Michaela loved the walks they took along the beach at sunset. She felt so incredibly comfortable with Alex. She loved this man and felt for the first time the Lord was showing her His plan for her life.

*****

One day in early October, Alex and Michaela were having Sushi at Stix Japanese restaurant. Engaging in their normal dinner banter when Alex asked, "How would you like to go to a military dining out?"

The question took Michaela by surprise, so she asked, "What is a military dining out?"

"I'm sorry, a military dining out is like a military ball. We wear our air force mess dress uniform, it's like a tuxedo but has shoulder boards for rank and we wear our medals over our left breast. The ladies wear long gowns like any other formal ball."

She replied, "Oh, that sounds so nice! I would love to go! When is it?"

Alex replied, "It's a week from Saturday. I thought we could leave about Noon on Friday and drive to Biloxi. I'll get us a room at the *Beau Rivage* hotel. The dining-out is Saturday night then we can drive back Sunday. That sound okay to you?"

"Yes, sounds great! And I've got a great gown that I can wear."

"If you say it's great, then I can't wait to see you in it!" Alex said with a smile and twinkle in his eye.

Michaela reached over and gave Alex a little love punch and a wink then said, "I guess you'll just have to wait and see!"

*****

They were at the *Beau Rivage* hotel getting ready for the dining-out. Alex was trying to get everything straight on his mess dress when Michaela walked out of the bathroom. Alex took one look at Michaela and his jaw nearly hit the floor as all he could do was stare at this *vision of beauty*. He mumbled, "Oh my gosh!"

After a few moments, he finally got his tongue untied and wandered over to her then took by the hand and said, "Michaela, you are stunning!"

With a slight blush and smile, she replied, "Thank you." She continued with, "You look incredible as well."

Alex with a wry smile simply said, "Thank you too."

Michaela asked, "So what are all these medals for?"

Alex shrugged his shoulders nonchalantly and said, "Oh, this, that, and the other, you know, stuff."

Well, Michaela didn't believe that for one second. She thought, she didn't know much about the military but figured they didn't hand out medals for nothing. She was eyeballing them when Alex broke her train of thought with, "So is my bowtie on straight? Also, is my cummerbund straight and look right?"

Michaela edged up close to Alex and straightened his bowtie just a little then leaned in and kissed him tenderly. After the embrace she leaned back a little as Alex had his arms around her hips, and she said, "Thank you for bringing me here."

They went to the dining-out and Michaela had the time of her life. All evening, it seemed like people were coming up to talk with Alex. At one point, Michaela whispered into Alex's ear saying, "You sure do know a lot of people!"

Alex with a smile turned and quietly said in Michaela's ear, "Not really. I only know about a quarter of these people." With a little grin, he said, "Rest assured most are coming over just to meet you!" He was smiling as Michaela leaned in with affection against Alex for a few moments until someone else stopped to engage in conversation.

During the evening, several of Alex's workmates and personnel within his squadron and group hung around them during the reception, at dinner, and afterward. Several teammates and more importantly their wives let Alex know that they really, really liked Michaela! Many warned Alex, "You better hang on to her, she is something very special!"

Alex always simply said, "Thank you, and you're right, she is special."

Michaela had a terrific time and told Alex so when the night was over and the next day on the drive home.

8

Best Birthday Ever

One night they were having a quiet dinner when Alex leaned over and said, "Michaela, do you have a passport?"

The question took her by surprise then she replied, "Why, yes, I do."

Alex paused for a moment then asked, "Do you have some vacation time?"

Michaela was getting more curious as she smiled saying, "Yes." She studied Alex's face for a clue of what he was thinking about.

He paused for a moment longer intentionally keeping her in suspense then said, "So you have a passport, which probably means you've been outside the country, right?"

"Yes," she said slyly.

"Can I ask you where?"

She replied, "Sure, I've only been outside the country one time and that was on my honeymoon. We went to Cozumel."

"Oh yeah, I've never been to Cozumel, did you like it?"

She answered, "Well, let me say it like this… I'll never go back!"

"Wow, I guess that's pretty definite!"

Michaela paused for a minute; examining Alex's face, she said, "What are you brewing in that mind of yours?"

Alex gazed at her for moment then said, "Okay, your birthday is coming up the first week of November, right?"

"Yes," she slowly replied.

"I want to take you somewhere special for your thirty-seventh birthday. Honestly, I haven't settled upon where that may be just yet, but it will definitely take a passport."

Michaela wasn't expecting that answer, and it froze her for a moment. She thought no one has ever done something that special for her birthday. She was completely quiet as she sat there smiling with a warm heart.

Alex interrupted her silence and asked her, "Is there anywhere special that you've always wanted to go?"

She quickly replied, "Yes, of course, but I will defer to your judgment. You have been to so many places in the world that wherever you choose I know I will love! Well, anywhere except Cozumel." They each busted up laughing!

Alex jokingly said, "Darn, I was going to choose Cozumel." He was laughing as Michaela leaned over and gave him a love punch!"

They were both still laughing when Alex said, "I have narrowed it down to three places, but I need to make a decision in the next day or so to get good airfare since we're still over a month out." He continued, "I'll let you know where we're going soon in case you might need some new clothes."

Michaela just sat there and smiled. Internally she was very excited but, on the outside, she tried to remain cool and calm.

A few minutes went by when Alex broke the silence with, "I would like to ask you something else."

Michaela glanced up at Alex with a quizzical look, thinking, *Where is he going with this?*

He hesitated for a moment then said, "Michaela, over Christmas, I would like to take you to Oklahoma to meet my parents and family. Would you want to go?"

Michaela, with a look of amazement on her face, placed her hand over her heart and said, "I would love that! I would love to meet your family!" Her voice cracked, and a tear came to her eyes.

"Great!" Alex gazed at Michaela and said, "I love you!"

At this, Michaela felt she had never been more loved than right now!

*****

Just as he had promised, Alex took Michaela to the firing range. He brought his own 9mm Baretta and he borrowed a friends' Springfield 308 and he had his friend take the scope off. They first went to the short range where they set up two targets at 30 feet. Alex instructed her in all aspects of the Baretta while it was unloaded. He let her practice holding and aiming the weapon prior to loading. He discussed breathing and the recoil of the weapon. Michaela was like, "Wow, there's a lot to know about the gun."

Alex replied, "You'll get used to it, but the most important thing is safety first." He continued, "Okay, I'll load your weapon and now it's ready to fire. Remember to always point the weapon away from people and never at someone else unless you intend to shoot. You take the right-hand target aim at the circle drawn on the chest of the outline of a person."

Michaela placed both hands on the weapon, took a long aim, and pulled the trigger. She said, "Did I hit it?"

Alex replied, "No, your round went high by about three feet." He said, "This time widen your stance, don't jerk the trigger but squeeze it, firm up your secondhand grip to reduce recoil. Try it again."

She aimed slowly and fired another round. "Where did it go?"

"Good shot, you hit him in the head around the left eye. So I assume you were aiming for the chest bull's-eye but see how far you brought down your round angle from your first shot." Alex continued, "You've got eight more rounds in this clip, so try it again."

"Eight more rounds?"

"Yes, I loaded several clips all with only ten rounds, a nice even number."

Michaela kept shooting until her clip was emptied. He pulled her target in and Alex said, "You know that's pretty good shooting for a first timer. You don't vary much left to right, all your rounds are on a north to south axis. Look, a couple rounds hit just above the head, one more on the head, two in the shoulder, three around the neck. I figure you were aiming at the bull's-eye, so you can see that you need to work on keeping the barrel down. By the way you fire this weapon, if I was going to buy you a handgun, I would probably get you a 380. It's just a little smaller round and weapon size with a little less recoil. I think you would be much more accurate."

Michaela added, "Okay your turn, let me see what you can do."

Alex slipped in a clip and charged his weapon, glanced over at Michaela, and winked. He aimed his weapon and fired off his ten rounds in quick succession.

Michaela with eyes extra wide said, "Wow, that was fast."

Alex reeled in the target and Michaela looked at it and said, "Oh my god!" She started counting the holes and got to ten. She looked at Alex and said, "They're all in the bull's-eye circle." Alex just shrugged. Michaela continued, "Well, I found out one thing…you can shoot!"

Alex reeled out another target for her and loaded the weapon. Under a little more direction from Alex, she shot better the second time around. They finished up at the short range and then walked over to the long range. Alex had the range personnel put up a man-target at only 100 yards.

He told Michaela, "That man-target is ours. I figured 100 yards was a good distance for you to learn. I had my friend take off his scope from this weapon because I wanted you to learn to aim the weapon without a scope." Alex continued, "This a 308-bolt action rifle, its range is 800–1,000 yards. It pretty much has a flat trajectory out to about 200 yards. Depending on conditions, the round will lose about 10 inches at 300 yards and about 3–4 feet at 500 yards. Shooting further, say out to the maximum distance would take more calculating than we need to explain today." He continued to explain, "Since we are only shooting 100 yards the shot will be flat especially today with no breeze."

Alex showed Michaela the bolt action to insert the round and how to aim. Michaela asked, "So do I go first again?"

Alex replied, "Since I've never shot his 308, I would like to check out it's aiming alignment."

She asked, "How do you do that?"

Alex said with a little laugh, "By firing the weapon." He then opened the box of ammunition and pulled out a cartridge." Michaela immediately said, "Wow, that's a big bullet!"

He jokingly replied, "Yep, and when it hits someone, it makes a terrible mess!"

Michaela stared at Alex and said, "Jeez, thanks for the visual."

He chuckled. "Well, that's what it's supposed to do!" Alex went on, "Okay, let me check out this weapon." He loaded the weapon, held it up for a moment, and fired. Alex slowly said, "It looks like it shoots a little right." He popped in another round, took careful aim, and fired. Again, he said, "Yeah, just a touch right."

Michaela was like, "You can see where that bullet hit? It's 100 yards!"

"Yeah, but let's look through our range scope here." As he did, he said, "Yeah, both rounds are on the right-hand side at the edge of the bull's-eye. This weapon definitely shoots about 3–4 inches to the right at 100 yards. Here, look!"

Michaela looked through the range scope and said, "Wow, you can see the holes real clear through this."

Alex said, "Yep, now it's your turn." He gave her instructions, hold the weapon firmly up against the shoulder, showed her how to aim, reminded her of breathing and squeezing the trigger, don't pull or jerk! He had her slip a cartridge into the chamber and close the bolt. She took careful aim and fired.

She quickly asked, "Where'd it go?"

"It was about 6 feet high."

"How do you know that?"

"I saw the dust fly on the embankment behind the target." Alex said, "This time keep a firm grip with your left hand on the stock and keep your elbows planted firmly here on the rest. Also, widen your stance just a little more, I think it'll feel more comfortable. Let's try it again."

She slipped in another round, closed the bolt, took aim, and fired.

Alex said, "Let me look through the scope, as I think that round barely missed the target high." He looked and said, "Yeah, it was close to hitting the target but just barely missed. Try it again."

Michaela reloaded and went through her routine and fired, she quickly said, "Did I hit it?"

Alex smiled. "Looking through the scope, he said you hit the upper right corner of the target about 2 feet to the right of the man's head. You know, for a rookie that's actually a pretty good shot. I'm proud of you!" He continued, "Try another."

Michaela took seven or eight more shots of which five hit the target. Of those five, two of them hit the man…one in the left shoulder and the other in the left arm. Alex gave her a big hug and said, "You did great!"

She kiddingly said, "Must have been the teacher!"

He chuckled and said, "No worries, you'll get better the more you shoot."

They laughed then she said, "Let me see you shoot this rifle."

Alex said, "Okay, we have a few cartridges left. You look through the scope and see how I'm doing. Also, this time I'm going to rest my elbows for better stabilization." Alex fired six more rounds then opened the bolt and laid the rifle down. He looked at Michaela and asked, "So how did I do?"

Michaela shaking her head looked up from the scope and simply said, "Amazing, that's unbelievable!" She continued, "Well, you adjusted for the slight pull to the right, all six rounds are right in the middle of the bull's-eye, that's crazy!"

Alex replied, "Well, the bull's-eye is a ten-inch circle."

"Maybe so, but your shots are clustered inside that circle." She went on, "That's incredible, how do you do that? That's 100 yards and you didn't even have a scope!"

He simply said, "I started shooting at a young age. First with a .22-caliber rifle then a 30-06, which is a little more weapon than this 308. I didn't have a scope until I was like thirteen years old so it's how

I learned. I guess I would say it has always been easy for me, it feels natural, no effort, I can't explain it any better than that!"

As they were leaving the range, Michaela said, "Thank you for bringing me here today, that was fun! You know you're a pretty good teacher!"

Alex laughed. "Well, you're a pretty good student." They laughed as they leaned in and kissed.

*****

Alex stopped by the complex office to get his FedEx packages. Sheryl met him, pausing for a second, she looked at him with a smile while raising her eyebrows said, "So how's it going with Michaela?"

Laughing, Alex retorted, "You know how it's going, you talk with Michaela a lot." He continued, "Actually, I should be asking you that question!"

Sheryl with a little grin simply remarked, "Oh, you don't have anything to worry about my friend!"

Alex was smiling as his thoughts drifted when Sheryl interrupted those with, "You love her, don't you?"

With a slight blush and grin, he whispered, "Yes, I do."

Sheryl leaned in and placed her hand on Alex's arm then quietly said, "She loves you too!" Alex smiling as his mind was wandering back to Michaela when Sheryl again interrupted his thoughts by asking, "I hear you're going to take her someplace for her birthday? Someplace that requires a passport to get there. So do you know where you're taking her too?"

"Yes, I do… I made all the reservations yesterday," Alex said.

Sheryl asked, "So where are you taking her?"

"Nope, won't work."

"What won't work?"

"I haven't told Michaela yet and I want her to be the first to know!"

Sheryl, nodding her head in agreement, simply said, "I can understand that. So when are you going to tell her?"

"Tonight, at dinner. I have a brochure that I will lay on the table as she's eating." Alex continued, "So if you want to know then call her tomorrow."

Sheryl, grinning, said, "Oh, I will."

Later at dinner, they were sharing some Thai takeout when Alex said, "Would you like to know where I've made reservations to for your birthday?"

Michaela, glancing up quickly at Alex with heart beating quicker in anticipation, a big smile coming across her face as she said, "Where?"

Alex laid a pamphlet down on the table. Michaela quickly read the cover, and it said "Costa Rica." Michaela, with a spark of energy and excitement, asked, "We're going to Costa Rica?"

He replied, "The reservations are all made. We are flying down on the Saturday prior to your birthday and will be there for eight nights."

Michaela, her mouth wide open in disbelief, finally said, "You're taking me to Costa Rica for my birthday!" The realization was beginning to set in as she said again, "You're taking me to Costa Rica for my birthday!" Her voice broke and tears appeared.

Alex nodded. "Yes, I am. You deserve it!"

Michaela, with a stare of disbelief, stood up, then Alex did as well. With tears flowing down her cheeks, she hugged Alex with great passion. She was still crying when Alex said, "Here, let me show you where we're going to actually be staying in Costa Rica."

Alex pulled out some more informational pamphlets and said, "We will be at the Westin Reserva Conchal right on the west coast so we should have awesome sunsets. It is an all-inclusive resort with a spa and has a Robert Trent Jones designed golf course that looks incredible. The resort has several restaurants and bars onsite, but we might be able to investigate the local cuisine off property too. Costa Rica has several volcanoes, obviously tropical forests, national parks, so we'll have many things to choose from while we are relaxing."

After Michaela had thumbed through the materials, she looked at Alex and quietly said, "This is the nicest thing anyone has ever done for me!" She smiled and said, "Now I can't wait!"

Alex quickly added, "Me too!" He continued, "One thing though, I have all these presentations for the meeting in December. I'm working on the materials as much as possible, but I may have to do a little bit of work while we are there. I figure if I have to then you can go to the spa and get a facial or something like that."

"A facial, hmmm, that actually sounds pretty good." She said, "The next three weeks are going to be so agonizingly long!"

*****

The weeks passed by quicker than expected leading up to Michaela's birthday vacation. Alex had turned in many late nights trying to move his projects along to ready them for presentation in December. Alex was feeling pretty good about the progress he had made. However, he still had a lot of analyses, evaluations, and writing of abstracts remaining yet.

Michaela had scheduled her routine follow-ups a week early just prior to Halloween. Her oncologist let her know that all the tests were still negative! This was great news as it moved Michaela to four years and nine months progression free survival. The doctor told her, "Everything is looking great!"

Alex prayed every day, Michaela prayed every day, and they prayed together as well. They each had great *faith*! Consequently, she was in great spirits and so excited for her birthday trip celebration.

Alex finished his October monthly reports and forwarded it to his team manager, Tim. A couple of days before leaving, Alex let Tim know that he was going to take a week of vacation.

Tim snickered as he told him, "Try not to work too much on your vacation time!"

Alex chuckled.

But Tim knew Alex all too well, plus he understood the almost insurmountable task that Alex had created for himself with all these presentations. He knew that Alex had been going through an extremely difficult time over the past couple of years and watched him dive head-on into work to ease his pain. Tim was a good friend, but still, Alex wasn't one to spill very much about his personal life. Therefore, Tim didn't know many details about his travails.

In addition, Alex really hadn't discussed his current relationship with Michaela to anyone. It simply wasn't his way; Alex was always one who could keep secrets. Alex was simply a very private person, and you add the fact that Michaela may have been even more private. That's an equation for anonymity, just the way Michaela liked it!

November 3rd finally arrived; they were so excited. Alex and Michaela flew through Atlanta to Liberia, Costa Rica. It was about a sixty-minute ride to the resort from the airport. Upon arrival, it was clear the place was spectacular. Michaela was so happy it made Alex's heart feel very warm simply seeing the glow on her face!

This was her birthday trip so Alex told himself that it was up to her to decide what activities she would like. She's in control, it's her birthday, and it's her choices. This made Michaela feel very respected and special.

The first day they went to a hiking area in the rain forest and had an absolute blast swinging on a zip line. Scenery, the waterfalls, the streams, the wildlife, the mountain views—all was great. On another day, they joined a group and went to the national park at one of the volcanoes. Michaela was enjoying herself like she had never experienced before.

The resort had a first-class golf driving range. Alex had arranged a couple of lessons for Michaela with the local pro. As Alex stood back and watched her getting lessons, he thought she is a natural. First, she has that competitive makeup, she's relentless when she is doing something she truly likes. Plus, she's a pretty good ball striker too! Even the pro said, "I can't believe the first time you ever swung a golf club was three months ago!"

Michaela said with a smile, "There's my teacher!"

Alex quickly replied, "Wasn't me, she's a natural."

The golf pro said, "Honestly, I think it's probably a mixture of both…she's doing very well!"

Michaela smiled sheepishly before saying, "He's been talking to me lately about the importance of course management and to not just hit the ball."

Golf pro said, "That is great!"

Alex jumped in, "Last time we played, she broke ninety and that was on one of the Robert Trent Jones golf trail courses in Birmingham."

"You know, that doesn't surprise me one bit. Keep it up," the pro replied.

Alex said, "Yeah, it won't be long until she's kicking my butt!" They all laughed, then the pro asked Alex, "I expect you play pretty well?"

He replied, chuckling, "Some days, some days not so much. But I manage to scratch out a handicap in the four-to-five range."

The pro asked, "Have you played here yet?"

"No, we have a tee-time for tomorrow morning," Alex said.

The pro, a nice guy, said, "When you've finished stop by my office, let me know how you guys did and what you think of the course. Also, since you are used to playing Robert Trent Jones courses, this one is no different. It is all risk-reward." He continued with a smile, "I think you understand what I mean."

Alex nodded with a grin. "Got it!"

They enjoyed eating light meals, getting a little sun but not too much. They especially enjoyed walking on the beach particularly right at sunset. Then they would sit in the sand and simply talk. Michaela liked opening up and talking about her dreams with Alex... something she had never done previously with anyone. He made her feel safe, respected, and special. She loved his calming influence; she loved his intellect, how he listened, and appreciated how he, too, liked solitude. She loved it when it was just the two of them, alone!

Alex did work on some of his projects while there, but he wanted to make sure the focus was primarily on Michaela! After all, this trip was for her! Alex arranged something a little special with the hotel for Michaela on the day of her birthday. They had a private dinner on the beach with candles. She was simply blown away!

While there, one of Michaela's favorite things to do was to stargaze. Her and Alex would walk down on to the beach after dark. Spreading out a couple of towels, they would enjoy a snack and wine as they observed the stars and planets. The ambient light was minimal, so seeing the different stars and constellations was clear.

Since they stayed up late stargazing, they enjoyed sleeping late and just frolicking in bed. Ordering room service breakfast served on the veranda of their suite was one of Michaela's favorite things. The resort had several restaurants, they enjoyed testing the cuisine at all of them.

They played golf the day after Michaela's lesson. The course was well-manicured, it was tough but fair for well struck golf shots, but it properly penalized one for off-target shots. Just like any Robert Trent Jones course, overall it was gorgeous with some spectacular views. As promised, they stopped by the pro's office after their round. When seeing them the Pro asked, "So how'd your round go today?"

Alex replied, "Pretty good, nice layout and beautiful views! Michaela shot a 93 and I had a 78."

The pro replied, "That's not bad on this course, not bad at all! And a 78 having never played it is really good."

"Well, thank you, that triple bogey I had was costly, but I was prouder of the way Michaela was striking the ball, she was impressive!" He continued, "We're going to play it again in a couple of days and hopefully do better since we now know the layout."

Together, Alex and Michaela felt peaceful, content, and at ease. The entire trip was so relaxing as they grew even closer. This trip validated all of Michaela's feelings that she did love him! It confirmed the same feelings within Alex.

On the flight home, Michaela told Alex, "This trip has been far and away the kindest and nicest thing anyone has ever done for me!"

Alex, with a smirk on his face, said, "You're welcome, but are you sure you really didn't want to go to Cozumel instead?"

Michaela with pursed lips began pinching Alex until he said, "Okay, okay, okay, I give...*not* Cozumel, got it!" They were each giggling and laughing like a couple of schoolkids.

Still smiling, Alex leaned his head back on the seat rest when Michaela whispered into his ear, "I love you!"

9

Her Cancer Returns

After returning from Costa Rica, Alex and Michaela were very busy. Alex immersed himself into getting his customer projects brought further along, many of which he completed. He reviewed the results with each customer and then in collaboration they developed the abstract and full poster. It was now about three weeks out from the meeting, and he still had about half the projects to finish up. The next weekend after Costa Rica, Alex went and performed some Air Force Reserve duty for a few days. He led his squadron during the day and at night analyzed data, plus wrote abstracts for the projects. It was truly the definition of burning the candle at both ends.

Michaela as well jumped back into her job to catch up on customer visits. Even so, she and Alex saw each other pretty much every day. Generally, in the evening for dinner. More times than not, it was takeout.

The weekend Alex was gone performing reserve duty Sheryl invited Michaela over for dinner. Sheryl was eager to hear all about their trip to Costa Rica, but more than that she wanted to hear how things were going between her and Alex.

After dinner, Sheryl poured some more wine and said, "Okay, how was Costa Rica?"

Michaela with a soft grin simply said, "It was great, we had an unbelievable time…we didn't want to come home!" She went ahead and told Sheryl about the trip. About all the different activities they

105

did and how beautiful the resort was and their walks on the beach. Michaela explained how Alex had made the whole trip about her... he would simply say this is your birthday!

She said, "Sheryl, his heart is so good, he makes me feel good about myself." Michaela continued, "I've always been a person who keeps my emotions in check and under wraps I guess until I feel I can completely trust a person. And quite frankly, those people have been very few and far between."

Taking a sip of wine, Sheryl asked, "Speaking of trusting someone, it appears that you trust Alex. You two are incredible together! It's almost like it was meant to be! That person that got you two together must be pretty smart!" She winked with a smile!

"Yay, yay, yay...don't hurt your arm patting yourself on the back!" Michaela quickly added while laughing out loud. They each busted up laughing.

There was a long pause when Sheryl said, "Michaela, I hope I'm not prying, and I know that you two have totally fallen for each other. You know that I know Alex fairly well, but you've been a lot more intimate with him, so what's he like for real?"

"Intimate?"

Suddenly, Sheryl realized that the way she asked the question that Michaela might be thinking she's asking her how Alex is in bed. Sheryl quickly said, "Oh my, I'm sorry. I'm not asking how he is in bed."

Michaela laughed, saying, "I didn't think you were, but just know that all is awesome on that front!" She winked at Sheryl.

Sheryl, with a sly smile, said, "Got it!"

Then after a moment of laughing, Sheryl continued, "What I meant to say was, what is he really like down deep, does that make sense? He is such a private person. I wonder if he has opened up to you."

With a slight smile, Michaela said, "Let me tell you, this is how I see Alex. Of course, you know that he is intelligent and hardworking, but also tender hearted, caring, he communicates, lives by high standards and is hard on himself in that respect. Alex is meticulous, a problem-solver, a leader who leads by example. As you know he is quiet, reserved, loyal, understanding, a patient person, he makes me feel very safe, he's always thinking ahead, and his mind always seems to be working overtime. I think that's where I help him be a little laid-back and relax and laugh in the moment. I'm not saying he doesn't relax, but sometimes he's needing a little help in turning it off. He has a subtle yet terrific sense of humor. He keeps his emotions buried, is sensitive, but tries not to show it. He cares and likes to help others, actually he puts others before himself. He's perceptive, he listens, and seems to organize life well if that makes sense. He's definitely a goal setter. Unlike me, he doesn't get too excited or too down, just keeps his emotions on an even keel. That part of him really helps me. I think we mesh up very well together. We each like our privacy and keep our emotions to ourselves, however because we now trust each other we have come to be able to talk about things openly. We have similar interests, he seems to understand me through all my different moods, he calms me! He considers my feelings and I adore that trait. No one else has ever done that for me. He respects me, makes me feel cherished, he brings out the best of me. He has tapped into the passion in me that I didn't even know existed. He's my best friend! He makes me feel like I'm priority one!

Sheryl was sitting there in awe as she was listening to Michaela detail how she felt about Alex. Michaela had finished talking, it was very quiet and after a pause Sheryl said, "Wow!"

With a little chuckle, Michaela said, "Well, you asked!"

"Yes, I did, didn't I." Sheryl continued, "It sounds like he opens up and tells you everything, no secrets."

"I think he does," Michaela said. She paused for a moment as Sheryl gazed at her with a quizzical look then asked, "What?"

Michaela continued, "You know, Sheryl, he told me a while back that he wouldn't keep any secrets from me and that I could ask him anything. After he said it, he paused for a moment then said, well anything except my early military career. I won't discuss some of my deployments with anybody."

"So are you curious what those deployments were about?"

"Maybe a little, but it doesn't matter now because that's in the past. I feel that he not only doesn't want to talk about them but maybe he can't discuss them either, know what I mean." Michaela continued, "I'm good with that, it's history now."

After a moment, Sheryl thought, "You know you're right and he's opened up to you about everything else so in the big picture of things it really doesn't matter."

There was a short period of silence then Michaela asked, "Have you talked with Alex since our return?"

"Talk? I haven't even seen him!"

Michaela replied, "Not surprising, he has been so unbelievably busy since we got back. I don't think he's gone to bed before 2:00 a.m. since our return. And keep in mind he's up every morning at five thirty. He gets in a quick workout before starting anything else."

Sheryl looked at Michaela affectionately and said softly, "You love him, don't you?"

"Love him? I adore him!" Michaela continued, "He's the best thing that has ever happened to me. Sheryl, thank you for bringing us together!"

"Oh, no problem, my pleasure," Sheryl replied.

"No, I mean it, thank you so much. He has been a Godsend for me!" Michaela's voice cracked; she had barely got out that last little bit when tears began to run down her cheeks. Sheryl leaned over and hugged Michaela while she wiped her tears then said, "I'm sorry, didn't mean to lose it!"

Sheryl countered, "That's okay, it shows me how much you truly love Alex."

Michaela hesitated for a moment then softly said as she was still wiping some tears away, "Sheryl, you don't know what I've been through the last few years! Please understand that Alex entering my life is more than a Godsend, he has literally saved my life. I don't know what God has planned for me, but I feel that whatever it is that Alex will be with me all the way!"

Sheryl holding her hand over her heart tenderly said, "Oh, that is so touching, I am so happy for you, I am! And yes, he will be there for you, always, I just know it!"

They continued talking for a few more minutes as they finished up their wine. Michaela was helping Sheryl clean up in the kitchen when she suddenly had a small pain in her left side and had to sit down.

Sheryl asked, "Are you okay?"

Michaela replied, "Yes, I'm fine. I haven't felt very good for the last couple of days… I'm just a little worn down."

"Are you sure?"

"I'm sure. I just need a little rest, and anyway, Alex will be home tomorrow afternoon," Michaela said.

*****

Alex returned home later in the afternoon the next day. Michaela made dinner for them, and Alex cleaned up the kitchen. They talked and cuddled on the couch as they watched a movie. They went to bed, and after a while, Alex was running his hand over Michaela's stomach, and he asked, "What's that?"

He continued, "There's a hard lump right there, and I think there's another one. Those weren't there before, were they? I think they are new. Are you feeling okay?"

Michaela replied, "Well, I didn't want to worry you while you were gone, but I haven't felt very good for the past couple of days."

"I don't like this. Something is not right. We need to get you in to see your oncologist tomorrow. Can you call first thing in the morning?"

She said, "Yes, I will, I had planned on calling anyway. I hope he's in this week being it's Thanksgiving."

Alex held her close as he prayed for her, "Please, Lord, let everything be okay with Michaela!"

*****

Michaela called her oncologist's office first thing the next morning. After speaking briefly with the doctor, he said, "I want to see you this morning!"

While she was in the shower, she showed Alex a couple more lumps that didn't appear to be there last night. Alex didn't say anything, but this concerned him greatly.

Alex asked her how she felt this morning, and Michaela said, "I still feel tired, and I'm hurting a little in my stomach." Alex knew this had come on pretty fast, so he was thinking privately that maybe it's something else and not cancer. He took her to the doctor's office and waited while she was being examined.

While he was waiting, Tim called and asked how the projects were coming along. Alex didn't say anything about him being in the doctor's office with Michaela; in fact, Tim didn't even know that Alex was even dating anyone. So Alex told him he was getting close.

Alex said, "I have two more projects to evaluate data then I can finish up."

He continued, "I received the numbers back from the statistician for several of the projects, and all is looking good. I'm going to take about eight to ten of the posters into the printer this week. I should be able to get the other six or so completed or nearly completed by the first of next week. Then all I will have left is to get them printed in time for the meeting in New Orleans. Time is getting short, but I have about two weeks still."

Tim said, "Well, congratulations, it looks like you're about to pull off the impossible! That is awesome!"

Alex with a chuckle replied, "Let's not count our chickens yet! I still have a lot of work to do." He said, "Hey, Tim, I got the poster numbers for the session and about half of them are on one aisle. All the customers will be there to help with the presentations." With a laugh, he said, "There's no way I could work fourteen posters!"

Tim laughed and made a crack, "Well, I guess we'll have to call that Alex's aisle!" This brought a chuckle to Alex.

Tim continued, he let Alex know which hotel our clinical team's annual reception will be located. He said, "We have a large ballroom as we're expecting quite the crowd!"

Alex replied, "Excellent, you know I think I'll probably have thirty-plus customers there myself."

They talked for a few more minutes before wishing each other a Happy Thanksgiving.

Alex once again brought his focus back to Michaela as he was wondering what was going on with the exam. She had been back there for more than an hour when the nurse came to the door and asked, "Are you Alex?"

"Yes."

She said, "Come on back, please."

Alex was taken into the exam room where Michaela was sitting. He reached over and held her hand just as the doctor said, "I don't like the way this looks, so I'm going to admit her immediately!" The doctor continued, "I've already ordered some tests and scans for today, then we'll do a couple more in the morning then see where we are."

All kinds of questions were rushing through Alex's clinically oriented mind, but he didn't utter a word. He just looked at Michaela, laid her head against his shoulder, gently stroked her hair, and kissed the top of her head.

Alex finally whispered, "Have *faith*."

Alex was with her all through the admission process and helped her get situated into her room. Michaela was going to have several tests and scans the rest of the day, so Alex went home to get some work done. Before he left, Michaela gave him a list of items to bring back later in an overnight bag.

Later, he brought takeout back for dinner. Alex brought some items back for himself, as he spent the night with her in the hospital room.

The next morning, they each got cleaned up, and hospital staff escorted Michela out for another battery of tests. The doctor said, "This will take a while in case you've got some other things to do."

Alex said, "Okay." He leaned over and gave Michaela a kiss after she sat down in the wheelchair then told her, "I'll be back after a while if that's okay."

Michaela sitting there reached up and gave Alex the biggest neck hug, then whispered into his ear, "I love you so much!" After a pause, she said, "See you later," as they wheeled her out the door.

Alex watched as the nurse wheeled her down the hallway. His mind wandered for a moment then he said a little prayer, "Lord, I don't know what your plan is for Michaela, but I love her and I want the very best for her so please keep her safe. But know that no matter what you have instore for her, I will be at her side the entire way!"

*****

It was midafternoon and Alex walked back into Michaela's room. A smile that would light up any room came across her face as she was so happy to see him. He asked, "How long have you been back in the room?"

She said, "Oh, about thirty minutes."

"Oh, jeez, I am so sorry, I wanted to be here when you got back."

"That's okay, I know you have a lot on your plate and besides you're here now, thank you," she replied.

He took her hand and said, "Thank you." Then he leaned over the side of the bed and kissed her. Alex asked her how she was feeling as she noted that she was hurting a little today. Alex squeezed her hand with affection as they gazed into each other's eyes. Alex was trying to show her strength as he felt she was feeling a little down. He was sitting on the bed when her oncologist walked into the room. A nurse walked in right behind him and began tending to Michaela.

The doctor looked at Alex and motioned to him and said, "Let's talk out here." They walked out of the room to the nurses' station where Alex leaned up against the counter. As he turned around to face the doctor, Michaela was in his line of sight. Standing with her doctor was his oncology fellow and a nurse at the counter. Alex could see that Michaela was staring at them with a look of concern.

There was a pause then the doctor glanced at his fellow and said, "I always hate this part!" As Alex glanced at the fellow, he saw the look of sadness on her face. This made him immediately think, "Uh-oh, this is not going to be good, brace yourself."

The doctor then said, "Alex, her cancer has come back in a big way!"

Alex asked, "Weren't her tests all clear a month ago?"

"Yes, they were but this uptick in her cancer is very aggressive maybe the worst I've seen!" The doctor was looking solemn when Alex asked, "So when have you scheduled the surgery?"

Doctor said quietly, "No, no surgery."

Alex, examining the look on the doctor's face, asked, "Chemotherapy?"

"No."

"Radiation treatments?"

"No."

The realization of what was coming next suddenly hit Alex. The doctor continued, "It's spreading rapidly all through her body, we can't do anything about it!"

Alex took a deep breath, trying to contain himself as he ran his hand through his hair and across his face. Tears were forming in his eyes as he tried to hold them in check. It was then that he glanced at Michaela who was closely watching his reaction from her bed. Alex took several deep breaths as he was staring at Michaela.

He finally looked back at the doctor and asked in a somber whisper, "How long?"

The doctor with a dark sadness on his face said, "It's extremely aggressive, and I don't think she'll make Christmas."

Alex dejectedly whispered, "Oh no."

The doctor replied, "I am very sorry!"

The nurse placed her hand on his shoulder as did the fellow. Alex reacted with a look of disbelief and shock. Tears were forming in his eyes again as Alex had so many things going through his mind. Alex glanced back at Michaela with a deep sigh of sadness as tears flowed down his cheeks.

Michaela was looking intently at Alex as he stared at her. She suddenly placed her hand over her heart. She could see the look of sadness on Alex's face, and she knew as she gasped placing her hand over her mouth. It was as if their eyes and minds were talking to each other.

Alex upon seeing her reaction rushed into the room and sat on the bed next to her. No words were spoken as he simply hugged her like never before. Upon seeing the tears in Alex's eyes, Michaela felt the great hurt in his heart and tears began rolling down her cheeks as well. They had a few moments of silence as they were oblivious to anyone else in the room. However, each of the doctors had followed Alex into her room.

When they broke their embrace, the team was standing there. Michaela with tears running down her cheeks and holding Alex's hand tightly looked at her doctor and in the strongest voice she could muster asked, "So, Doc, how long do I have to live?"

The doctor said somberly, "I am so sorry, but the cancer is spreading so rapidly all throughout your body and there's nothing we can do." He continued, "It has spread so rapidly it's difficult to believe. Your ovarian cancer is now stage IV, grade III and we see it in the entire abdominal area, the liver, the spleen, your intestines, lining around the lungs, and lymph nodes. We're also seeing it in the brain too. We can't do surgery as it's everywhere and spreading. Treatments like chemotherapy and radiation will not do any good. It's too advanced. I can't hardly believe it has been this aggressive this quick. Frankly, in all my years I've never seen one this aggressive."

Michaela, squeezing Alex's hand even tighter, asked again, "So how long?"

Directly looking at Michaela, the doctor said, "I told Alex that I don't think you'll make it to Christmas." The result of this announcement felt like all the air had just been sucked out of the room. At this, Michaela leaned against Alex, held him tightly, then she had such an outpouring of heartache and sadness. The release of emotions and grief was difficult to witness!

After she collected herself, her doctor gently explained, "Your fatigue will increase sharply, you'll begin having quite a bit of vomiting and nausea, weight loss, and your pain will begin to increase as well. We can try and manage the symptoms as best we can as they arise and intensify!"

Alex added, "I will obviously help with all aspects of palliative care and caregiving," as he was hugging Michaela.

All was quiet; there was a somber mood in the room as no one knew quite what to say next when Alex broke the silence with, "Okay, enough of this defeatism!" His take-charge attitude took everyone by surprise as he looked at Michaela and simply said, "I don't go down easy and I'm at your side the whole way!" She hugged his neck so hard!

He continued, "I don't think God brought Michaela and me together for no reason. I feel there is a *miracle* wrapped into this situation somewhere!"

The doctor engaged with, "I like your enthusiasm and positive outlook, but I'm open to any suggestions."

Alex looked at the doctor and told him the company he worked for and that he was within the Medical Affairs group. The doctor was surprised as Alex continued, "You know, Doc, there may be some experimental agents at some other institutions that you don't know about."

The doctor replied, "That's always possible. Any ideas how we proceed?"

Alex responded, "Yes, first I can call our Oncology Medical lead for any ideas, secondly, I can reach out to our Oncology Medical leads who call on MD Anderson and maybe Johns Hopkins. Next, can you gather all of Michaela's medical info together in case we need to forward them somewhere. Lastly, if we need to fly somewhere this weekend such as Houston for an appointment at MD Anderson then we will make that happen."

Her doctor replied, "That's a good plan, plus I have a couple of colleagues that I know at MD Anderson I can call now."

The doctor went out to call his colleagues while Alex reached out to his company's Oncology Medical lead in headquarters. Alex and the lead talked for a while as he described what was going on, the cancer, and prognosis. He was very empathetic to Alex, and he continued, "I have some close colleagues over at Sloan Kettering here in New York. Do you have her records?"

Alex replied, "Her oncologist and I have already discussed that, and he can pull them together today. We are moving this along very quickly for obvious reasons."

The company oncology lead said, "Alex, let me make some phone calls and I will call you back shortly."

Michaela's oncologist walked over to Alex and said, "I contacted a colleague at MD Anderson and he's reaching out to another oncologist there on staff."

Alex replied, "I discussed the case with our lead and he's contacting some colleagues at Sloan Kettering and possibly some other places." Alex went ahead and said, "I'm calling my colleagues in Houston and Maryland too."

It wasn't long until Alex's oncology headquarters lead called and provided him with a name and phone number to call at Sloan Kettering. Alex passed the information along to Michaela's oncologist.

Alex talked with each of his medical affairs colleagues in Houston and Baltimore who work with MD Anderson and Johns Hopkins, respectively. They each provided their recommendations for specific physicians and even reached out to them as well. They gave their permission to let Michaela's doctor call them too.

Alex assisted Michaela's doctor with collecting together copies of her records, and he ended up forwarding them by FedEx to MD Anderson. After Michaela's doctor spoke with an oncologist at Sloan Kettering a copy of the records was sent there as well. Now all there was to do was wait while oncology specialists at MD Anderson and Sloan Kettering had an opportunity to review the records and provide a recommendation.

Michaela was discharged. After getting home, Alex immediately sat Michaela down on the couch and said, "I know you're feeling down right now and asking yourself why me, but I will *not* allow you to drift into melancholy. Look, Michaela, I meant what I said, I feel that God brought us together for a good reason. Furthermore, I believe God will grant you a *miracle*, I believe that because we have *faith*!

Michaela was gasping for a breath as tears were flowing down each cheek simply reached out and hugged Alex with such steadiness then said, "Hold me, please hold me, I'm scared!"

Alex quietly said, "It's okay to be scared, but just know I'm here to be your *strength*!"

She quietly murmured, "Ohhhh!" She hugged his neck.

Alex then got down on one knee, he held each of her hands as he peered deeply into her eyes and with the utmost sincerity he said, "Michaela, I want you to know that wherever this journey takes us that I am with you all the way. I will be here at every step and at every moment. This is our journey, together… I am with you! Michaela, I love you! I love you, I do, so passionately! I *will* be here for you no matter what! We simply must pray and keep the *faith*!"

Michaela was breathless, tears flowing almost uncontrollably she hugged Alex's neck with all her might! Then Michaela placed her hands on each side of Alex's face and kissed him tenderly. Still holding Alex's face, she said, "I love you too, you make me so happy! I can't hardly believe that God brought you into my life!" Alex's heart was so incredibly touched!

*****

The day after discharge, Alex asked Michaela, "What would you like to do for Thanksgiving tomorrow?"

She thought for a moment then said, "You know what I would like is a traditional Thanksgiving meal."

Alex thought about that for a few seconds then replied in a forceful voice, "Michaela, you want a traditional Thanksgiving meal, then by golly, that's what you're going to get!"

"So what are we going to do?" she asked.

He replied, "You are not going to do anything unless you want to help, but I'm going to fix you Thanksgiving dinner. It'll be my first time, so I'm warning you now."

She laughed then smiled and said, "Hmmmm! This is going to be interesting."

Alex went to the store and gathered all the items for his menu. Early Thanksgiving morning, he began to prepare his meal. He cooked a turkey, made the stuffing from scratch, and made a sweet potato casserole. He included deviled eggs, green beans, cranberry salad, giblet gravy, dinner rolls, and had a store-bought pecan pie. This was the first time Alex had ever fixed a Thanksgiving meal and it made Michaela very happy.

Michaela told Alex, "This was terrific, you did great, thank you!"

Alex teased her and said, "Well, I hope you like turkey because that's what you're going to get for the next three to four days!"

Michaela belted out a laugh. "I love turkey!"

Alex tried to keep Michaela busy and engaged in activities to keep her from thinking about her prognosis. He worked to keep her in good spirits.

Alex would work on his projects late into the night after she had gone to bed. He would get some more work completed early in the mornings as well. By the end of the weekend, Alex had all his projects completed and was working on the assessment phase for the final two. He emailed data to his statistician so he could evaluate the information on Monday. Alex dropped a couple more projects off at the printers and by Tuesday afternoon was down to his last two that needed to be finalized. He could finally begin to see the light at the end of his proverbial tunnel.

During this time, Alex continued to do all he could to keep Michaela's focus off her cancer. They watched movies and, in the evening, gazed at the stars while sipping on a glass of wine. Michaela's pain level had escalated a little but was still within very tolerable limits.

The week went well, and time passed faster than expected. Alex had all his projects completed and had forwarded the last two to the printer by Thursday afternoon. Alex had an end-of-week phone call with Tim. Besides catching up on standard topics, performance measures, monthly report, he also let Tim know that he had completed all the projects for the meeting presentations next week.

Tim said, "That is awesome!" He continued, "You know after this meeting there are going to be some of our colleagues nationally that will probably be pissed off at you for setting the bar so high!" Tim continued, "But most will be congratulatory and probably ask you how in world did you do that much. So be ready for all kinds of reactions."

Alex simply shrugged his shoulders and told Tim, "Well, you know how people are and you know me, I can only control what I do, not what others do, say, or think. However, I'm always here to assist anyone, you know that."

Tim responded with, "Oh, I agree but just wanted to make you aware just in case." He continued, "Let me say what you've accomplished is nothing short of remarkable, way to go! I'm proud to have you on my team!"

*****

The oncology physicians at MD Anderson and Sloan Kettering had reviewed all the records for Michaela. Even though Michaela and Alex were willing to fly to Houston or New York or anywhere else for further assessment it wasn't needed. Alex took Michaela into her oncologist's office where a conference call had been set up. On the phone were the oncologists from MD Anderson and Sloan Kettering. In succession, they each provided their feedback and agreed that the aggressive nature of this cancer was astounding. After discussing the particulars of the case, they agreed that it has expanded into so many of her organs and other spaces. Apologetically, they agreed that they didn't think she would make it to New Year's.

However, they each noted that they had access to this new drug which was in early phase II trials. They noted this agent wasn't being studied for stage IV ovarian cancer, but they thought because of its mechanism of action that it could possibly help. They discussed adding it to other chemotherapy and see what develops. All the physicians concurred, and they decided to have the study drug forwarded to Birmingham.

Michaela was trying to follow the medical discussion but finally turned to Alex to ask, "So what does all of this mean?"

Alex hesitated then responded with, "Your prognosis has not changed as they still believe the first of the year. However, they would like to initiate chemotherapy anyway with the addition of a new phase II trial drug. So bottom line is that there is a small ray of hope by adding the new agent…they simply don't know."

The physicians all chimed in with virtually the same response, "Alex summarized our thoughts pretty well!" They continued,

"Michaela, we are very sorry that we can't do anything more for you but our current state of innovation in oncology medicine just hasn't advanced to the level of effectiveness one needs to destroy this aggressive cancer."

Her oncologist asked Michaela to come back Monday and noted they will get started with her first round of chemotherapy, which would include the new agent.

Michaela with a shaky voice asked, "So what are my chances that this will work?"

Each physician noted, "Well, again, we hate to say it, but we don't know if it will work at all, but it is the only thing which may give you a fighting chance. That's merely a respectful way of saying that we are hoping for the best."

Contemplating this new information, Michaela with a somber whisper stated, "Let's give it a try, nothing to lose!" Alex admired her strength as he thought privately that he was going to do everything within his power to make her life the best it can possibly be no matter what happens.

*****

Arriving home, Alex would not let Michaela slip into a depressive state of mind. He told her that they would be in this together no matter what happens. He continued to explain all the areas covered by palliative care.

Alex told Michaela, "The areas we will manage that fall under palliative care are your pain, your anxiety, your spirituality, manage any nausea and vomiting, and very importantly your nutrition and hydration. I'm going to make your quality of life the very best I can. I will help you with sleep and fatigue. Your comfort and sense of well-being are important as well. We will put together a care plan and work with your doctor. We will engage a caregiver service in the event I must be out of town. I know I haven't covered everything, but we will be ready and address things as they arise. Bottom line is that I will be here for you!"

He continued, "We will pray for a *miracle* to happen as I personally feel that the Lord didn't bring us together for nothing. I have *faith* that something great will occur on your behalf!"

All Michaela could do was hug Alex as some tears flowed and nothing was said. Internally, Michaela felt so blessed to have Alex in her life. She curled up on the couch with her head in Alex's lap. Alex stroked her beautiful locks as they remained quiet. After a while, she fell asleep. Alex covered her with a blanket while laying her head on a pillow after taking off her shoes. He just let her sleep!

Over the weekend, Alex worked to pull together all his posters for the national meeting in New Orleans. Plus, he and his co-presenter completed the final tweaking of their power point slides for their platform presentation. In addition, he and Michaela talked a lot about her care plan. It was Alex's focus to plan every aspect of her days and weeks to concentrate on her health, spirituality, and overall status.

Alex intended to do things that Michaela either liked to do or always wanted to do but couldn't. He felt that if she was engaged in doing things that she liked it would help to keep her in a more positive frame of mind.

During their discussions, Alex asked, "Is there anywhere you have always wanted to visit but never could?" He continued that thought with, "My notion is that we could go places as long as you felt like it."

Michaela was thinking that is ever so sweet and it reaffirmed her love for Alex. After a bit, she replied, "Thank you for offering, maybe there are some places that we could visit." She continued, "You know, Alex, when I lived in the north Atlanta suburbs, I always wanted to go stay at Chateau Elan Winery and Resort. Can we go there?"

He replied, "Absolutely! I've been there a couple of times, and it is wonderful. It would be my pleasure to take you there."

She continued, "You know where I would like to go?"

"No, tell me?"

"Can I go with you this week to New Orleans? I've never been there."

A little shocked, Alex said, "You've never been to New Orleans? Well, of course, you can go! I should have thought of that already, I'm sorry."

He continued, "I was going to fly down but we can drive. I'm leaving Wednesday morning and coming back Saturday evening. Does that work for you?"

"Yes, it does, I would love to go with you. Actually, I want to be by your side as much as possible." He took a deep breath as this made Alex's heart feel very warm; he loved this woman so much!

Michaela continued, "Let me think about some other places and of course it will depend upon how I feel. In fact, you've been many more places than I, so maybe you can come up with some places to visit? That is if I'm up to it."

He said, "Okay, I'll start thinking on it."

A couple of moments passed when Michaela spoke again saying, "I know we had planned on going to Oklahoma over Christmas to meet your family. I truly want to meet your family so very bad, but I want to wait until I am fully in the clear from my cancer. I'm not trying to hurt your feelings and I hope you understand."

"I absolutely fully understand what you're saying!" Alex replied, "Don't you worry about a thing!"

10

Coming to Grips

On Monday, Alex took Michaela in for her initial chemotherapy treatment. Her oncologist stopped by the infusion center and they had a discussion.

The doctor stated, "Your treatment has the extra drug which is being infused. Honestly, we are unsure how this cocktail will affect you. Of course, we hope it slows down the cancer growth and reduces it as well. But we don't know what adverse events and symptoms you may have to endure. Be aware of the potential for increased nausea and vomiting and it may accelerate your hair loss. Frankly, we just don't know with this cocktail. I wanted to be up front with you so that you can prepare yourself. Alex knows how to treat any symptoms which may arise. Plus, he and I have spoken, and he has some good ideas to help."

Alex looked at Michaela and said, "I've worked up a whole nutrition plan which I ran by the group's dietician first, and the doctor approved it. It is a plan very high in protein, some fruits and vegetables, and low-fat dairy. We are going to cut out as much sugar as possible, only drink decaffeinated coffee, cut salt intake, and unfortunately cut out alcohol so there goes our wine."

Michaela asked, "Why wine?"

"Because the alcohol is metabolized by the liver and your liver has enough problems to deal with right now. Your chemotherapy agents and the cancer taking up residence in parts of it are enough for it to work on right now."

Michaela with a little snicker said, "Yeah, I guess you're right!"

Alex continued, "For proteins, we're going to have a lot of chicken, fish, and boiled eggs, plus I'll be mixing you some of my special protein shakes. At first, two shakes a day then later on more. We absolutely must keep weight on you!" He went on to say, "Some key things we'll have are asparagus, Brussel sprouts, avocadoes, oranges, bananas, peaches, pears, strawberries, figs, apricots, raisins are all some of the fruits and vegetables. For carbohydrates, we'll focus on rice, noodles, pasta, potatoes, beans, and honey. Also, we'll add more cheese, milk, and yogurt."

She said, "Okay, I like all of those foods, so what are the foods that I will need to avoid?"

Alex responded with, "That's a good question! Everything deep-fried is out, nothing grilled or barbecued, things like bacon, ham, and sausages are out as well."

"You know, that doesn't sound too bad. It actually sounds healthy!"

Alex replied, "That's exactly what it is…a balanced diet which is healthy." He continued with, "Really no diet can improve your chances with cancer even though there are urban myths about a vegan, or some special diets may help but they do not. The keys are to eat a balanced diet with lean protein and try to keep your weight up and to be sure to drink plenty of water."

Michaela smiled at Alex then raised her hand and they gave each other a high-five followed by her saying, "We got this!"

"Yes, we do!"

*****

Later in the day, Alex took Michaela home after chemotherapy where she laid down for a nap. Alex went out to perform some errands. He stopped by the printers to get his last two posters for the meeting and then to the grocery store. Finally, he stopped by the complex office to speak with Sheryl. He and Michaela hadn't seen her for several days, but Michaela had called her to give her the news about her cancer. Alex walked into the lobby, Sheryl walked up to him and simply placed her arms around him with a warm hug. After a few moments, she eventually said, "Alex, I am so sorry!"

Alex said, "Thank you."

With some tears running down her cheeks, she was able to ask, "How did her chemotherapy go today?"

"It went well, I took her home and she laid down for a nap. I've been running some errands." He continued, "Sheryl, I have a request."

"What is it?"

Alex said, "She is going with me this week to New Orleans."

"Oh, that's great, she'll like that! I'm glad you're taking her."

"Thanks, but I ordered a really nice wheelchair, which should be delivered later this week. When it comes can you store it in your apartment until the day that we may need it?" He continued, "I want to be prepared just in case we need it, but yet I don't want her to see it to think that it's inevitable. Does that make sense?"

"It absolutely does, and you are so thoughtful to do it this way to take her feelings into consideration first."

Alex didn't say anything; he simply smiled.

Sheryl continued, "So when are you guys leaving for New Orleans?"

"We are leaving out Wednesday morning probably around eight o'clock." Continuing, Alex said, "She doesn't know it, but I've made reservations for us Wednesday evening at Antoine's Restaurant. Also, I have reservations at Brennan's Restaurant for Friday night. I hope she feels up to it both evenings!"

Sheryl replied, "Oh, I'm green with envy. I've always wanted to eat at both of those places. From what I hear, they are great! She'll love it!" Sheryl closed with, "I'll take care of the wheelchair for you, no worries, you guys have fun!"

"Thanks, Sheryl!"

*****

They arrived in New Orleans and got checked in to their hotel, the Marriott on Canal Street. After getting situated, they laid down for a bit.

A little later, Alex was contacted by several of his customers, and he met them in the lobby where he gave them their posters. He was glad to give these away, as fourteen posters was simply too many to tote around! Returning to their room, Michaela was up watching the traffic on Canal Street and looking out toward the river. Alex asked, "How do you feel?"

Michaela responded, "Pretty good, that little nap helped. What time are our dinner reservations?"

Alex said, "We're on for seven o'clock. It's about four blocks over to Antoine's. Then I thought after dinner, we might circle back through Jackson Square to walk off some of our dinner on our way back to the hotel."

"That sounds good. Is that where the St. Louis Cathedral is?"

"Yes, you guessed it, it sure is!"

Alex continued, "At Antoine's we have to get the Oysters Rockefeller for an appetizer. They are known for them, and I love them…they are great!"

They got dressed up, and as usual, Michaela looked absolutely stunning. She confessed that she was hurting a little but not too bad. She admitted that she got a little nauseated on the drive down, but some crackers and water along with the short nap helped that to subside. As they walked through the lobby of the hotel, Michaela was amazed at how many people stopped to say hello to Alex. Finally, as they left the hotel with Michaela holding Alex's arm, she leaned into him and said, "I feel pretty good right now." Alex gave her a little love squeeze but remained silent as he had a warm feeling in his heart.

She held his hand tightly as they walked and talked the three to four blocks it was from their hotel to *Antoine's*. They were exactly on time, and Michaela even noticed that a couple more people saw Alex and greeted him while they were escorted to their table. Alex definitely took notice that many sets of eyes stopped to gaze at Michaela as they meandered through to their table. All Alex could do was smile as he agreed…she is incredibly beautiful!

Of course, they ordered the Oysters Rockefeller and Michaela sticking to her diet plan had a fish dish with vegetables. Alex ordered the beef tenderloin filet grilled to perfection. For dessert, they shared an Antoine's specialty, the baked Alaskan with decaf coffee. After an elegant dinner with intriguing conversation, they took that stroll over to Jackson Square. The evening had a slight chill, but Alex had carried her wrap earlier so Michaela was comfortable. Plus, she pressed up against Alex often to feel his warmth. Holding hands, kissing a little, walking close to each other as she leaned on Alex for support, they strolled back to their hotel.

Once they climbed into bed, Michaela said softly, "Thank you for bringing me here!" She continued, "Dinner was fabulous, and the walk was just right!"

About all Alex could do was smile, kiss her, and say, "I'm glad you came too!"

He continued by saying, "Tomorrow I'm afraid it's going to be a very full day for me. I've got all those posters just after lunch and will share the podium with a colleague for our presentation early. So you know, tomorrow evening is our national clinical team's annual reception. It is always very well attended, and I will be extremely busy shaking hands and talking to friends, customers, and colleagues alike. A large ballroom at the hotel has been secured and it will be packed, I can almost guarantee it! I will check on you during the day, but you'll be on your own if that's okay. I will be back here late in the afternoon to refresh myself and give my feet a short rest before I go to the reception. Now, if you want to go to the reception, that's okay, as I can get you in even though it's by invitation and badge only. I'll let you decide." He added, "One more thing, if you're up to it I think there is a shopping area just a couple of blocks toward the river. You could ask the concierge. The walk is short but be careful not to overextend yourself and get too tired."

Michaela with her head on the pillow said, "Thanks for asking, I'm not sure if I'll be up to a large, crowded reception like that. I know you'll be busy, and I don't want to slow you down. I might go shopping. We'll see how I feel. Anyway, thanks for looking out for me!"

She looked so calm and serene as she laid there with a beautiful smile on her face and her gorgeous blue eyes beaming. Then she glanced up at Alex and quietly said, "Alex, I love you!"

With this Alex said nothing, he kissed her, smiled broadly, then simply wrapped his arms around her and cuddled until they each fell asleep.

*****

Alex was up early the next morning getting ready for the day and being as quiet as possible. He didn't want to wake Michaela. Alex had prepared some protein shakes with his special blend of greens and fruits the evening before and had them in the refrigerator. He had written a note the night before about the protein shakes and to feel free to order some room service. He signed it, "Have a nice day and call me if you need me."

When he left, Alex placed a card where Michaela would see it after she awoke. It wasn't much, simply a short, handwritten note which said,

Michaela,

I'm going to love you through your weakest moments to your strongest ones. I'm going to love you when you're happy, and I'm going to still love you when you're sad.

I'm here, and I'm not going anywhere. I want to love you, each and every day. I want you no matter what happens. I'm going to be here loving you every second of the day and with every breath I take.

Love,
Alex

Michaela found his card and after reading it, she simply sat there and cried! A few minutes later, she wiped her tears and started to pray. "Lord, I don't know or understand what you have in store for me and my life, but bless you, O Lord, for bringing Alex into my life. I Love him so very much."

The day sped along quickly. The early platform presentation went well to a packed room. Alex interacted with dozens of friends and colleagues during the day. All the posters presented looked great and Alex's partner customers were appreciative and thankful for his efforts. Alex's team manager, Tim was so proud that one of his people had this many presentations at one meeting.

Toward the end of the afternoon, Alex had talked with Michaela several times during the day. She noted that she had slept in late and drank one of the shakes. Michaela had ordered a small lunch making sure that she stayed within her diet plan. After lunch, she curled up with a good book and read, as she didn't feel like going anywhere.

Alex took the shuttle bus back to the hotel from the convention center. After entering the room, he immediately took his shoes off to relax his feet. He gave Michaela a kiss and asked how she was feeling.

Michaela replied with, "I've been a little tired all day, just haven't had the energy to do much."

"So did you get a lot of your book read?" he asked.

"Yes, I did. Have only twenty to thirty pages left."

Alex asked, "Was it good?"

She replied, "Aahh, it was so-so." Michaela asked, "Your feet hurting you?"

He said, "Jeez, right now they're killing me. Those concrete floors at the convention center are so hard to walk on with leather soled dress shoes."

"When do you need to be at the reception?"

"Oh, not until six thirty. Some of us have been requested to get there early."

"Great, that gives us two hours to blow off."

Alex asked, "Is there anything you need me to get for you?"

"No, just some of your time."

This made Alex smile all over. He broke the silence with, "Did you do anything else today?"

Michaela said, "I talked with my boss, and they placed me on a six-month medical leave of absence with full pay."

"That was nice of them!"

"Yeah, it was, they are holding my job for me." After a few moments, Michaela laughed and said, "Look at me, I'm still wearing my night gown under my robe." She sprawled out across the bed then glanced at Alex and opened her robe. With a little grin and a wink, she said, "Can you think of anything we could do for the next hour or so?"

Alex undoing his tie and unbuttoning his shirt said with a little smile, "Oh, I think we can think of something!"

*****

Alex got showered, dressed, and went to the reception. As expected, people started to pile into the ballroom around seven. It was a very large ballroom, but by eight to eight thirty, the place was jammed. Alex was mingling during the event talking with his customers, friends, and colleagues. Everyone was having a tremendous time. The appetizers, food, and beverages were delicious and plentiful. Alex was talking with his manager and some senior management, who were present, as all were impressed with the client attendance. It was confirmed that this was the best national clinical team reception to date. Frankly, it truly was amazing, and customers were still talking about the reception months later.

Alex did get an opportunity to step out for a few minutes to call and check on Michaela. She noted that she had ordered some room service and was all laid up in the bed watching a movie.

When Alex returned to the room, Michaela was sound asleep. He was quiet then snuggled up close to her, which she reciprocated.

*****

The next day, Alex went to several continuing education breakouts and talked with customers and colleagues alike. He continued to check on Michaela throughout the day. This day she did manage to get out of the hotel and did a little shopping. She didn't stay out long as she knew they were going out to dinner, so she took a nap in the afternoon as she was feeling a little queasy. Michaela was drinking two of Alex's special protein shakes a day. Her food intake was by her diet plan, but her portions were indeed small the past couple of days. Yet it was clear to Alex that she was going to be a fighter!

They were getting ready for their evening when Michaela asked, "So where are we going to dinner?"

He said, "We are going to one of my favorite restaurants in the entire U.S., it's called Brennan's. They are famous for their Bananas Foster for dessert, which they flambè at the tableside. The rest of their menu is some great cuisine as well. I've invited eight of my customers, so we have a table for ten. I think you'll like them all, they are terrific people."

As Alex was tying his tie, Michaela took a step back and asked, "So how do I look?"

With a kidding gesture and a wink, he slowly examined Michaela up and down then with a grin he simply said, "Yeah, you look okay." He was trying to keep a straight face when she began to pinch him until he swung around, and they embraced. After a short laugh, they kissed and then Alex said, "Michaela, you always look stunning!"

She said, "Thank you" as she was straightening out his tie knot.

They walked hand in hand once again from the hotel to Brennan's, which was only about three blocks. They were right on time for their reservation as was the rest of his party and all were seated. This group of eight customers were those in which Alex partnered with on the poster presentations for the meeting.

Alex introduced Michaela to everyone and told her where they each worked. The group was having an enjoyable time talking and laughing all during dinner. When choosing dessert, Alex spoke up and suggested the Bananas Foster noting that they are world famous here at Brennan's. They all agreed, and Alex ordered three for the table, which they prepared at tableside. Delicious doesn't begin to describe their taste!

Prior to departing, one of Alex's customers, Gail who was also a good friend, leaned over and whispered to Alex, "Michaela is truly charming and so elegant, plus she is incredibly beautiful…where did you meet her?"

Alex simply said, "She's my neighbor and we've been dating for quite a while, and you are right she is charming, smart too!"

Gail, in a low voice said, "You know all night I haven't been able to take my eyes off her. She has the brightest blue eyes I have ever seen, so radiant!"

All Alex could do was smile as Gail was right.

Again, Gail looked at Alex with all sincerity and said, "She is definitely a keeper, and we can tell that she loves you so much! Her body language toward you speaks volumes!" She continued, "As a woman, I think I'm supposed to be a little jealous of her, but I can't be. She is not only one of the most beautiful women I've ever seen, but her skin is utterly perfect!

After a short laugh, Gail jokingly said, "Well, actually I'm probably supposed to hate her, but I can't." As she continued to laugh, Gail went on to say, "Of course she is delightful, radiant, and I must talk with her sometime."

"Why is that?" Alex asked.

"Because I want to learn how she takes care of her skin," said Gail.

"Maybe we can all get together some time in the foreseeable future as I'd love to get to know her better."

Alex thought for a moment and replied, "I agree, we should do that!"

"Great, you guys can come down to our lake house on a weekend," Gail responded.

Alex said, "That sounds good."

Gail finished up with, "Good, then she can explain to me what she does to her skin to keep it so silky smooth, soft, and radiant. You know, it appears as if she's not hardly wearing any makeup. If so, that would mean her beauty is natural. That would be incredible!" She continued, "Does she wear much makeup?"

Alex, smiling, answered with, "I don't think she does. I know she doesn't take very long to get ready, but you'll just have to ask."

At that, Michaela had been talking with a couple of the other guests and she walked up and said, "Very nice to meet you, Gail."

Gail returned the compliment with, "Yes, great to meet you as well. Also, we were just talking, and I've invited you two down to our lake house sometime."

Michaela, grabbing Alex by the arm, responded, "Oh, that would be nice."

The group was beginning to break up and depart while Alex was paying the bill. They all gave Alex a hug and a big thank-you for a wonderful evening. While Alex was finishing up, Michaela had noticed where Brennan's serves breakfast. While their waitress was still there, she asked Alex, "Can we have breakfast here in the morning?"

That question took Alex a little by surprise, but he smiled and said, "Yes, I think that's a good idea."

Alex turned to the waitress and asked, "Can you make us some reservations in the morning?"

She said, "Give me a moment and I'll see what's available." The waitress returned in a couple of minutes and said, "How does eight forty-five sound?"

Before Alex could say anything, Michaela spoke up quickly and said, "We'll take it!"

Alex looked at the waitress and simply replied, "Well, you heard the lady, eight forty-five works."

They all left the restaurant and Alex walked Michaela one block over to Bourbon Street. They strolled down Bourbon back to Canal then down Canal Street to the Marriott. Their final night in New Orleans was memorable!

*****

The next morning, they were all packed. Alex had the bell stand store their luggage while they went to breakfast. Breakfast at Brennan's was just as incredible as the dinner the evening before. Michaela savored every bite and let the whole experience engulf her emotions. She was feeling that she probably wouldn't get this opportunity again anytime soon, if at all. The emotions of the moment overcame her, and tears began to roll down her cheeks. Alex quickly noticed the look on her face and her tears then he asked, "Are you okay?"

She reached over and took hold of Alex's hand and affectionately whispered, "Yes, thank you for bringing me here!"

Alex squeezed her hand and with a little smirk he said, "Yeah, the food is pretty good here," then smiled.

She leaned in and squeezed his hand a little harder and added, "You know what I mean, here to New Orleans, with you!"

Grinning, he admitted, "I know what you meant, and you are welcome. I've enjoyed every minute of our time! I wish I could articulate better how much I truly cherish being in your presence!"

Michaela, with a warm smile, said, "You just did."

After breakfast, they walked back to the hotel where they retrieved their luggage and car. On the drive home, Michaela showed just how much this trip had drained her energy. Alex was still crossing Lake Pontchartrain when he noticed that Michaela had dozed off… sound asleep. She slept most of the drive home.

During the drive home from New Orleans and while Michaela was sleeping, Alex's Manager, Tim, had called. Tim congratulated Alex once again on his repertoire of presentations as they were all terrific. They discussed how the team's reception was literally the talk of the meeting afterward. They continued by thinking through different and potential strategies for the upcoming year. As their conversations began to wind down, Alex said, "I need to discuss one more matter with you."

Tim answered, "Oh yeah, what's that?"

Alex said, "This is more informative than anything else. You know that when it comes to my personal life that I am extremely private. You recall that I hadn't discussed anything about Cynthia with you or really anyone else until all was said and done! So along those same lines I wanted you to know what I am dealing with, well let's call it a personal problem. I have no idea how long this personal problem will last, but I am going to attempt to limit my away from home travel to as little as possible. I plan on attending our Year Beginning Management Meeting in January. However, unless absolutely necessary to travel, most of my customers I can phone, at least for a while. I've already discussed this with my Air Force supervisor, and I'll perform my annual duties in lump timeframes later in the year. Well, that's about all I have to say on the matter at this time."

Tim pondered on what Alex had just related then replied, "As usual it sounds like you've thought this through. And as much as I would like to know more about your personal problem not as your manager, but as your friend, I won't delve into that topic until you're ready to tell me."

Alex chuckled and said, "Look at it this way, you're going to have more funds available in your team budget because my expenses will be lower for some time. Although, I have no idea how long that may be."

Tim could hear the sadness in his voice, so he simply said, "You do whatever you need to do, got it!"

"Thank you, Tim, that's important to me! Don't worry, I'll be getting all my monthly and budget reports completed as usual. You probably won't even see a decrease in my performance output, but I will have some personal things consuming my time."

*****

Monday morning, Alex took Michaela in for her next chemotherapy treatment. He sat there with her as she received her infusions. They talked about spending the past few days in New Orleans and how they each had such a wonderful time.

Michaela told Alex, "It was nice to meet some of your friends and customers." Yet what she was really thinking was that everyone she met whether it was friends or customers showed a great amount of respect for Alex. She could see it and hear it in the way they interacted.

On this day, Alex could tell that Michaela was feeling uncomfortable and probably in a little more pain than usual. But he didn't want to ask her as he attempted to keep her mind on other things besides her pain. Before each infusion they said their prayers, always ending by asking God for a *miracle* to heal Michaela.

They played cards and talked while the drugs were infusing. One of the things Alex had on his mind was when to take Michaela to Chateau Elan Winery and Resort. He had promised her he would, but now, the question was not necessarily when, but soon. This morning Michaela had shown Alex several clumps of her hair that had come out. Now, she was going through her second treatment. Alex was thinking that she very well may lose her hair sooner than normal. He knew that most people going through chemotherapy will lose their hair between four and six weeks. But with Michaela's chemo cocktail who knew, yet it was starting.

During her infusion the doctor dropped in and took a seat.

He asked how she was feeling and what were some of her key symptoms. The three discussed her current diet and weight and he said to double her protein shakes per day. He and Alex analyzed and discussed her current plus potential future pain management. He told them her fatigue and tiredness would continue to increase so keep that in mind before attempting any activity. You may want to go ahead and procure a wheelchair. Alex didn't tell them that he already had a wheelchair. The doctor said that he would like to perform some more tests and scans next week after her third treatment. Finally, the doctor told Michaela that she was looking a little better than he had expected this week. As the doctor was leaving, Michaela thanked him for stopping by, as did Alex.

Alex said to Michaela pardon me for a moment, I will be right back. At that, Alex walked with the doctor out of the infusion room and part way down the hall. Her doctor told Alex that she looked better than what he expected today. He complimented Alex, saying, "Whatever you're doing, keep it up!" The doctor continued, "Her attitude seems to be positive so try and keep her in that frame of mind. Plus, let me say that she adores you! It's written all over her… the way she looks at you when you're not looking and the way she touches you! So keep it up! Also, here is a card for a caregiver service who can assist if you need to be away for any reason."

"Thank you, Doctor, we'll see you next week."

*****

Michaela could tell that Alex was thinking hard about something, so she asked, "Whatcha thinking about?"

Alex replied, "Well, I was thinking about when to take you over to Chateau Elan."

This answer caught Michaela off guard because she had forgotten all about her request to go there. It made her feel good that he not only remembered but was working to live up to his promise.

He continued, "If you're feeling up to it, how would you like to go over to Chateau Elan later this week? We are about ten days out from Christmas, so I'll bet the place is nicely decorated. One thing, though, there is an onsite winery and I personally like their wine. However, keep in mind that you shouldn't be drinking any wine. So instead of drinking wine, I'll make you an appointment at the Spa if you would like."

Michaela simply smiled at Alex and, with a small tear in her eyes, said, "You're always thinking ahead and putting me first." After a couple of sniffles, she replied, "This week would be fine. I wish I could have some wine, but at least a facial would be a nice compromise."

Smiling, he replied, "I'll take care of it!"

*****

This week's round of chemotherapy treatments hit Michaela hard! She went to sleep early that first night and was rather fatigued for the next couple of days.

Alex stuck to her diet plan and increased her protein shake intake just as the doctor recommended. During this time, Michaela was now staying in Alex's apartment full-time so he could keep a close watch on her. The nice part was if she needed anything from her apartment it was only a few steps away. They would watch movies and he would take her for a short walk when she felt up to it.

By midweek, her hair was coming out in large clumps, so Alex assisted her with cutting the rest of it off. Michaela had prepared for this day as she had already purchased and or made several headwear and turbans. She cried on Alex's shoulder; she was sad her long dark-brown locks were once again gone as he held her in a tight embrace. After a bit, she modeled some of her head turbans prancing around like a runway model asking, "So how do I look?" Standing there all sassy with her hand on her hip and chin up.

Alex laughed, stood up, and pulled her toward him with his arms around her waist, and gazing into her eyes, he said, "You look just beautiful!"

That night after Michaela had gone to bed, Alex was sitting quietly. He was worried about Michaela. She had lost a couple of pounds, which he knew was significant. She needed to keep her weight up. Her energy level was low, fatigue, and tiredness was becoming more prevalent. He was thinking about what foods he could add to her diet plan to increase energy. On the positive side, he felt that she had a good attitude. Although, at times he could read the fear in her eyes. They prayed every day and their *faith* remained strong. Alex still felt in his heart there was a *miracle* embedded within their situation somewhere and that God would provide when *He* was ready.

Alex sat there quietly in solitude; his heart was hurting for Michaela as his anguish boiled up inside of him. It had reached an overflow point and all this built-up pressure was finally released... he began to cry. Tears flowed for a couple of minutes and then he started to pray.

"Dear blessed Lord, I don't want to complain, And I know others suffer too, but I really need you. Jesus, you are the Great Healer. I humbly request that you send your Spirit to heal Michaela. Relieve her pain, restore her health. Lord, please know that no matter what happens we are your children and our faith in you is secure. Christ heals all wounds. He relieves all pain, and he dries my tears. You are our salvation. Free Michaela from her sickness and pain, by the grace and mercy of Almighty God. In Jesus's name, amen."

After the prayer, Alex had concern written all over his heart as he fell asleep.

*****

Alex and Michaela went to Chateau Elan Winery and Resort, which is along Interstate-85 northeast of Atlanta. Alex had retrieved the wheelchair from Sheryl's apartment and placed it into the trunk of his car, just in case. That first evening, they enjoyed a quiet dinner and a short walk around the grounds. On all their walks, Michaela held Alex tightly as he would steady her with every step they would take.

The next day after breakfast, Alex had arranged a spa treatment for Michaela. While she had a facial and relaxed with a light lunch, Alex visited the winery building where he picked up several items. The day was comfortable for a December afternoon, so Alex grabbed a blanket, and they went to the driving range. He hit a large bucket of balls while Michaela sat and watched. Alex asked if she wanted to hit a few but she insisted that she simply wanted to sit and watch. He noticed that she was beginning to look a little fatigued, so they headed back to their suite.

That evening they had dinner served in their suite for a quiet, romantic evening. They were lying in bed watching a movie, but each fell asleep long before the ending. When they awoke the next morning, heads on their pillows looking at each other quietly when Michaela broke the silence as she whispered, "I love you!"

Alex moved closer, gently kissed Michaela, and then simply held her close and whispered back into her ear, "I love you too!" After a bit, they got themselves cleaned up, had some breakfast, and checked out of the hotel. Although short, Michaela had a delightful couple of days.

She let Alex know in her most honest way possible how appreciative and grateful she was that he brought her here. Michaela said, "Alex, I had always wanted to come here but never did, so thank you so very much for making this a beautiful weekend and a dream of mine come true!"

Alex simply gave her a hug, a light kiss, and a soft-spoken, "You're welcome!"

*****

It was Monday morning and time for Michaela's next infusion. As the doctor noted last week, today he had ordered a series of tests and scans prior to receiving her chemotherapy. Afterward, they proceeded to the infusion area to begin this week's treatments. Alex was there with Michaela, and they played Trivial Pursuit. On this day, Michaela felt particularly fatigued and was looking forward to getting home so she could rest. While they played, Michaela brought up the fact that she could not travel this Christmas to meet Alex's family. She reiterated once again how important it was to her and she was so looking forward to meeting them one day.

They were there for a little over three hours when her doctor came into the room. He sat down with a grim look on his face and said, "I have the results of the tests and scans. Before we discuss, let me ask, are you hurting in your hips at all?"

Michaela replied, "Why, yes, I am, but it's not been anything that I can't handle, why?"

Doctor continued, "The cancer has spread into your bones, especially your pelvic area. It has also spread throughout your abdominal cavity and around your lungs. But your liver, spleen, and brain all look about the same. It's puzzling, and I'm sending copies to each of the doctors in Houston and New York to review."

Alex asked, "So what are your thoughts?"

He replied, "Not sure, the new drug in combination with the other chemo may be slowing the growth in some areas. However, it doesn't appear to be slowing it down at all in other areas."

"Recommendations?" Alex asked.

"I'll discuss with my colleagues in Houston and New York to see if it would be advisable to increase the dose of the study drug. They've had more experience with it and its dosage ranges. Secondly, keep doing what you've been doing. I want you to track her weight daily. Take the weight measurements in the mornings. I would have thought that her weight would have dropped off much further and faster, so it wouldn't hurt to add another protein drink each day."

Alex, looking at Michaela, said, "We can do that!"

The doctor started to depart when he turned to Alex and said with a grin, "One of these days, you're going to have to tell me what's in your special protein drink."

Alex smiled and replied, "Be glad to."

He continued with, "Each day, I vary the different combinations of ingredients, so the flavoring changes from drink to drink. However, I put both turmeric and ginger into every single shake. Those two ingredients are supposed to have anti-inflammatory properties. Other ingredients I vary in combination are vanilla, chocolate, and strawberry protein powder. Then I use whole milk, dark chocolate, almond butter, Greek yogurt, strawberries, blueberries, bananas, peanut butter, raw cocoa powder, avocado, vanilla extract, mango, pineapple, dried dates, beets, almond milk, baby spinach, heavy cream, caramel toppings, honey, cooked bacon, raisins, wheat germ, ice cream, mint extract, as well as many other ingredients. I group different items together to make a variety of shake flavors. I figure if they don't taste good then she'll have a more difficult time keeping them down, so I try and make them taste good."

The doctor responded with, "You'll have to break down your different combinations for me sometime. I'd love to keep them on file for others and get some input from the dietician. I can tell you right now that everything you're using should promote weight gain. I like the idea of the turmeric and ginger in each one…good idea, doesn't hurt! Keep it up!"

Alex, privately, was very concerned about Michaela. Her cancer had spread into some areas but had slowed in others; he couldn't figure out what this meant, yet. He took Michaela home and once again she was utterly exhausted from the day. Alex helped her get ready for bed and she went to sleep almost immediately.

Michaela wasn't hungry for the next couple of days, but Alex did get her to consume the protein drinks. The drinks seemed to soothe her nausea as well. Her pain had begun to escalate especially in her abdominal and pelvic regions. The week was the toughest yet for Michaela, but Alex stayed by her side to tend to her every need. By the weekend, she was able to eat some real food, so Alex ordered some takeout. She drank her protein shakes every day and Alex kept changing and experimenting with the different flavors. Michaela said they were all very tasty except for the one with spinach, kale, and avocadoes together with mint chocolate ice cream. That one was her least favorite, but she still drank it.

The weekend nights were clear, so they went out and looked at the stars. They loved doing that, especially Michaela, as she could sit and gaze at the stars for hours on end. Alex wouldn't serve wine, of course; he would serve protein shakes. So they would sit out on their blanket and toast each other with protein shakes. On one of these nights, Alex asked, "Michaela, is there anything else you would like to do or have me do for you?"

Thinking for a moment, she said, "Maybe if we get some warmer days we can go out for some more picnics."

Alex responded with, "We can do that! Anything else?"

She thought for a minute and smiled then said, "You know what I would like?"

"No, what?"

"I have always wanted to read many of the classics."

"The classics?"

She replied, "Yes, the classic novels! I've always wanted to read so many of them but never seemed to have the time. Novels like *War and Peace, Romeo and Juliet, For Whom the Bell Tolls*, and so many more!"

Alex thought for a second and said, "Okay, I'll read them to you!"

This took Michaela a little by surprise then asked, "You will?"

"Absolutely, I'll get some novels from the library and begin to read them to you in the evenings, on picnics, whenever."

All Michaela could do was hug Alex, smile, and think I'm in love with a terrific man!

*****

On Monday, the day before Christmas, Michaela went in for her fourth chemotherapy treatment. She was progressively feeling a little more poorly every couple of days. The doctor dropped in again and told them that after consultation with the other physicians they all decided to increase the dose of the study drug. He continued with, "The infusion you're getting today has the increase in dosage. They felt that this is probably at the upper limits of any efficacy and they're not sure of the toxicity at this level. So be prepared for additional side effects and document them as they arise. We need to report all adverse events because this is a phase-2 study drug. One thing you don't have to worry about is hair loss, as yours is all gone, even your eyebrows."

Michaela, with a slight smirk, said, "Gee, thanks for reminding me, Doc!" With that, they all had a nice chuckle.

The doctor continued, "I like the headwear and turbans that you've been wearing to cover your head, very stylish."

Michaela replied, "Thank you, I made these myself."

The doctor said, "Really, you know you could make these and sell them! Our patients here would love these. I've heard several patients have asked the nurses if they knew where you had bought your headwear. I'll pass it along that you make your own."

Michaela thought out loud, "Now that's an idea. Alex, please remind me later, we need to stop by the fabric store to pick up some more cloth."

"Will do."

After leaving the infusion center, they did indeed stop by the fabric store. Michaela bought several different pieces of cloth that she was going to use to make a few more headwear turbans. By the time they got home, Michaela was completely exhausted. Alex, once again, helped her change into some nightwear, and she went straight to bed.

Christmas day was not particularly fun for Michaela as she felt terrible most of the day. She spent most of it in bed. When she awoke, Alex had some protein shakes prepared for her to drink as they were very helpful to calm her nausea.

Alex talked with his family on Christmas day but did not let anyone know what was going on with him nor did he mention Michaela. That had always been his way, this was his burden to bear.

The week was nearly identical to the previous week. Alex tried to keep Michaela busy and entertained to the limit that her body could tolerate. Yes, of course they went out stargazing many times when the night skies were clear. This gave Alex an idea and it was the perfect time of year for it. He went to several stores and bought a few items that were on Christmas clearance. He had an idea on how to use these items in the near future as the opportunity arose.

Alex was keenly aware that this was the week in which the physicians projected Michaela would not live through. That thought brought a sense of torment to his mind, so he did all he could to focus on her and worked hard to keep her in a positive frame of mind! He and Michaela had open conversations as they didn't keep anything from one another. They openly discussed their feelings, their fears, their joy, their possibilities for the future, and the cancer. But their love for each other is what shown through the most, especially to others it was most apparent!

Privately, Michaela tried to keep her *faith* and had *hope*. She felt that since she had made it to New Year's, that a *miracle* would indeed enter her life. She would say her prayers each day. On this day, she prayed this prayer:

"Father, I come to you today with faith so small I cannot see a way. I want to believe you are able to do more than I ever imagine. I want to walk by faith and not by sight. God, please bring a miracle into my life. I know that you can do the impossible, and I am trusting in your promises. Thank you for being a God who sees and hears my every need. In Jesus's name, amen."

She continued to say her prayers as her *faith* held true. She and Alex would say prayers together as well. It didn't take much for Michaela to keep a good attitude with Alex beside her every step along her path. She was so immensely grateful that Alex was by her side. This gave her strength and great joy!

*****

Michaela had her next chemotherapy treatment the day before New Year's. All went as before; she was infused with the increased dose of the study agent as the nausea was manageable the last time. Her doctor asked her to come back in a couple of days for more tests and scans. He told her that for some reason, she was holding up very well for someone who had outlived all the experts' predictions.

She went to her appointments and had the tests and scans performed. Alex took along a couple of protein shakes for her to drink during and after her tests. After waiting a bit, the doctor called them into his office. He started out by saying, "I have two completely different sets of news."

Michaela and Alex were listening intently.

The doctor began by saying, "First the bad news. I have the results of your scans and the cancer has continued to grow in all areas of your body. The abdominal cavity, liver, spleen, lungs, intestines, bones, and other areas. To be honest, with cancer growth such as yours about 99 percent of the time that person has already passed away. I don't want to sound morbid, but really, I'm in disbelief. I've been doing this for twenty years plus and have never experienced someone like you before. Which brings me to the good news, which is you're still alive! I know your symptoms are bad, and I wish I had an answer for why you're still alive, but I don't. I kind of feel that it is a combination of things, your attitude, your diet, maybe the chemo, Alex's special protein shakes, probably spiritual too... I just don't know. Actually, it's probably all the above! So all I can say is that you should feel blessed that you are still with us no matter what the reason!"

Alex and Michaela were feeling both happy and sad. Their emotions were waning back and forth unable to say anything for a moment then Alex finally had the nerve to ask, "So what's the next move, Doc?"

The doctor with a heavy sigh and looking a little puzzled replied, "Well, let's keep doing what we've been doing both the chemotherapy and all your actions. I'm going to be discussing these test results with my colleagues in Houston and New York. We might be able to increase the dose of the study drug a bit more. Based upon our examinations she is living on borrowed time. Now, Michaela, I don't mean for that to sound harsh, but you are an anomaly all to yourself."

Michaela was holding Alex's hand firmly as she listened to the conversation and attempted to absorb all the information. Yet she was unable to speak.

Michaela looked as if she was frozen in time, so Alex replied for them both saying, "We'll be here next week for her treatments, and we will keep doing all that we've been doing."

The doctor finished up with, "She's lost a couple more pounds, so if you can drink more of your special shakes a day then that would be great, drink as much as possible." Alex nodded as if saying "Roger that!"

Michaela didn't say a word on the drive home. She sat there with a blank stare on her face. Alex could tell that the emotions and a load of thoughts were racing through her mind like a whirlwind. He wasn't about to interrupt her, he figured she would speak when she was ready. They arrived home, and Alex helped her up the stairs. She clung to him tightly as they slowly walked down the breezeway. Once in Alex's apartment, she sat down on the couch, still not uttering a sound. After hanging up their coats, Alex sat down next to Michaela and gently grasped her hand.

After a few moments, she turned to Alex and whispered in a wimpy tone, "Oh, Alex."

Then burying her face into his chest all her pent-up emotion came pouring out! She began to cry uncontrollably; she was leaking tears like Niagara Falls, and in only a few moments, Alex's shirt was soaked. Alex was holding her tightly, rubbing her back, not saying a word, simply letting all those emotions spill out. After several minutes, sniffling heavily, Alex handed her a couple of tissues as she broke the embrace. Her head bowed as she wiped away tears and a runny nose. She finally mumbled between sniffles, "What's going to happen to me?"

A question, a question that Alex could not answer!

He hesitated not knowing what to say. What could he say, Michela, his love, was slowly dying and his mind, though searching, had no answers.

He placed his hand under her chin and gently raised her head up, peering deeply into her eyes he delicately kissed her on the lips. Still gazing into her eyes, he softly said, "Honestly, I don't know what's going to happen, only God knows that! I'm sure he has a plan, but he hasn't revealed it to us or if he has, we don't understand it yet."

Michaela with tears flowing and wiping her runny nose said, "So what do we do?"

Her emotions were beginning to overcome Alex as well, he had tears flowing down his cheeks too! Somewhat collecting himself, he replied, "Listen, Michaela, I don't know where all of this will lead us. The only thing I can say is we must continue to live in the present. What is past is now history, it can't be changed. Our future is unknown at this time even though I still feel there is a *miracle* involved somewhere in all of this. So what can we do? Simply have *faith*, and we will continue to do everything we possibly can day-to-day!

He continued with, "And lastly, I will be by your side every step of the way because I love you!"

Alex, holding Michaela's face in his hands, said, "Michaela, I love you unconditionally, which means I'll be here for you no matter what!" He then gently kissed her on the lips.

Michaela, having quick respirations and heart beating ever so fast, threw her arms around his neck and kissed Alex with all the passion that she could muster! Slowly releasing her kiss, she stared at Alex and whispered, "I love you, what did I ever do to deserve you!"

Alex gazing into her eyes placed his hands on each side of her face once again and replied, "It's not a matter of deserving each other, I think God brought us together for a reason! Look, we each have had extraordinarily difficult pasts that God probably felt it was our time to each have some happiness. At least that's my take on things. We must keep the *faith*!"

Michaela with a sweet smile and tears rolling down her cheeks said, "Alex, let me tell you, I have never been happier in my whole life than I have been with you! Just seeing you makes me smile, sitting next to you or holding your hand makes my heart and soul feel all warm inside."

She paused to wipe away tears then continued, "I don't know what I would have done without you coming into my life! And yes, I agree that I think we were brought together for a reason, which is still beyond my comprehension. Just know with all my heart and soul, I love you! Yes, I love you so very much!"

Alex, completely silent, simply hugged her and held her so close that he could feel her heartbeat! Oh, how he loved her with every morsel of his being. He then said a quick prayer to himself, asking God to have the strength to persevere.

*****

It was early January and Alex had his annual performance review with his manager, Tim. He reviewed Alex's performance numbers and provided his assessment for the year. Bottom line, Tim noted Alex had an extraordinary year. So many solid customer relationships and collaborative medical evaluations culminating in national presentations and publications. After some further discussion, Tim asked, "So what's your encore for this year?"

This gave Alex the opportunity to explain some of his short- and longer-range goals to define a number of objectives that he will be including in his strategic medical plan, and finally some thoughts on his direction to expanding his customer base. He also told Tim that he had several newly initiated projects. He felt that he would have several presentations this year at four to five national meetings. Alex assured Tim, "If I can pull this off it will add up to several more than I had all this past year."

Tim stated, "Well, that will certainly keep you as a top performer!"

Alex quickly replied, "You know I don't care where I stack up against my peers! All I can do is do the best I can the rest is up to you."

Alex continued, "Can I take a moment to provide some feedback on what I thought about your performance this year?"

Tim replied, "Why, yes, that was my next question. I always want your honest feedback! With your experience in leadership and management, I always want your inputs, so never be shy."

Alex said, "Tim, you have put together a terrific team of solid and high performers! That, of course, is obvious. Additionally, your assessment of new talent as recognized by the strong performance of your latest hires shows that your evaluation of people is particularly keen to say the least! The biggest thing when someone has a team of excellent performers is to ensure they all have a grasp of the overall team strategy and purpose. The overarching goals should be clear. And let me say that you do this very well. Also, it's important that high performers need their autonomy, as that's part of what instills performance pride in what they do! However, the new people will always need a little more direction, training, and quite frankly a little handholding until they can move into a more of an autonomous state. You do this very well. You don't look over people's shoulders so to speak. You have a good grasp of the differences between management and leadership. So after saying all of that, I can say good job and keep it up!"

After a pause, Tim said, "Wow, well, thank you!"

"You know me, I teach leadership courses in the air force so I can quickly spot good leadership, yet on the other hand, I can also spot the other kind as well."

They each had a good laugh on that note!

Alex continued, "Senior management always requests feedback so what I just said is what I plan on sending up our chain of command to Bob and Tom. When I get it ready to send, I will forward you a copy."

Tim said, "Thank you, that's nice!"

Alex retorted, "Not really, it's simply the truth."

Tim continued, "Let me ask something else. You have the leadership experience so what can I do better for the team?"

Alex thought for a moment, "Now that's a good question! You provide strategic guidance both for the team and individually which gives us focus and purpose. You congratulate when appropriate, and on the other hand, you tactfully point out problems or areas needing improvement. In addition, you talk to each of us at least once every two weeks. So where can you improve?"

There was a lengthy pause as Alex considered this question. After a moment longer, Alex said, "Here's what I think, you should try to have more field-time with your people. I know with a dozen people it's difficult, but ride-a-longs or face-to-face time is invaluable. Plus, it assists you to better understand the customers and what their needs may be when you're face-to-face. Having those in-person meetings with key clients could become invaluable when in discussions in headquarters. Thus, my recommendation would be to set a goal of one ride-a-long with each team member per quarter. Thoughts?"

Tim replied, "I like that! I've wanted to get out more now that we have a full team. I believe a goal of once per quarter would be possible. That's four per month. Thanks!"

"You're welcome, and no thanks are necessary. You have a very strong team and in my unvarnished opinion, trying to be as unbiased as possible, you have the strongest team of the entire medical affairs group! Frankly, I think it's obvious, just look at the performance numbers and results. After all, it should be about relationships, outcomes, and results!"

Tim replied, "I agree with you on that. You know there are some who don't think like that."

Alex quickly replied, "Well, all I can say is that there will always be those who disagree, but in the end, results matter!"

Tim was thinking in silence when he finally said, "You know, I'm really glad you're on my team!"

"Thank you! Me too!"

*****

It was late in the afternoon; Alex had been working in his office most of the day while Michaela slept that afternoon. He knocked off and noticed that she was still sleeping. Alex wrote out a quick note and taped it to the bedroom door just in case she woke up. He was running up to the complex office as he knew that he had some FedEx packages.

Alex strolled to the office where he collected his packages from Sheryl.

Sheryl asked, "Do you have a few minutes to talk?"

"I do, Michaela is sleeping, what's up?"

She said, "I was just wondering how you were holding up? And I wanted to ask you how she is truly doing. I talk with her every couple of days, but not sure if she's telling everything."

"Well, I don't know what she's told you, but what would you like to know?"

Sheryl continued, "Alex, I don't know how to ask this, but is she living on borrowed time if you know what I mean?"

"I know what you mean, and the answer is yes. She is about a week past the time all of her oncology specialists predicted was her life span."

"So is that good or bad?"

"Both, the cancer has metastasized throughout her body. Truly the doctors all said that patients with this amount of cancer within their bodies would have already passed away by this time. That's the bad part, but the good part is that she's still with us. The woman is incredible! She has such strength!"

Sheryl said, "Oh my, I hadn't realized it was so advanced!"

"Don't you dare tell her I told you this much…it makes me feel that I'm compromising some privacy."

She replied, "I understand, don't worry! You really love her, don't you?"

"Yes, I do! I would do anything for her!" Alex continued, "I try to be strong and focused on her, but sometimes my emotions do overtake me. It is so difficult to watch someone like her simply evaporate away piece by piece."

"You're going to be with her till the end?" she asked.

"Of course, I am, but we also have *faith* that the good Lord has a *miracle* in store for her!"

Sheryl paused for a moment then asked, "You know, ever since you two got together she and I have caught up a number of times. But I was just thinking, you and I have not. Tell me how you feel or what you think about that pretty lady?"

Alex took in a long breath, and after a brief pause, he looked at Sheryl and said, "So, do you have the rest of the night? What I know and feel about that incredible woman would fill a novel!"

Sheryl continued, "Well, I have some time."

Alex agreed and said, "Okay, here are my Cliff Notes version of what I think about this beautiful lady! Michaela is very reserved, deeply emotional, has great intuition, and once she trusts you, is extremely passionate! She is very loyal to those around her, can be intense, and I wouldn't want to cross her! She is intelligent. She can overcome more obstacles than most women and that is very apparent throughout her life. She has a knack for assessing situations and she can be stubborn and take care of herself. She desires authenticity and genuineness which is one reason why I think she likes me. She likes to have deep conversations to gain emotional investment and I've found out that she shows commitment and devotion once she falls in love! I can attest to that. Initially, she was afraid of getting hurt, but once she learned to trust me and knew that I'm loyal, she was all in emotionally. She likes our intimacy and is intense and passionate, you can take my word on that! Wink, wink! Michaela has a full imagination, can be assertive, is honest, relentlessly faithful to those she really cares about. She is a homebody, and her space is sacred to her. She feels uncomfortable around large crowds. She's not shy about being clear on her likes and dislikes. I feel that she is devoted to me which makes me feel that she is fully committed and would stick by my side through all challenges. Just like I am for her! Michaela is genuine, she is supportive of me, she's honest, and I trust her. She has compassion, empathy, and is forgiving. She has a big heart but doesn't show it unless she trusts you. A great mind and spirit. She has a good grasp on financial matters. She is kind and willing to compromise or meet me halfway if we disagree. Obviously, she is classy yet down to earth, she's inspiring, yet very private. She likes her anonymity. Oh, also she shows gratitude and has a great sense of humor. She's a good listener and communicates her feelings to me. She understands that true love requires sacrifice and service, always. She understands that falling in love can be easy sometimes. However, staying in love is a whole other story…it takes effort and work! And she puts in the effort and work! I will finish with this…when we were down in Costa Rica, we were having a discussion about love one night on the beach. After saying I love you to each other, she told me something that has stuck to me like super-glue. She said, Alex, I chose you not because you are the better guy, but because you make me a better woman! I can tell you, at the time it literally took my breath away and melted my heart!"

Alex paused for several seconds then said, "Well, that's the Cliff Notes version of what I think and feel about Michaela. You see, I love her more than anything!"

He laughed and after a moment said, "You know we've been playing several games of late either at home or during her infusion sessions. We play gin rummy, dominoes, and some others. We also like to play Trivial Pursuit, and I like how she is competitive. She kicks my butt more than I win. In Trivial Pursuit, I know the areas of geography, history, science, and sports well, but she kicks my tail in the areas of entertainment and arts and literature. We have a blast!"

There was a long pause, then Sheryl interrupted the silence with, "Oh my god!" She was quiet for a moment with her mouth half-open trying to grasp all that Alex had just said.

Alex looked at her knowing that she was still trying to process his spoken assessment of Michaela. He broke the silence with a little laugh then he said, "Well, Sheryl, you asked what I thought. That is what I think and how I feel about her."

As a final point, Sheryl said, "You have shown me a couple of things. One is you truly love Michaela, and the second is that you have a detailed understanding of that woman."

He replied, "Thank you, I feel that I do but right now it's taking all of my energy to be her *strength*!"

She took Alex by the hand and softly said, "And you are doing a great job, showing your love!"

After a moment, Alex added, "Well, I need to go, she may be awake by now and will wonder where I am."

"Before you go let me ask you something else."

"What's that?" Alex asked.

"Michaela has been spending most of her nights with you, correct?"

"Yes, that's right, actually every night," Alex said.

"Have you two talked about her apartment at all? She's not spending any time there in her one-bedroom where you have a three-bedroom. Understand where I'm going?"

"Yes, I do understand what you're asking, and the answer is no, we haven't discussed anything about her apartment. However, it is a conversation that needs discussion. Tell you what, I will look for a chance to broach the subject with her."

Sheryl replied, "Thanks, since she's staying with you, I thought she could save some money. Also, I want to invite you two over for dinner tomorrow night if she feels like it. Maybe we can play a game or something."

"Why, thank you, Sheryl. I will ask her and let you know. But I do need to get out of here, so I will see you later."

Alex left and was carrying his packages down the sidewalk as Sheryl watched him. She was thinking, he is quite a man.

*****

Michaela and Alex went to Sheryl's for dinner the next evening. When Alex called Sheryl to confirm they were coming over he provided her with some ideas for dinner based upon Michaela's diet plan.

Michaela was feeling pretty good this evening although the walk up to Sheryl's, though only four buildings away, did fatigue her. She held onto and leaned on Alex the entire walk to Sheryl's. Sheryl had prepared an excellent dinner with a potato soup starter and a main course of roasted salmon with smoky chickpeas over a bed of greens.

It was an excellent dinner. Alex had brought along Michaela's after dinner protein shake, which she sipped on during their game.

After dinner, they engaged in some conversation while beginning to play a game of Trivial Pursuit. Michaela liked playing this game because she won more often than Alex. Alex would generally get frustrated with the entertainment, arts, and literature questions. He used to joke that he would get questions from those topics in which he would have no idea about the answer. Then say, she would get questions in that area like, who painted the Mona Lisa. He would exclaim, really are you kidding me! Doesn't everybody know it was Leonardo da Vinci. Michaela would tease him back that she gets questions like which element is the symbol Hg for (Mercury), or in which country is the Indus River (Pakistan), to him easy questions. They so enjoyed jabbing at each other back and forth...it made them laugh and relax.

Sheryl watched their bantering which made her smile and happy. She knew that Michaela probably wasn't going to be around long, so it made her feel so good that she was enjoying her last days. Sheryl witnessed the true love that emanated between the two of them, it was heartfelt. She thought, there was no question that these two were meant to be together.

As they finished the game and their conversation began to wind down, Michaela leaned in and draped herself over Alex. She gave him a kiss on the cheek and asked, "You feel like carrying me home?"

Alex looked at her and knew she wasn't kidding. He had a tight hold on her hand as he whispered, "I'm sorry, this was a long evening for you, you must be exhausted. You hurting?"

She replied, "Yes, I am hurting a little but don't worry about that. Sheryl, I had a wonderful time, and dinner was awesome, thank you!" She went on, "Alex, I'm very tired. I wasn't kidding about carrying me, hope you don't mind."

Alex locked on to her eyes and said, "No, I don't mind but there's no need."

Michaela, looking a little puzzled, replied, "I don't understand?"

Alex glanced at Sheryl and asked, "You have that chair back there?"

Sheryl answered, "I sure do, let me go get it."

Michaela looked at Alex and asked, "What chair?"

Alex winked at her and said, "I bought this some time back and asked Sheryl to keep it here until it was needed. Well, it appears like it's needed."

Sheryl came down the hallway pushing this beautiful new plush leather wheelchair. She rolled it right up next to the couch where Michaela was sitting.

Sheryl said, "Alex got this for you, and I have these two pillows that you can use in the chair. Something soft to sit on and to support your back better."

As Michaela moved over and took a seat in the chair, she quietly said, "This is comfortable!" She paused then looked up at each of them as tears formed in her eyes, she whispered, "Thank you!" Tears began streaming down her cheeks.

Alex kneeled next to the chair, didn't say anything he simply held her hand. After a few moments, Michaela said, "I'm scared!" Trying to fight the tears and talk at the same time she managed to get out, "Alex, I don't want to be a burden."

He quickly responded, "Look here, Michaela, you will never ever be a burden to me! You hear me?"

With that, Michaela lost it; she buried her face on Alex's shoulder and the tears flowed. Alex simply wrapped his arms around her and held her tight.

His eyes tearing up as well; he glanced over at Sheryl who had a tissue wiping the tears from her eyes and cheeks. She was feeling so sad as she placed her hand over her heart. Sheryl had not been around each of them together like this so the love they had for one another was on full display. Sheryl was literally overwhelmed.

Alex was still holding her when he softly said, "Michaela, you have a right to be scared, but just know that I will always be with you to help carry this load. I am scared too, but we must keep the *faith*, together okay."

Michaela couldn't respond since she was crying so much. All she could do was to nod her head up and down as if saying yes. Sheryl was standing off, tears were flowing then she said, "Excuse me for a moment." She walked down the hallway toward her bedroom and shut the door.

Alex knew what she was doing, the emotion of the moment was simply too much for her. She was crying almost uncontrollably; Alex could hear her sniffling even through her closed door.

He continued to hold Michaela in complete silence while she cried. After a bit, Michaela finally began to get ahold of herself and looked up at Alex with her sad, teary big blue eyes, and she softly said, "Thank you!" She then kissed him tenderly on the lips. He gave her another big hug and whispered, "We better get home." She nodded in agreement.

He got her to crack a smile when he said, "Look, now you've got your own wheels with one manpower!"

Alex gathered their coats, and he walked down the hallway to knock on Sheryl's bedroom door. As he did, he said, "Sheryl, we're leaving now."

Sheryl came out, still wiping the tears from her eyes. They walked back into the front room where Alex told her, "Sheryl, thank you for dinner and the evening was great!"

Michaela quickly agreed, "Yes, it was, thank you, we'll have to do this again."

They all said, "Good night and we'll see you later," as Alex wheeled Michaela out the door and down the breezeway to the sidewalk back to Alex's apartment.

*****

A couple of days went by, Michaela couldn't do much as she was fatigued and her pain persisted, yet she never complained, simply endured. Alex thought what a survivalist; he knew she had that internal fortitude and *faith*, although she understood her reality as well. They would say their prayers each and every day.

One evening, Alex assisted her with getting ready for bed and tucked her in when she asked, "Alex, would you read to me tonight?"

He grinned as he said, "What book would you like to start with?"

Michaela smiled and replied, "I see you picked up a copy of *War and Peace*. I've always wanted to read that one, can we start with that one?"

Alex beamed as he said, "Of course! That's a good one. *War and Peace* by Leo Tolstoy, let's do it." He continued, "It's long, you know."

She laughed. "I know, that's why I never read it!"

She asked Alex, "Have you read it?"

"Yes."

"What's it about, can you give me a quick overview?"

Alex replied, "I sure can. It's set during the Napoleonic era of the early 1800s in Russia. It follows the lives of four to five aristocratic families: princes, princesses, counts, and countesses in that society. It discusses Napoleon's invasion of Russia and the Emperor Tsar Alexander. I'd call the book part soap opera, part history, and part philosophy. I found it to be quite readable, yet most people don't read it because it is dauntingly long."

She asked, "Will you read it to me?"

"Of course, I will!"

Alex then kissed Michaela on the forehead and began to read *War and Peace*. She liked the way Alex read. He wouldn't just read it in a matter-of-fact way but put emotion into the verse where required. It made Michaela smile, laugh, and helped to get her absorbed into the story. This, of course, made Alex very happy. He would read to her as many pages as it took for her to doze off. Sometimes it would be ten pages and other times it might be thirty pages. Didn't matter how many, Michaela loved the fact that Alex read to her, and she also was enjoying the book immensely.

*****

It was a beautiful January day with the temperature in the midsixties. Michaela was feeling pretty good, so they decided to go out on a picnic. They packed a picnic basket along with a couple of blankets and set off for a quiet day somewhere. They were out for one of their Sunday drives a few miles outside of Birmingham. Leisurely driving down a county highway, relaxing and talking when all of a sudden, Michaela yelled out, "Stop! Pull down that lane!"

This took Alex by surprise, and he quickly slowed and turned down the lane where she was pointing. As he turned and pulled down the lane about fifty yards, he stopped. When he did, they were looking at a field with a running creek meandering down the middle. There were large elm, oak, and pecan trees lining its banks. It was a scene just as Michaela had described to Alex several months ago. A gorgeous field in this tight valley. Alex looked up the lane and saw a wooden bridge across the creek then leading up to a home partially hidden by trees. Alex thought to himself, this is a beautiful place. He then said to Michaela, "I'm pretty sure this is a private lane."

Michaela was staring at this beautiful area which was straight out of her dreams. She glanced over at Alex and asked, "Oh, can't we have our picnic here?"

Alex was privately thinking that it does look kind of like a Norman Rockwell setting.

He continued to think that this is private property, but Michaela loves it, maybe we can go ahead and if caught ask for forgiveness. With that, Alex told her, "Sure, let's go ahead." He pulled the car up a little further and off to the side as far as he could.

Alex spread their blanket out and helped Michaela out of the car and down to the blanket. He had spread it out in a good spot not far from the creek nor the car. They had a nice picnic, of course with tuna salad and egg salad sandwiches. He brought some boiled eggs, yogurt, and a couple of his special protein shakes. Alex brought a light jacket for Michaela, and he wrapped her in a blanket as well. Michaela was admiring the beauty of this field and its babbling brook. They talked for a bit and then Alex began to read some more from *War and Peace*. He had read approximately thirty pages when a vehicle pulled into the lane. The driver drove on down and stopped his vehicle just past where Alex was parked.

As the car stopped, Alex looked over at Michaela and whispered, "Well, the party might be over. Rest easy for a minute."

Alex stood and walked over toward the road. As he did, he could see a man and woman in the vehicle. As he reached the road the gentleman exited his vehicle.

Alex knew he needed to be extra charming as the man approached him, he said, "Hello, good afternoon, I'm Alex."

The guy said, "Hello, I'm Will, and that's my wife, Sara."

Alex gave a wave as he said a little louder, "Hello, Sara."

Will continued, "Looks like you guys are having a little picnic here."

Alex admitted, "Yeah, this was such a beautiful spot we couldn't pass it up. I figured it was private property, and I apologize for not asking permission. However, we would have picked up anything we brought and leave the area just as we found it."

During the time that Will and Alex were talking, Sara was looking over at Michaela. Sara noticed that she was wearing one of those head turbans like people wear during chemotherapy. Examining her closer, she could see that Michaela appeared to look a little gaunt even wrapped in the blanket.

Will replied, "I appreciate what you said, and I know that you're not hurting anything but—"

Just then Sara called over to Will and said, "Could you come here a moment please?"

Will walked over to Sara as she was seated in the vehicle. After they spoke for a moment, Will turned around and said, "Alex, can you come over here for a minute?"

Alex walked the few feet over by Sara's window. Will said, "We talked about it, and why don't you go ahead and stay as long as you want, just be sure and clean up the area, okay?"

Alex replied with a "Thank you, that's very kind. And yes, I will make sure we don't leave anything."

Sara asked, "What's her name?"

Alex said, "Michaela."

Sara continued, "Did you already eat your picnic food?"

He answered, "Why, yes, we did. For the last thirty minutes or so I've been reading a novel to her."

Hearing that, it made Sara's heart feel so good as she said, "You're reading her a novel, so which one are you reading?"

Alex said, "*War and Peace* by Tolstoy."

Sara with an astonished look on her face simply said, "Wow, *War and Peace*, that's a lot of novel!"

Alex replied, "Yeah, I've been reading it to her for about a week now, and we are around halfway through it."

Sara wanted so much to ask more questions, but she didn't. She merely said, "That's a very nice thing you're doing!"

He replied, "Thank you, but she's worth it!"

This gave Sara such a warm and fuzzy feeling as she thought he really loves her. Sara then turned to Will and said, "Let's go." Then she turned back to Alex as they drove away, "You guys have fun!"

"Thank you," Alex replied.

Alex walked back over to Michaela and said, "They are some nice people."

Michaela asked, "What did they say?"

Alex smiled. "We can stay, now, where did I leave off?"

Before he began reading, he first asked Michaela, "How you holding up?"

Michaela, with a broad smile on her face, said, "I'm doing great!" She gazed off into the trees and listened to the water flowing in the babbling brook.

Alex returned to reading the novel, occasionally glancing up at Michaela to see a calm, relaxed, and pleasing smile on her face. He knew that this place made her feel all warm inside, and she didn't appear to have any pain. At least it didn't show. Alex read for a couple more minutes when he heard someone coming. It was Sara and she was carrying something. Alex paused from reading and stood up just as Sara approached.

Sara said, "Hello again, I thought you might like some hot chocolate so here is a thermos and a couple of cups."

Alex replied, "Wow, thank you so much and yes we love hot chocolate!" He continued, "Sara, this is Michaela."

"Very nice to meet you," Sara said.

Smiling and replying in her sweet voice, "Nice to meet you too and thank you for letting us stay, your place is so lovely, serene, and calm. It's almost like a Norman Rockwell painting or something!"

Sara thought right then what a beautiful lady, and it made her take a more in-depth look at her own property. After those thoughts, she turned and said, "I'll leave you now. I just thought you might like some hot chocolate. When you leave, just put the thermos at the front door if you don't mind. And it was very nice to meet you both." At that, Sara strolled back up the lane toward the house.

As Alex started to pour the hot chocolate, Michaela said, "You know Alex that was very nice of her."

"I agree."

They sat there for a little longer sipping on their hot chocolate while Alex began reading a few more pages from the novel. In all they stayed about thirty minutes longer before they decided to call it an afternoon. Alex helped Michaela back to the car first and got her situated. He then went back and packed up all their picnic items and blankets, plus ensured the area was spotlessly clean. Alex had a few of his personalized thank you cards, and he enclosed a business card. He took a moment to write a short note of thank-you on the card and placed it and his business card in the envelope. They drove up to the house where Alex placed the thermos and card by the front door.

As he got back into the car, Michaela asked him, "Do you think they would let us come back some time? I love this place, it's like I'm getting to view my own dream."

That touched Alex's heart but all he could say was, "I don't know, but I think we could try our luck again!" She liked that answer as she squeezed his hand and leaned over and gave Alex a kiss on the cheek. With that, Alex raised her hand and he gently kissed the back of her hand.

On the drive back home, Michaela was quiet, and then she placed her hand on Alex's shoulder, and in a soft, heartfelt voice, she said, "Thank you for today!"

It wasn't what she said but the way she said it that made Alex's whole body feel warm and fuzzy as he was barely able to respond with, "You're welcome!"

*****

Alex took Michaela to her chemotherapy appointment. During her infusion this week, they played dominoes and then a few hands of gin rummy. Michaela didn't feel very well, but she was a trooper and hung in there. She drank her protein shakes that Alex had brought along.

As usual, Michaela's doctor stopped by the infusion area. They talked about her symptoms, her weight, and the results of her morning blood tests. He let them know that they did increase the dose of the study drug just a bit. He told them that he wanted to get some more scans next week. The doctor noted that based upon the next scans a decision would be made as to whether to continue the chemotherapy or not.

Alex asked the doctor again for the best caregiver service. He said, "I have a company Year Beginning Managers Meeting in Orlando next week. I really need to be there even though I don't want to leave Michaela. I would like to take her along with me and we discussed it, but she's clearly not up to it. They all talked for a few more minutes as the doctor provided the name of a good caregiver service.

As the doctor was leaving the room, Alex said, "I'll be right back, Michaela, I'm going to walk with the doctor a moment."

Walking down the hallway, Alex asked, "So, what do you think, how long?" Shaking his head, the doctor simply said, "With her, I really don't know! By every measure she should have already passed away. I don't know what it is that is keeping her alive but spend every minute you can with her. You have kept her in an excellent state of mind and incredibly your nutrition tactics have worked so far as her weight hasn't dropped much. Yet the cancer is everywhere! I don't see how her body is even functioning. She should be very constipated from the drugs and the cancer in her intestines, but she says she hasn't been. So bottom line is, still I don't know how to answer your question, and at the risk of sounding morbid, she should be dead."

Alex replied, "Thanks, Doc, for being honest. For the lack of constipation, I monitor that closely with her. I vary the use of multiple stools softening agents and depending on the diet a little magnesium citrate."

The doctor replied, "Well, whatever you're doing it seems to be working so keep it up. A blockage now could be a trigger to her detriment. Plus, she should be almost to the point of literally screaming in pain, yet she takes very little pain medicine. She is truly an anomaly! A couple of months back, I had a patient with a similar cancer to hers. However, that patient's cancer wasn't spread even half as much as Michaela's, but her pain level was unmanageable, and she passed quickly."

*****

They arrived home, and Alex carried Michaela up the stairs. He assisted her in changing into some pajamas, and she proceeded to take her usual after treatment nap.

While Michaela was sleeping, Alex hung up some large, sealed photos that covered the wall in both the shower and tub area. What Alex did was take a couple of his photos from their trip to Costa Rica, measured the shower wall and tub wall, and then took the photos to the printers. The printer blew them up to Alex's measurements, and they were plastic sealed to be waterproof. Alex took these pictures and stuck them to the walls in the shower and the tub. He cut out for the fixtures so they would slide right through holes in the pictures... it was impressive. The photo in the shower was one of a beautiful waterfall they visited in the jungle while in Costa Rica. While the picture in the tub was a photo from the beach at their hotel looking out across the ocean at sunset.

When Michaela rose from her nap, she saw the pictures in the bathroom. She stood there for the longest time and stared, and her mind drifted back to their time in Costa Rica. She reminisced about the wonderful experiences they shared on her birthday trip. It made her heart zing with joy, and on the other hand, it seemed like it was a million years ago. She stood there and recollected many moments in time shared in Costa Rica. It began to bring a little tear to her eyes. She then walked into the kitchen where Alex was making dinner. She came up behind him and put her arms around his waist and quietly said, "I love you!"

Alex reached around with his arm and held her close as he continued to stir some food on the stove. He kissed her on the side of her head and asked, "You sleep well? Feeling any better?"

"Yes, I feel much better! And by the way, I love the pictures in the bathroom. Thank you." She hugged him tightly.

After a few moments, she asked, "So what's for dinner?"

He answered, "We're having baked salmon and some vegetables."

As they were eating dinner this night, Alex said, "Michaela, I have something to ask you, or really it's more like I have something that I would like for you to think about."

"Okay," as she closely studied Alex's facial expression.

He continued, "Don't take this wrong, but think about what you want to do with your apartment. You live here, I have a three-bedroom and who knows what's going to happen down the road. I would like for you to live here even if you didn't have the cancer. However, you need to think about it, and I will gladly support any decision you come to."

She thought to herself that was timely as she had already been thinking about her apartment for some time but didn't know how or when to broach the topic with Alex. And here out of the blue, it feels like he's been reading my mind.

After a few moments, Michaela said, "I've been giving it some thought over the past couple of weeks. Let me work some things out and we'll talk more."

"That sounds good."

*****

It was a very nice clear night, so they went out stargazing. Alex hauled Michaela down in her wheelchair. When they got to their spot, Alex sat in the chair with Michaela on his lap. He took care to cover her well with a warm blanket. They gazed at the stars and easily engaged into their routine of talking to one another. Between each other, they could always be honest and discuss their feelings. This evening was particularly difficult because it was the first time Michaela had talked about her life running short! Her acknowledgment of her probably impending death hit Alex particularly hard. Through his tears, he was able to tell Michaela to keep the *faith*... God hasn't thrown in the towel yet!

Michaela thought, *Alex always has such an easy going way about him, and he just makes me feel good about myself in addition to feeling so comfortable with him.*

They had been sitting there for a couple of hours when Alex noticed that Michaela had fallen fast asleep right there in his arms. He stared at her with amazement, gave her a light kiss on the cheek, and was thinking, *She is so beautiful!* He scanned every detail of her face and thought to himself, *She's not wearing any makeup whatsoever and her beauty still radiates even in the dark. Amazing, simply amazing!* At that, Alex felt it was a good time for a prayer, so he began praying.

"Almighty Father, have your mercy on Michaela. Please, Lord, bless her with your healing to survive this terrible affliction called cancer. She has suffered enough with this cancer and through her whole life, yet she remains faithful. Dear Lord, I humbly ask for your protection and power of healing for Michaela in Jesus's name. Amen."

*****

During this time, Alex continued to work on his various projects and periodically would talk with customers. He would evaluate medical data for individual customers. In conjunction with a fellow customer colleague, he had just been notified that their manuscript had been accepted for publication. This was another way in which Alex was a trusted partner with many of his customers. Although challenging, Alex managed to look after Michaela while continuing to perform his company duties. He did much of his office work late at night after Michaela had gone to sleep. Alex was putting off his Air Force Reserve duties at this time, but he would be catching up with those duties in a few months.

At the end of the week, Alex had arranged for a caregiver service to come by the apartment, and he went through her routine. He showed her how to make his special protein shakes. He had typed up each of the different protein shake recipes. Alex let the caregiver know that he would mix a different shake for all six to eight each day, never duplicating a shake. Alex had developed recipes for fifteen different shakes. Thus, he instructed the caregiver to be sure to change them up. He had stocked the refrigerator with plenty of fresh ingredients. Sheryl had agreed to come by after work each evening to make dinner while Alex was gone.

One afternoon, Alex stopped into the office and talked with Sheryl, he asked, "Can you take Michaela to her chemotherapy infusion appointment on Monday?"

Sheryl was thinking for a moment when Alex continued, "Hey, look, Sheryl, I realize that seeing Michaela there in the cancer center getting infused with other patients around may be a little overwhelming for you. So please don't feel any obligation to take her as a lot of people couldn't handle the situation."

At that, Sheryl continued to ponder the question then looked at Alex and said, "Yes, I will take her."

Alex drew in a deep breath of relief and said, "Oh, thank you so very much! I didn't want her to have to go with the caregiver. She needed someone there that she knew. I was even prepared to take a later flight to be there for her!"

Sheryl looked at Alex and after a pause said, "Alex, I'm not like you. I've not been around a medical environment with a lot of sick people. I hope I can deal with it all."

He replied, "Don't worry about everybody else, focus on Michaela. You do that and take a couple of games along to play during the infusion process. It will pass the time."

"Okay, that makes sense," she replied.

"Also, the doctor may want to perform some more scans and do the normal tests. So you might be there for a while. Is that okay?"

Sheryl again replied, "Yes, that will be fine, I've got coverage at the office."

Alex went on to say, "Based upon the results of the tests and scans, the doctor will most likely brief Michaela on her test results and the plan forward. I'm going to tell you right now. I'm sure Michaela will want you to stay in the room while the doctor gives her the results. You need to get a grip on yourself because the information the doctor provides will probably be extremely difficult for you to hear, but you need to be strong for her. You understand?"

"Oh, Alex, I don't know if I can do that or hear it…it'll probably be bad news. I can't do it, I can't."

"Sheryl, take a deep breath, it's okay. If you don't think you could stand hearing the test results and what the doctor has to say then simply excuse yourself for a few minutes. But realize Michaela may ask you to stay. Also, I can discuss with her the fact that you might not be able to handle any medical updates. I'm sure she'll understand, but I also know that she'll like for you to be with her, so have courage."

"I can try."

"That's all I ask! You see courage is simply doing something even though you're scared!"

Sheryl paused for a few moments then asked, "Alex, tell me the truth, how bad is Michaela's cancer?"

Alex grimaced and silently stared at Sheryl for several moments seemingly to formulate his thoughts then finally replied, "Bad! She's a month beyond what the specialists predicted for her life. Basically, she should have already passed away. Frankly, they don't know what's keeping her alive as she is ate up with the cancer!"

Sheryl putting her hand over her mouth was in disbelief and said, "I knew she was bad, but I had no idea!" As she began to form tears in her eyes, she asked, "So how long does she have?"

"They don't know."

Sheryl pondered this update from Alex then she quietly said to him, "I don't know how you do it! How long have you known that she's going to die?"

"Two months."

"Two months! Are you kidding me!" She went on, "How have you kept it together this whole time?"

"It's up to me to be her strength and help her with her *faith*! Also, I have a feeling there is a *miracle* wrapped up with Michaela here somewhere, I truly believe that!"

Sheryl nodding her head back and forth from side to side said with a quiet murmur, "You are amazing!"

Alex quickly responded, "No, not really. I'm just doing what any *man* would do to take care of the woman he loves unconditionally!"

Sheryl was quiet, her heart rate picked up considerably as all she could think was…he is remarkable! He loves her so much!

*****

That night after dinner, Alex read more of the novel *War and Peace* to Michaela. At times, they would pause the reading and discuss what was happening in the story. They would think what it must have been like to have lived during those years. Alex reminded her that this was during the time that Napoleon had invaded Russia. He noted that just like the German army in World War II, Napoleon found out the winters in Russia are brutal on armies. Their supply lines were stretched too far and then the snow and cold took its toll. Thus, that's what they call Napoleon's long, painful, and bloody retreat from Russia. Alex proceeded to read a few more pages when Michaela interrupted him and said, "You know, I like this book, it's a good story!"

Alex agreed, "Yes, it's a great story that most people don't read because the length of the book overwhelms them!"

"Well, I think it's good," she replied.

"Agree," as Alex continued to read a few more pages until Michaela dozed off. Alex in marking his page noticed they only had about 150 pages left of the original 1,100 plus.

*****

It was early Monday morning; Alex was packed and about ready to head to the airport. He told Michaela that he would be staying at the Renaissance Hotel Orlando the one across from SeaWorld. He wrote down the hotel's phone number just in case. Alex reminded her that he would call her several times a day and for sure each evening. Michaela placed her hand on the side of Alex's face and said, "I love you! Please be safe!"

Alex, holding her hand against his face stared at her then said, "I hate leaving you at this time! I think the caregiver has everything straight. Sheryl will be by each night to make dinner. I want you to take it easy, and I'll call you every chance I get. I will also try and skip out on Friday's meetings and leave Thursday night. I will let you know if I can because I don't want you to be scared when I come in very late. One last thing, I love you too!"

*****

Sheryl took Michaela for her infusion, tests, and scan appointments on Monday just as she had promised. She and Michaela played a couple of games during her infusion. Just as Alex had informed Sheryl, the doctor came by to discuss her results and the plan going forward. At first Sheryl didn't know if she could stand to hear this, but her compassion for Michaela and curiosity took over so she stayed.

Her physician told Michaela that the cancer had continued to advance and grow...basically, it's everywhere. It has attacked her bones, it's advancing into the brain, almost fully encompassing her lungs, and so much more. He complimented her on surviving this long and it appears that Alex has kept your quality of life as high as possible. The doctor smiled and said, "You're incredible, you're a walking anomaly or miracle, and no I don't know how long you have. Just enjoy every day you can."

Sheryl hearing this could do nothing but hold Michaela's hand tightly. She was now fully aware and understood better what Michaela had been going through for some time let alone Alex. It made her heart feel so sad as it brought out emotions that she had yet to feel in her life. Sheryl was very much afraid for her friend!

On this day, Michaela had brought ten of her handmade headwear with her to the infusion center. Before the doctor left her side Michaela said to him, "Here are some of my homemade headwraps or turbans. I want you to have them for the office and you give them out to your patients at your discretion!"

Shocked, her doctor simply said, "Thank you, these are great! It would be my honor and pleasure to give these out!" He continued with, "You know, I still say you could sell these for a pretty penny! Women would snatch these up so fast!"

Michaela replied, "Maybe so, but at this point if I can provide just a little bit of happy time in another woman's life during a difficult period then that's reward enough!"

The doctor softly replied, "I understand!"

*****

Alex called Michaela that evening, and they discussed the latest test results as he had talked with her doctor late in the afternoon. Alex told her to not focus on the test results, just keep doing what we've been doing. That is to get rest, drink your shakes, eat when you can, get more rest, and take your pain medications if needed. He told her to continue to pray as we had been all along. Keep the *faith*!

Michaela asked, "So how was the meeting today?"

"Same as always, we had an opening combined meeting of all groups with talks from senior leadership and then a reception this evening. I walked out of the reception for a moment to give you a call. It's good to see a lot of friends and colleagues from around the country."

Michaela continued, "Today I had a chance to talk with Sheryl about my apartment."

Alex was listening intently.

Michaela asked, "Do you still want me to move in with you?"

"Of course, I do!"

"Thank you, this is what I've come up with and Sheryl will assist. She will give me a break on my rental contract because of my ailment. I would like to move a couple pieces of furniture into your spare bedroom. Some of my other items like my bedroom suite, living room furniture, breakfast table, and the barstools, Sheryl believes they will sell quickly to people in the complex or maybe new renters."

Alex replied, "I think that's a good plan and please feel free to put anything you want to keep anywhere you want in the apartment! You see it's now *our* apartment!"

Michaela said, "Sheryl let me know that the complex's maintenance man could assist with moving my items into *our* apartment. You two can get the pieces of furniture I want to keep. The rest would simply be clothes and kitchen stuff mostly."

She continued, "Also, I wanted you to know that I've engaged an attorney who specializes in wills and estates. I told him my circumstances and he's going to meet me on Wednesday here at the complex office."

Alex said, "That's great, I think that's a good idea. I've been wandering about that for a while. Thanks for telling me!"

There was long pause, and Michaela said, "I've had a long day, and I'm very tired so I'm going to climb into bed."

"Okay, get some rest, and I'll call you in the morning."

Michaela had a moment of silence then, in a very soft tone, said, "Alex, have I told you lately that I love you? Well, I do!"

Her voice and words skewered Alex right through the heart. He was a little choked up as he could hear the pureness in her voice then he quietly replied, "I love you too! Good night!"

*****

One evening during the week, Alex, Tim, and several other teammates met after dinner and had a cocktail. Alex never was one to talk very much during these little get-togethers as he mostly enjoyed being with his friends and colleagues. And this time was no different. He would mainly listen unless directly asked a question.

His teammates were having a great time, lots of laughing, and side conversations within the group.

Sitting next to Alex was Tim who at one point leaned over and tried to quietly ask Alex, "How's your personal problem coming along?"

Alex was pondering his response as he was a private person and Michaela was even more so. She loved her anonymity. He looked at Tim and answered with a short, succinct response, "I still have it, no change!"

Tim examined his face for some form of further clarification but it never appeared so he simply replied, "Well, let me know if I can ever help."

"Thanks, Tim, you're a good friend!"

At that, Tim let the crew know that he had some work to do in the room, so he excused himself. After he left, a couple of Alex's teammates jumped over into Tim's seat and started talking with Alex. Everybody was laughing and having a good time. Sitting next to Alex to each side were two of his close friends and teammates, Lynn, and Maggie. They had been close friends for several years.

After a few minutes, Lynn leaned over and quietly said to Alex, "I heard what Tim asked you, is there anything you would like to talk about? If so, I'm here to listen!"

As she said it, Maggie overheard Lynn's comment as she had slightly heard Tim's question earlier as well. Maggie who was sitting on the other side of Alex heard what Lynn had whispered to them also. She said, "Alex, I agree with Lynn, is there anything you need to talk about? You know we're here for you and we'll listen!"

Lynn chimed in with, "I heard Tim say that you've been having a personal problem for some time now. Is that right? Anything you want to talk about?"

Lynn and Maggie were sitting there reiterating their willingness to listen or help Alex in whatever way they could.

Alex pondered their inquiry for several moments, grappling with how to answer an honest question from two very close friends. He was thinking and they could literally see the wheels a turning in his brain.

Then Alex said, "I appreciate you asking and your concern but this problem I'm wrestling with is ongoing, and I made a promise for privacy, plus in this matter anonymity is of the utmost importance. So as much as I appreciate each of you and your precious friendship, in addition, as much as I would like to tell you more, I can't! So please, I'm asking, let's just drop it right now if that's okay."

They could hear from his softened voice response that he had something heavy weighing on his mind. Plus, they had noticed that he had gone off many more times than usual to make private phone calls. They each didn't know what was troubling him, but out of their respect for Alex, they let it go.

Lynn and Maggie each said, "If there is ever a time that you need to talk, please feel free!"

Alex, with a strong feeling of gratefulness, simply said, "Thank you, I appreciate your friendship and that means more to me than you know!"

At that, the three of them clinked their wineglasses in a little toast to friendship.

*****

The next evening, Alex retired to his room after dinner. It had been a long day and he was worn out! Before bed he had called Michaela. They talked for about fifteen to twenty minutes. She told him that Sheryl had fixed her dinner this evening, but she wasn't very hungry. She let Alex know that she had been feeling pretty poorly all day and was looking forward to his return!

Michaela said to Alex, "I miss you reading to me, it always makes me feel so calm and peaceful and my pain leaves me when you read." This made Alex's heart feel so warm and that he was needed.

He asked her, "You know we'll be finishing up this novel over the weekend for sure. So which novel would you like for me to read next?"

Michaela considered his question for a moment then said, "I don't know, do you have some ideas?"

Alex thought for a moment then replied, "Yes, how about *To Kill a Mockingbird*, or *Romeo and Juliet*, or *For Whom the Bell Tolls*, or *Frankenstein*, or *Robinson Crusoe*, or *Horatio Hornblower*, or *The Mysterious Island*, or maybe *Ivanhoe*. There are so many choices, it depends on what your interest might be."

Michaela replied, "So many choices! Okay, of the books you just mentioned, which one do you think I might like the best, next?"

He spoke up with, "You know, before I recommend the next book, I have a question."

"Okay, ask away!"

He continued, "I'm sure you've had to read some novels during school, so what books have you already read?"

She thought for a moment then replied, "That's a good question! Let me think a minute."

Alex was listening intently as he could almost hear the wheels in her brain turning! She finally spoke up and said, "It's been a while, but I've read *The Scarlet Letter*, *The Adventures of Huckleberry Finn*, *Moby Dick*, *The Great Gatsby*, *Pride and Prejudice*, *Little Women*, *The Portrait of a Lady*, *The Red Badge of Courage*, *The Call of the Wild*, and *David Copperfield*."

"That's a pretty good list right there," Alex replied.

She continued, "I remember a few more. I've also read, "*A Tale of Two Cities*, *The Hunchback of Notre Dame*, *Gulliver's Travels*, and *Wuthering Heights*."

"Wow, that is a good list! You've probably read more of the classic books than most people! That's pretty good! No, actually really good! Let me ask, which one of those did you like the best?"

Michaela thought about that for a moment then said, "I liked *The Portrait of a Lady*."

"That's a good choice. Also, I would say that you've read many of the standard reading novels which is great, but the *Portrait of a Lady* is not one that is generally a must read. Can I ask you why you liked it?"

She said, "That's easy. She was independent and stuck to her beliefs even after she was tricked into marriage. But her strong character made her stay even though she could have taken an easy way out!"

Alex didn't say a word, he simply nodded his head in agreement as he thought privately that your morals, your character, your integrity, and standing tall to endure the rough road shows what kind of person you are versus the individual who takes an easy way out when life gets tough! Alex thought, *Her liking this says a lot about Michaela!* This made him smile.

Hearing all the books that she's already read in her life allowed Alex to trim his list of potential next novels. He continued to think about her question, "Which one next?"

Alex mulled it over for a minute longer then said, "I think you'll like *For Whom the Bell Tolls* by *Ernest Hemingway.*"

"What's it about?" she asked.

He said, "It's set during the time of the Spanish Civil War in the late 1930s. An American volunteer joins a band of republican guerillas to oppose the Nazi and Italian Fascist fighters in a mountainous region of Spain. The American and one of the guerillas named Maria fall in love. And that's all I'm going to tell you. We'll just have to read it!

She teased Alex, "Oh, you're so mean, tell me part of the story and then don't finish it!"

"Yep, that's right," he responded with a little laugh. "Don't want to spoil it!"

They talked for a couple more minutes before each called it a night. She asked Alex to please come home as soon as possible. With that request, Alex could hear her desire, her fear, and her yearning to be with him all wrapped up in her appeal.

He had no more than hung up the phone from talking with Michaela when his phone rang again. Alex immediately thought, *This is a busy night!*

Alex answered, "Hello, this is Alex."

The voice on the other end said, "Alex, this is Sara."

"Sara?"

"Yes, you and Michaela had a picnic on our property a few days ago. I brought you down some hot chocolate."

"Oh, yes! Sara, how are you?"

"Good. First, thank you for taking the time to write the note… that was nice and very thoughtful!"

"You're welcome," Alex said. "And thank you and your husband for allowing us to have that simply marvelous afternoon."

Sara continued, "Will and I have talked about you guys over the last few days, and we agree that if you would like to come back here for more picnics then please feel free to do so at any time.

This took Alex completely by surprise as he responded with, "Wow, thank you, that's so nice of you! I might add, Michaela absolutely loved it there! Additionally, she's always had a dream to have a home in a place just like that or a very similar setting. This will make her feel very happy! Thank you again for giving her this opportunity to enjoy the beauty of your place!"

"Our pleasure!" Sara added, "Can I ask you something else?"

"Absolutely," Alex replied with a sense that he knew what was coming next, so he braced himself for the tough question that he expected.

She carried on with, "I couldn't help but notice that she was wearing one of those turbans on her head that patients wear because they've lost all of their hair probably caused by the treatment for cancer. She looked underweight, a little gaunt as well. In addition, I noticed she had gorgeous features and a radiant complexion! Plus, may I say that she has the most beautiful blue eyes that I've ever seen!"

"Why, thank you! Of course, I think she's beautiful too!" Alex replied.

"I'd like to ask one last thing?"

"Sure, what's that?"

"Does she have cancer?"

Alex inhaled deeply and had a long moment of silence as he pondered with how to respond.

Recognizing his long pause as a feeling of being uncomfortable with the question Sara spoke up with, "You don't have to tell me if you don't want to."

Alex replied, "No, it's not that," as he toyed with how much he wanted to say. After a few more seconds, he finally conceded to himself that it would be okay to answer her questions. With that, he said, "Sara, to answer your question, yes, she has cancer!"

She continued, "Is it bad?"

"Bad? Its horrific!"

This gave pause to Sara then she finally asked, "So do they think they can cure her?"

"No."

Sara thought oh my and followed with, "So is her prognosis bad?"

"Yes! She is terminal."

This revelation wasn't what she was prepared for as she quietly blurted out, "Oh my gosh, how long?"

Alex continued to let her know some details by saying, "Without a *miracle*, she's not predicted to live much longer. All her specialists had predicted that she would be gone about a month ago. So right now, she's really living on borrowed time."

This disclosure all at one time quite literally took Sara's breath away. She really hadn't expected that answer and didn't know what to say! After a few breaths, she finally stumbled with her words enough to say to Alex, "I am so sorry, I don't know what to say."

Alex simply said, "That's okay, most people don't."

He continued with, "If I may, I do have one request, just pray for her!"

Sara responded with, "That would be our pleasure!"

Sara reiterated her invitation by saying, "I want you to know that you are more than welcome to bring her here for a picnic and a day of solitude anytime you would like!"

Alex softly said, "Thank you!"

Once again, not long after the call with Sara his phone rang one more time. This time, it was Sheryl. She let Alex know that today Michaela wasn't feeling too well. She also said, "I'm sure her pain level was much higher today even though she wouldn't admit to it."

Sheryl said, "Quite frankly, she is missing you something fierce!"

Continuing, she asked, "When do you think you can get back? Alex, she needs you by her side! You see, you are her strength!"

Alex thought about this for a moment then said, "Let me see what I can do."

*****

Immediately after Sheryl's call, Alex called Tim and asked, "Is there any way to leave the meeting tomorrow at the end of the day skipping out on Friday?"

Alex continued with, "I wouldn't ask but my personal problem is needing some assistance."

Tim replied, "I think it'll be okay."

Alex asked, "Do you need to seek counsel from Bob?"

"No, I'm going to go ahead and authorize it!"

Alex said, "Thank you so much. I'll change my flight plans and go to the airport after the meeting is over at five o'clock."

Tim said, "Just quietly sneak out… I've got your back!"

"Thank you, this means a lot!"

Alex called Sheryl back after talking with Tim. He said, "Sheryl, I've been given the okay to leave after the meeting tomorrow instead of Friday. So I'm changing my flight to tomorrow night. I will be getting home very late so I'll be quiet and don't let Michaela know as I will surprise her the next morning."

Sheryl replied by softly saying, "Oh, bless you, she needs you so badly!"

*****

Alex flew out of Orlando back through Atlanta and was able to get on the last flight into Birmingham. He took every precaution to ensure that he was extra quiet when he arrived home well past midnight. He did not want to startle or awaken Michaela, so he slept on the couch.

The next morning, he was as quiet as possible, and he fixed breakfast for Michaela. When he thought she was awake he took her breakfast in bed. When Michaela saw Alex, she beamed with joy! Still with a look of surprise, she asked, "Where did you come from? When did you get home?"

"Very late last night," he said as he put the breakfast tray down and sat on the edge of the bed where she promptly threw her arms around his neck and planted a big kiss!

"I'm so happy you're home!"

Alex grabbed the tray and said, "I made you some breakfast."

With a soft smile, she reached up and placed her hand on the side of Alex's face and tenderly said, "Always thinking of me!" Then with a smirk, she said, "Sure, I'll take breakfast. Thanks, this looks good."

Alex was silent but watching her closely as she ate, and after a few moments, he softly asked her, "So how are you feeling?"

With what appeared to be a calm over her face, she said, "Better now that you're here."

Alex was quiet while she finished her breakfast. He took the tray away and back to the kitchen to clean up. After a bit she came into the kitchen and sat down. In a couple of moments, she said, "I didn't even hear you come in last night!"

"No worries, I was trying to be very quiet so not to disturb you or scare you!"

It made Michaela feel good to see him home as she watched him clean up and put dishes away. As he was finishing up, he said, "Guess who called me yesterday?"

"I don't know, who?"

"Sara, that lady who brought us the hot chocolate when we were having a picnic on their property."

"Oh yeah, what did she say?"

"She said that we can go back there anytime to have a picnic, that it was just fine with them."

"That is so nice!" Michaela was silent for a moment then asked, "So can we go back there? I loved that place!"

Alex replied, "Absolutely, anytime you want."

She noted, "I think tomorrow is supposed to be nice weather… could we go tomorrow?"

"If you'd like, certainly we can do that…we'll pack a nice picnic basket and go on out there just past noon."

11

Endearing Love

It was a beautiful Saturday afternoon! Alex and Michaela went out to her favorite picnic area on Will and Sara's property. The serene surroundings provided such calm to Michaela that she forgot all about the pain she was braving. She loved sitting there quietly watching the trees gently sway in the breeze while listening to the water gurgling down the creek or what she called the babbling brook. To her, the tranquil setting gave her such a feeling of peacefulness.

Alex didn't disturb her while she was quiet and relaxed all unto herself. He quietly took out their picnic supplies and prepared lunch. Alex had as always brought along a couple of her special protein shakes for her to sip on.

They ate their lunch and talked for a few minutes. One thing they discussed was that her doctor was stopping her chemotherapy treatments altogether this week. She was wondering what this meant for her, and as she put it, what it meant for them long-term. Alex said to her, "I really don't know what it means for us or what God has in store for us. We'll simply have to trust in the Lord."

Michaela thought, *Alex had such a way about him which helped to keep her positive. He would simply say that we must keep the* faith!

After a bit, Alex opened their current novel, *War and Peace*, and began to read. She loved the way Alex would read to her as he would put such emotion into the words. To her, he had a way of bringing the story to life! Alex read to her for almost two hours stopping from time to time to take a drink of water. He could tell Michaela was enjoying herself as she looked so relaxed and more important to Alex she appeared to not be in any pain. It wasn't long after this observation that he read the last page of the novel *War and Peace*. When he finished, he looked at Michaela with a smile and said, "The end."

She kept quiet for a few moments then she said, "Thank you, that was great! That truly is one of the greatest novels of all time and the way you brought it to life by interjecting feeling into the words, wow! Thank you!"

Alex replied with, "My pleasure for sure!" He looked at Michaela affectionately and said, "On to our next novel, right?"

Michaela followed with, "Right, it was *For Whom the Bell Tolls* if I remember correctly?"

"That's it, we'll get it started tomorrow."

They were sitting there quietly enjoying the silence except for the running water in the babbling brook. Michaela moved close to sit next to Alex then took hold of his hand and quietly whispered, "Alex, I love you!"

At this, Alex put his arm around her shoulder and held her tightly as she snuggled close. It was getting on into the afternoon and beginning to cool off a little, but this day had been beautiful for a February day!

He was holding her close when Alex softly and tenderly said, "Michaela, I think I fell in love with you the first time I saw you face-to-face in the office that day. When I saw you that first time up close so beautiful and radiant, I honestly felt that my life would forever by changed. From that first date and week, I was consumed with making every date as special as I could by being different. Yet most of all I wanted to just be myself and have fun plus ensure you had fun as well. At the time, I couldn't believe that we only lived five doors apart and hadn't bumped into one another. I didn't know but I figured other guys were seeking your attention as well. Thus, all I could do was to be myself and be honest. I still can't hardly believe that I'm sitting here loving the most beautiful person alive! As we have come together, I have come to love you more and more with everything inside of me. Honestly, I don't know if we'll live happily ever after, but I will try to make it as close as possible. Michaela, I love you!"

This from Alex made Michaela feel all warm inside as goosebumps covered her body. She hugged him tightly as they remained quiet, wrapped in each other's arms. Michaela was thinking what a beautiful admission of feeling from the man that she loves. After a few quiet moments, Michaela spoke up with, "Alex, just so you know, I've never had any other suitors. It was always just you! Frankly, you had me from our very first date at Copeland's. When you told me that you don't kiss on the first date, right then you held my heart in your hand? You had me right then! Like I said, it was only you! When I feel the love I have for you, my heart fills with such delight and joy! Such joy that literally touches the very depths of my soul. I love your lips, your smile, your wit, your gentleness, your embrace, your eyes, your intellect, your patience, and your touch that simply melts my heart. I feel that we are connected even when we are apart. I love the way you share your feelings and fears with me. I truly feel that we have melded together. My primary desire is to love you because my heart knows how much you fill my soul!"

When she finished, she had tears running down her cheeks and Alex held her ever so tightly. Alex knew that their love for each other was an unbreakable bond no matter what happened in the future!

*****

The next few days were difficult for Michaela, as being out for so long on Saturday had sapped a great amount of strength from her body. Alex was there to assist her in every way she needed.

During this time, Alex with some help from the complex's maintenance man was able to move a couple pieces of furniture out of Michaela's apartment into his. Plus, he moved all her clothes and bath items. He boxed up her kitchen items as well.

Sheryl was helpful too. She put out the word on her furniture items and all the pieces sold very quickly. Michaela was now totally out of her apartment, and as promised, Sheryl let her out of her remaining lease. Plus, even though she was several days into February,

Sheryl did not try to collect for those additional days, she let them slide. Sheryl also returned all of Michaela's security deposit.

*****

Alex would get Michaela settled in during the day watching a movie while he did work in his office. Alex had discovered that she liked to put puzzles together, so he bought several for her. One day they had made a run to the fabric store to get some more cloth and supplies. She would spend a couple of hours each day making her head turbans. Michaela really enjoyed making them plus she felt that they might bring a little joy to someone else. This made her happy which helped to keep her in a positive frame of mind.

It didn't matter what she did during the day—watch movies, work on a puzzle, or sew a new turban, she fatigued easily. While working in his office during the day, Alex would always keep one ear open for Michaela. He could hear her doing certain things to pass her time. When he couldn't hear her, he would glance around the corner to check on her. More times than not he would see that she had fallen asleep on the couch. At this, Alex would cover her with the soft blanket and give her a light kiss on the cheek.

Alex would fix dinner. Sometimes they would get takeout, but they had to be careful since some foods wouldn't settle right with Michaela. She would drink her protein shakes during the day, which helped to keep her stomach settled. Alex had started with the next novel, *For Whom the Bell Tolls*.

She absolutely loved him reading a novel to her. He would put such emotion into his reading that she felt a part of the novel's story. This provided her such a feeling of relief and calm that he completed the novel quickly. While he read, she could feel herself being engrossed in the characters. At the end of this novel, *For Whom the Bell Tolls*, she told Alex, "You are right, I did like that book!"

She continued with, "Okay, what's the next one?"

Alex again thought about it for a moment then finally said, "You know, I was thinking about reading *The Iliad and the Odyssey* by Homer, but it's a difficult book to read."

Michaela said, "I've heard of it, but what's it about?"

He continued, "*The Iliad* is about the Greek hero Odysseus, the king of Ithaca, and *The Odyssey* is about the Greeks' journey home after the Trojan War. I've read them and like I said it's a difficult read." Thinking a moment longer, he said, "Another is the collection of books about *Horatio Hornblower* by C. S. Forester, but I don't have all of them, so I don't want to start those yet. I think since I already have it, we'll read *To Kill a Mockingbird* by Harper Lee.

Again, she asked, "Okay, I've heard of it too, but what's it about?"

He said, "The book addresses things like racial inequality, talks of tolerance, and there's prejudice. The author is originally from southern Alabama, and I think she modeled the novel loosely on her observations growing up there prior to World War II."

He continued, "This will be heavy reading as it discusses some of the societal issues of the day, so I just decided that the next one we read will be a detective novel named *The Hound of the Baskervilles* by Sir Arthur Conan Doyle.

*****

They had begun to settle into a routine as Michaela had become more and more fatigued. Alex had begun to feel that if God was going to interject a *miracle* it had better happen fairly soon. Because Michaela had begun to sleep more during the day. Then she would be awake a little later than usual at night. This afforded them the opportunity to go out and gaze at the stars. He would help her into the wheelchair, and they would stroll through the parking lot until they reached their viewing spot. Alex would always pick her up and get seated himself and she would sit on his lap. He would always bring a blanket so she would stay warm. They would talk freely about different topics affecting them and others. Alex would bring out their novel and read a few pages using a small flashlight. Many times, while stargazing, Michaela would fall asleep on his lap with her head nuzzled against his neck. At times like this, he would get her back into the apartment, trying not to wake her up. Carrying her to bed and tucking her in as gently as possible. Each and every night, he would take a few moments to say a prayer for her!

Alex tried to keep her days busy as much as possible. He didn't want her to be bored, but on the other hand, she wasn't able to do many things either. One day, she thought she felt good enough to go to the movies, so they went to an afternoon matinee. She made it about three-fourths through the movie before she asked Alex to take her home...they left immediately. By the time they arrived home, Michaela was totally fatigued and went straight to bed where she fell asleep almost instantly.

During the rest of February and into March, Alex took her out to their picnic spot. She would thoroughly enjoy herself, but they weren't able to stay very long, and each time was a little shorter. Alex continued to read to her quite often. They had finished the novel *To Kill a Mockingbird*. She liked that novel, but she noted to Alex that she didn't like it as well as the first two novels. After Alex had finished the next novel *The Hound of the Baskervilles*, she said, "I liked that one! Who wouldn't like a good detective story?"

After the Sherlock Holmes detective story, Alex thought another change of pace would be good. So he selected *Ivanhoe* by Sir Walter Scott. Alex told Michaela that it's about a Saxon knight named Sir Wilfred of Ivanhoe who has devotion to the Norman king, Richard the Lionheart. Upon returning from the Crusades, he found some skullduggery going on. Plus, of course, it has a love interest embedded into the story. Upon hearing this, Michaela said, "Oh, that sounds good, when can we start?"

"Immediately, as I have this book on hand," Alex replied.

*****

Michaela was no longer receiving chemotherapy or the new agent in phase II trials, but she was still seeing her doctor regularly. It was now early March, and she had gone in this day for some more tests and scans.

Once again, the doctor briefed them with the results. He quite literally said, "Honestly, no improvement. I would normally tell you that you are much worse and there's no hope, but you're still around! I'm sorry to be so blunt, but you are a walking contradiction. On one hand, you have me completely stumped, yet on the other hand, I am quite proud of you! Although I'm not so sure why. I know you and Alex have great *faith*, so you have me beginning to believe there's a higher force at work on your behalf."

Michaela squeezed Alex's hand tightly as he was attempting to show her strength and that there is always hope. Alex could feel her heart racing, and he knew by gazing into her eyes that she was scared. Alex said nothing simply held her close. He tried to show her strength outwardly, but Alex was just as scared as she was. In truth, he had no idea as to what to do for her. Thus, all he knew was to continue to pray and have *faith*.

The doctor was quiet while he watched their interaction. it made him sad as he knew that these two extremely fine people would one day suffer major heartache. The doctor continued with, "Your weight is down thirty-plus pounds to around ninety-five pounds. The protein shakes seemed to be working for a while, but your weight loss has accelerated in the last three weeks or so. I want you to drink and eat as much as you can, including the protein shakes. I'm fearful that any more weight loss would become detrimental to your outcome, understand?"

Her doctor paused for a few moments allowing everyone to gather themselves when he asked, "I've noticed you haven't said much about your pain. So can I assume you are somehow keeping it in check or able to deal with it?"

Michaela answered with, "I hurt all over pretty much all the time, but when Alex is physically close to me, when he reads to me, or simply looking out for me it helps to keep me from focusing on my pain."

The doctor was quietly thinking, he didn't want to say anything out loud, but he was astonished! He's never had a patient live this long with this much cancer throughout a person's body and organs. In amazement, he privately thought Michaela should be screaming in agony! Yet obviously, she's not, and sometimes, she even manages a smile...remarkable! She surely is an anomaly without explanation!

Before they left the office her physician noted that he had already alerted hospice care, and he provided the contact information to Alex. This made Alex feel quite concerned and fearful for Michaela. Basically, because Alex knew full well where hospice care would end. Yet he did all he could to not show his distress.

Right before they left the doctor's office, Michaela donated another fifteen headcover turbans, which she had made for the office. Her doctor and staff were blown away by this gesture. It really made Michaela's day when his primary nurse said these headcovers are so beautiful and the patients love them! They all said, "Thank you very much for these, they are so beautiful!"

Alex could see the joy in Michaela's eyes upon their responses to her donation. She loved making these headcovers and further enjoyed donating them for others to use.

One could hear the humbleness in her voice when she smiled and softly said, "You're welcome."

There was a moment of silence then Michaela spoke again with, "By the way, I'm working on several more, so I'll bring them in the next time I'm here."

This made the nurses and staff all smile and say they were looking forward to seeing the new headcovers. At the same time, this made the doctor consider how many more times he would actually be seeing Michaela, but he kept his thoughts to himself.

*****

Alex continued to read the novels as they finished up *Ivanhoe*. He asked her, "So what did you think of this novel?"

"It was exciting, and I love the way you read it!"

"Anything else?"

She thought for a moment and answered, "Yes, I'm glad Rebecca survived, and of course, it wouldn't be a great ending if the love interests didn't live happily ever after!"

Alex smiled and said, "You mean the Lady Rowena and Wilfred of Ivanhoe."

"But of course!" she said with a smile. She went on, "I liked that novel a lot! Good choice."

Alex was smiling at her compliment when she asked, "So what's next?"

He had already been thinking about the next novel and had decided for a change of pace and told her, "I'm going to read *Twenty Thousand Leagues Under the Seas* by Jules Verne."

"I've heard of that one too!"

"Yeah, you may have seen a movie made about it some thirty years or so back. It's a science fiction adventure about Captain Nemo's underwater ship, the *Nautilus*. The book takes the reader through many adventures with Captain Nemo and his *Nautilus*."

Alex began reading it that very evening while Michaela was putting some final touches on some of her new head turbans. She enjoyed this novel, so Alex read to her during the day and the evening which allowed them to finish it quickly.

During the course of the day, Michaela still liked to spend a little time working on puzzles. She would work on her headcovers and sometimes watch a movie. She fell asleep many times during the movies and Alex would let her nap.

At times, Alex would take Michaela out for a stroll in her wheelchair. They would stroll around the complex and would generally stop into the office to chat with Sheryl.

*****

Since they had just completed the Jules Verne novel, they were ready to move on to Alex's next selection. This next book he chose was *Les Miserables* by Victor Hugo.

Again, Michaela said, "That's a classic too! I've heard of it but have no idea what it's about."

Alex said, "It follows the life of a convict named Jean Valjean. The book tells the story of his life but also how the lower classes of people in France lived in their society set in the nineteenth century. It has some historical aspects to it as well. I think you'll like it!"

Alex read this novel over the next couple of days, so they went through it pretty quickly. While reading, Michaela had finished several more head turbans and she now had about twenty more finished. She said to Alex, "Next time we go to my doctor's office, don't let me forget to bring these headcovers. I want to donate them too."

Alex smiled and said, "I think that would be wonderful! I'm so proud of you!"

This brought a blush to Michaela's cheeks, but she stayed quiet.

They had completed the novel, *Les Miserables*, another one in which Michaela said, "I really liked that story too! Alex, you have the best taste in books."

Alex laughed as he said, "That's funny, everything we've been reading are classics, basically some of the best books ever written!" He continued to chuckle.

Michaela smiled and replied, "I know but it's the way you read them! You put such heart and soul into each story it makes me feel as if I'm part of the story itself. The best way I can describe it is that your reading style brings each novel to life! Makes me feel that I'm one of the characters in the stories!"

He was quiet and just shrugged his shoulders as it gave him a warm heart to think that what he was doing made her feel good!

*****

It was early April and Michaela was spending most of her time in bed. When she felt like getting out, Alex would roll her around in her wheelchair through the parking lot or up to the complex office. Around the apartment, Alex would carry her to the couch so they could watch a movie. He would carry her to the table even though she was mostly drinking her shakes. Alex was also carrying her to the shower or bathtub, which ever she preferred that day. She enjoyed soaking in the tub with some bubble bath looking at the large picture of the beach and sunset from Costa Rica thinking about days gone by.

Alex was getting more and more concerned on a daily basis. A week into April and Michaela's weight was down to eighty-five pounds. This scared Alex yet he wouldn't let on to Michaela. All he did was continue to love her unconditionally!

It had become more difficult and rarer for Michaela to feel good enough to go out and view the stars. Alex could tell this caused her to have a high level of sadness. Thus, one night after Michaela had gone to sleep Alex dug out the Christmas lights he had purchased over the holidays. They were all white lights some larger than others and some would blink. He hung them from the ceiling in the bedroom. Alex left them on so when Michaela woke up that next morning, she was amazed! She laid in bed and gazed at her bedroom stars. Some were brighter than others while some lights were larger and twinkled.

Alex thought he heard her from his office rustling around so he stepped into the bedroom. He quietly looked on as she was focusing on the lights hung around the ceiling. Alex could see that tears were running down her cheeks. He paused for a few moments then made his way over and sat down on the edge of the bed. Alex gently took hold of her hand but remained quiet.

Michaela finally glanced at Alex and softly said, "I love them they are beautiful!" She smiled as she continued, "It must have taken you most of the night to get all of these up!"

Alex simply shrugged his shoulders.

She pulled Alex close and gently kissed him as tears were rolling down her cheeks and then whispered, "Thank you!"

Everyday life was getting tougher and tougher for Michaela, so whatever Alex could do to make life as easy and normal as possible kept her mind off her thoughts that she was indeed dying. Although, during these days, they did engage in discussions of her death. Neither one wanted to believe that it would actually happen. Together they had continued to pray and have faith that the good Lord would step in at some point. Yet they discussed the reality that it appears she was going to pass away soon. This was a very uncomfortable discussion

for them to have but it was them! It was the way they were together…
honest and always able to lay out their feelings!

*****

It was time to start another novel but instead of simply asking
which one was next she thought she would ask something a little
different.

Michaela gazed at Alex and, after a moment, asked, "We've read
quite a few novels and the ones you have chosen have been superb. I
know there are many more to choose from, but I was wondering, are
there any books that you have read that have a strong message about
life?"

Eyeing Michaela, he was contemplating on her question when
he finally said, "You know, that is a very good question. Let me see,
what books have a profound message for life?" Alex continued to
think about this question when he answered, "Michaela, many of the
books that we have read have a legitimate message about life. Some
point out how difficult love can be while others show the pitfalls of
adultery. A few books point out greed, or selfishness, or how power
obscures responsibility while many point out societal issues during
different points in time."

He went on to say, "At first I thought you may be asking about
self-help books, but I feel like that wasn't what you meant. Then I
thought maybe something like the books on Thomas Jefferson or
James Madison to better understand our Founding Fathers and the
true direction our country should be taking. Then I thought, 'No,
that's not what you were aiming for either.'"

This was an excellent question as Alex kept pondering when
suddenly he blurted out, "Michaela, I've got it, of course, I should
have thought about this before."

Michaela, smiling and now very curious, said, "What is it?
You've piqued my curiosity!"

He went ahead and said, "It's a book that I've studied many
times throughout the years. I'm almost embarrassed that I didn't
think of it right off."

She asked, "So what is it?"

Alex said, "It's *The Art of War* by Sun Tzu."

Michaela looked a little puzzled at first when she answered, "I've heard of the book but don't really know what it's about. It sounds like a military book of some kind."

Alex responded with, "You just made the same assumption that most people think. Yes, it is a military book, yet it's so much more. Let me explain."

Michaela was thinking internally, this should be interesting as she nodded to Alex.

Alex continued, "Sun Tzu was an ancient Chinese military Strategist from the 5th century BC. He developed principles and sets of skills related to warfare and military strategy and tactics. But what many don't understand is that the principles laid down by Sun Tzu apply well beyond military thinking. His strategies apply to business tactics, legal strategy, lifestyles, sports, and relationships."

Michaela stared at Alex for a moment then asked, "So military strategy also applies to relationships as well?"

Jokingly, Alex said, "You've got it!"

"Okay, you're going to have to explain this one in more detail!"

Alex continued with, "You ready, here it is. It's a series of tenets to go by. I want you to think about each one and how it would apply within a relationship. The first thing we should always remember is in relational leadership we are here to serve others first. Remembering that serving your partner comes first so here we go, rule #1 is *Choose your battles*. Rule #2 is *Timing is essential*. Rule #3 is *Know yourself and your partner*. Rule #4 is *Have a unique plan, gather information to help make better choices*. Rule #5 is *Understand others moods and have the ability to listen*. Rule #6 is *The best way to win is to not fight at all, you don't tear down others*. Rule #7 is *change represents opportunity*. Rule #8 is *success breeds success*. And rule #9 is *No one profits from prolonged warfare, don't let fights go on and on*. That's it, so what do you think?"

Michaela sitting there feeling a little overwhelmed finally let Alex know, "Wow, that's a lot to think about! I can definitely see how they would be good points to go by, but I would need more time to study and learn the particulars of each point." After a moment, she continued, "You know, as you read those, one can see how they would and should apply in relationships."

Alex, smiling, said, "You are exactly right! There are people who study Sun Tzu and they are still learning key points to go by in life. This includes myself!"

Michaela thinking about it a moment said, "You know, Alex, hearing you talk about some of those key points actually explains a lot about why you are the way you are! I mean, you live by those points which helps to make you such a good person. You think of others and place them first, meaning me! I love you so much! Thank you for sharing."

Alex was silent, not knowing what to say as he had goosebumps popping up all over. It made his heart feel warm inside. He was quiet when Michaela broke the silence with, "What book do you have in store for me to hear next?"

After another moment of silence, Alex looked her way and answered with, "You know, I'm not sure yet. I haven't decided although I do have several on hand… I'm still thinking about it!"

Alex didn't say anything, but he had been thinking about reading *Anna Karenina*, another novel by Leo Tolstoy. However, he thought the story line might not be pleasing to Michaela at this time.

After a little more thought, he finally decided. Alex looked at Michaela and with a smile said, "Tonight, we will start *The Count of Monte Cristo* by Alexandre Dumas.

Michaela with a tired grin replied, "You know, I've heard of that novel. What's it about?"

Alex answered, "Well, it's set in the post-Napoleon years in southern France. The main character is a little-educated man named Edmond Dantes. He was a sailor, had a great fiancé named Mercedes, was about to be promoted by the ship's owner, a Monsieur Morrel, and life was looking great. Then his best friend, Fernand Montego, who is in love with Mercedes, and a couple of compatriots falsely accuse him of treason. Dantes is sent to an infamous island prison, which makes escape impossible. His best friend then marries Mercedes. Dantes meets an old man, a fellow prisoner, who is very educated and teaches him about science, other languages, history, and many other things. He also tells him where an enormous fortune is hidden on a small uninhabited island named Monte Cristo. By chance after many years in prison, the old man dies, and an opportunity arises in which Dantes is able to escape. We'll just have to read the book so you can understand what happens next.

"Does he get back with his old fiancé, Mercedes?"

"You'll just have to wait and see," Alex said with a snicker.

Michaela gave Alex a little love punch in the shoulder and with a smile leaned in and hugged him. Then recoiled a little and gave him a kiss. She looked at him with those soft-blue eyes and a little smirk and said, "You sure you don't want to tell me what happens?"

Standing firm, his eyes glancing away he simply teased, "Nope! You're going to have to find out the old-fashioned way…by reading it! Or I'll read it to you!"

Michaela nodding with a sweet smile gave him another little punch and replied, "Did you know you're mean?"

"Who me?" He smirked.

She said, "Please, I can't wait."

Alex replied with a grin, "Okay, it's about revenge, justice, hope, and a little mercy. How's that? That's all I'm going to say!"

Can we get started tonight?"

"Yes, that's exactly what I was thinking," Alex replied.

After a few moments of silence, Alex could see that Michaela was thinking about something else. He let her mull over her thoughts for a few moments then he interrupted her with, "Whatcha thinking about?"

She hesitated then said, "You know, we never did watch one of your favorite movies!"

Alex thought about that for a moment and replied, "You're right, I forgot all about that. We need to watch *Goodbye Mr Chips*, the 1939 version. I'll see if I can find it tomorrow and we'll watch it tomorrow evening. How does that sound?"

"Perfect," she replied.

This evening, Michaela was looking forward to starting the novel, *The Count of Monte Cristo*. She was very fatigued, so they started early. Alex began to read the novel in his usual way putting emotion and feeling into every verse and scene.

Michaela loved it!

*****

The next day, Michaela had Alex roll her wheelchair up to the complex office. They spoke with Sheryl for a few minutes when Michaela's attorney arrived. He and Michaela met for about an hour privately.

Alex waited for her patiently to finish as he talked with Sheryl part of the time. This time was agonizing on Alex as he knew that they were finalizing her last wishes and disposition of assets. They had finally finished and Sheryl with a coworker had gone in to witness and sign some documents.

When Michaela finally came out of her meeting, she was utterly exhausted! Alex took her immediately home and assisted her into bed to rest for the afternoon.

Alex worked in his office all afternoon being quiet enough to not awaken Michaela. It was early evening before she awoke and called out for Alex. He went to her immediately. Sitting on the edge of the bed, Alex took hold of her hand and asked, "How you feeling? You had a nice nap!"

Michaela squeezing his hand tightly said, "I was really tired today after the meeting, actually exhausted. I'm sure glad you were here to carry me to the bed as I don't think I could have made it myself. Plus, earlier I was really hurting so after you tucked me in, I then took a couple of my pain pills."

Taking a deep breath, Alex asked, "How do you feel now?"

"Oh, I'm still hurting, but it's back down to a level that I can endure."

Alex simply grimaced as his heart hurt for his beloved!

She then said, "Can you carry me to the bathroom? And run me a bubble bath?"

Alex smiled and replied, "Of course." He continued with, "What do you feel like doing after your bath? Also, are you hungry at all? I can fix you a protein shake."

Answering, she said, "Yeah, I'll take a strawberry shake while I'm in the tub."

Alex ran her a nice hot bath with plenty of bubbles and carried her to the tub. He turned on some soft music and went to the kitchen to make her protein shake.

Michaela soaked and enjoyed some quiet time for a while then called out for Alex, "I'm done now." Alex dried her off and carried her back to the bed where he put some pajamas on her. When done Michaela threw her arms around Alex's neck and gave him a big hug. She didn't say anything, and he didn't either. They simply held each other in silence. No words were necessary, the love between them was engrained into their soul.

Michaela broke the silence as she said, "You know what I want to do?"

"No, what?"

"I want to watch that movie you like, *Goodbye Mr Chips*."

Alex asked, "You up for it? You think you can make it through the whole movie without dozing off?"

"I don't know, but I'd like to try!"

With that, Alex said, "Hold on to my neck," as he then carried her from the bed to the couch. After helping her get comfortable, he started the movie, and they snuggled. Michaela as usual laid her head against Alex's right shoulder and held his hand.

Incredibly, she was able to stay awake as she was engrossed during the entire movie. At different parts of the movie, she was wiping away tears. At its conclusion, Alex could tell that Michaela was both sad and in awe while wiping away a few tears. She was silent and after a moment, Michaela said, "That was so good! I can see why it's one of your favorites. I was so sad when his wife died, they had something special. But his acting was superb for the whole movie. I loved it!"

Alex replied with, "Yeah, I think this was Greer Garson's first movie. And Robert Donat won the Academy Award for Best Actor.

He won the award over some of the most iconic performances in one year ever as many thinks 1939 was the single greatest year for movies. So him winning Best Actor was a great achievement. Yet Greer Garson was nominated for Best Actress in this her first movie but lost out to Vivian Leigh for *Gone with the Wind*. Pretty impressive, huh!"

She leaned against Alex, still wiping the tears and softly saying, "I loved it!"

Alex held her for a bit then carried her to bed. He laid next to her for quite a while as they talked for a short time prior to her falling asleep in his arms. Alex rose and tucked her in tightly and gently kissed her cheek. He kneeled next to the bed and prayed. Before leaving the room, he turned on the strings of lights representing the stars in our galaxy.

*****

Alex was working in his office one afternoon when his office phone rang, it was his boss, Tim. They hadn't talked for a couple of weeks, so they took a few minutes to catch up.

Tim let him know that his quarterly report for the first three months of the year was very impressive. Tim noted, "You know, Alex, for someone who is handling a personal problem, plus being pretty laid back with customer engagements, you had an extraordinary quarter!"

Alex answered, "Thanks, I've been trying to keep caught up with all my customers and projects. I've got a handful of new customers, so it's been a challenge. Most of my office work I get done between 9:00 p.m. and 1:30 a.m. now."

"Wow, now that's burning the midnight oil, literally!"

"Yeah, but that's just me, kind of normal. I've been pretty busy during the daytime, so late night affords me the time to stay on top of things," Alex said in a soft, sad voice.

This got Tim to thinking and afforded him the opportunity to ask Alex, "So how is your personal problem coming along?"

After a long pause, Alex finally said in a low voice, "I'm afraid my personal problem may work itself out in the next few weeks."

Tim didn't say anything, as he could tell by his response that it was very hurtful and that he was struggling with something significant. Tim wanted to ask more about his situation, but he felt his pain, so he wanted to respect his privacy and wishes.

There was an extended period of silence when Tim finally broke in to the quiet with, "Alex, let me throw something out to you."

Alex replied, "Okay, whatcha got?"

Tim continued, "You've been selected to do a secondment [internship] at headquarters in New York."

"Oh, wow, that's quite an honor!" Alex quickly responded.

He continued with "So when would it start and when do I need to let you know?"

Tim answered, "I would say just after June 1st, or in about six weeks. And I would say that you probably need to let me know within the next couple of weeks if possible."

Quietly, this timeline brought chills to Alex. He felt that Michaela was really going downhill fast which had him very worried for her and he was scared. Alex simply didn't know how to handle all of this at the same time. He suddenly was feeling so overwhelmed, but he knew he had to keep it all together for Michaela. He was thinking that his first allegiance was to Michaela no matter what! Finally, he managed to collect himself enough to tell Tim that he would like to take the secondment and that it was a great honor.

Alex said, "Tim, it is a great honor to be selected but since I don't have to provide an answer right this minute give me some time."

Tim replied, "That's reasonable. I know that you're struggling with something else right now, and you probably need some time to work some things out, so let me know when you can."

"Thanks, Tim, that's fair! I'll let you know as soon as I can!"

After hanging up the phone, Alex sat there and contemplated this new offering. He thought a secondment with upper management in headquarters is an incredible opportunity. Alex was thinking he would like so much to accept. Yet on the other hand his first responsibility right now was to Michaela especially at this critical juncture when she needed him the most at her side. He kept thinking privately that he loved this woman more than anything and no matter what other opportunities may come along he is devoted to her first 100 percent. So at the end of the day, it was Michaela first all the way! In his mind, this wasn't even up for discussion. He understood that he had a few weeks before having to provide Tim with a final answer, so he said to himself simply let life play out! He thought, *God has a plan just have* faith.

*****

Once again, that evening, Alex read from their current novel, *Count of Monte Cristo*, to Michaela until she fell asleep. He could see that she was thoroughly engrossed in the action and intrigue of this novel. She even said that she loved it!

When closing the book this evening, he noticed that they were about three-fourths the way through this particular novel. Alex thought that they will finish this one in the next couple of nights.

He wondered if they would need another novel. Michaela had begun to spiral down very quickly. She had not even gotten out of the bed for the past couple of days except when Alex assisted her to the bathroom. She attempted to drink some protein shakes but could only take in between two to three total. He knew her weight was down just by carrying her as she was looking so very gaunt. It was breaking his heart, but he didn't dare let on to Michaela. He tried to be her strength! But in reality, he was getting extremely worried about Michaela, and he was beginning to feel in his heart that he may be losing her soon.

*****

Michaela felt a little stronger this day, so he took her in for her doctor's appointment. Not knowing at the time, but this will be the last time she would see her doctor and his staff. Alex pushed her everywhere in her wheelchair.

Her doctor only did a cursory examination on this day as he knew her life was growing short. Her weight was down to a lowly seventy-eight pounds. Even the office nurses could tell that an ashen look was beginning to come over her so that the end of her life was drawing near.

The staff huddled around Michaela for a few minutes as she was one of their very favorite patients. Frankly, they simply adored her! They had watched her go from one of the most beautiful statuesque women they had ever seen to a person who was simply evaporating before their eyes! Many knew it, and it was too difficult of a situation to take for several as they simply walked away to wipe the tears from their eyes.

While the nurses were talking with Michaela, her doctor pulled Alex aside. He said, "Honestly, she has been a miracle to last this long, but I truly believe that her time is getting very short! Do you understand?"

Alex, taking a deep breath, replied in a soft voice, "Yes, I do."

Tears began to flow from Alex as he now felt the weight of the world upon him. He was feeling a little alarmed and had to sit a moment as he was visibly shaken.

The doctor staring at Alex was surprised as this was the first time he had seen this man with great character and strength looking so sorrowful and nearly defeated. The doctor had dealt with literally thousands of families, but the devastation that had been beset upon these two people was hurting him even more than anyone had that he could remember in recent times.

While Alex was sitting there in silence deliberating his own actions when he asked if there was anything else he could do the doctor interrupted his thoughts with, "Alex, I firmly believe that you will need to call Hospice within the next couple of days. Do you understand? I don't want you to wait too long as hospice will help to manage her final days and hours more effectively."

Alex with tears running down his cheeks simply said, "Yes, I got it."

He pulled himself together and wiped away his tears then stood up and said to himself, "Okay, it's time to go back out there, pull it together, have strength!"

Alex and the doctor walked back in to where Michaela was sitting in her wheelchair talking with the nurses and staff. All could tell that she was doing her best to put on a strong front, but Alex could see that she was getting exhausted.

Alex approached her chair while working up a smile, saying, "You ready to go? I'll bet they need to get back to work."

Michaela said with a smile, "Before we go, I have a bag of headcovers for the staff to share!"

One of the office nurses took the bag from Michaela. She looked through the bag and said, "These are beautiful! How many are there?"

Michaela replied, "I think there are twenty-five or twenty-six, I'm not sure."

The nurse called over to the doctor and said, "Look at these."

The doctor quickly glanced through the bag and agreed, "Yes, these are gorgeous! Thank you so much. We'll provide these to patients as they need them. We will also be sure to let people know that you, one of our patients, made these beautiful headcovers and turbans. You know, you have quite a talent!"

This brought a big smile from Michaela as she softly replied, "Thank you, it's my way of giving back and saying thank you to you and your staff!"

This interaction brought a big smile and warmth to Alex's heart. He knew it made Michaela very happy, and he could tell by the smile on her face that her donation made her feel appreciated.

12

Hospice Begins

Over the next couple of days, Michaela was feeling worse and worse. She was nearing the point of not wanting to eat or drink anything at all. She needed to be carried anywhere from the bed as she was growing weak. She was still able to converse and put on a great face when she was awake. However, Alex could see that she was turning a little more ashen each day. He had seen this look in people through the years and knew full well that the end was nearing.

With Michaela looking more ashen each day, Alex knew it was time to begin to pull things together. On this day, he called Sheryl and, in a somber voice, said, "Sheryl, you really need to stop by tonight and see Michaela!"

At first, Sheryl didn't really understand what that tone in his voice meant. She replied, "Sure, I can stop by after work can I bring anything?"

Alex reiterated, "No, just bring yourself."

This time, Sheryl recognized the subdued tone in his voice as she took a deep breath then whispered, "Oh my!"

She continued with, "Alex, is it bad?"

He simply replied, "Just come."

"I will be there!"

Later in the afternoon, Michaela and Alex sat on the edge of the bed and talked! Michaela was honest with Alex and more importantly she was honest with herself.

Michaela sat quietly on the bed holding Alex's hand and leaning up against him when she said, "Alex, I know I don't have much longer! I can feel the life force draining from me almost daily."

At this, Alex hugged her tightly as they each had tears streaming down their faces. They looked at each other and started to laugh when Michaela said, "Look at us!" She wiped the tears from Alex's cheeks; he then reached up and wiped them from hers as well.

Michaela placed her face next to his and whispered into his ear, "Thank you so much for loving me! You know that I adore you!" Alex stayed quiet as this warmed his heart yet at the same time his heart was beginning to break.

After a few minutes, they managed to collect themselves enough to talk. Michaela with the saddest look on her face said, "Alex, you need to call hospice care the first thing in the morning. I know this hurts, but it's what needs to be done."

After a few moments, he answered, "I'll take care of it."

Michaela continued, "I want you to know that in the event of my death all arrangements have been made. Everything from my funeral to disposition of assets my attorney has my instructions."

She went on and said, "As far as everything here in our apartment just donate my stuff except for my jewelry. Collect all my jewelry together and my attorney will be in contact. He's going to sell it and donate the proceeds to a charity I designated."

Alex was sad but smiling as he said, "I think that's great!"

Michaela said, "Don't worry he's going to take care of my car as well." She looked at Alex with sad eyes and softly said, "I didn't want you to have to deal with anything afterwards."

"I understand," he replied softly even though his heart was being ripped apart at the thought of losing her.

There was a moment of silence when Michaela spoke up, "You know, this will be my last night here as we'll probably be going to hospice care tomorrow."

Alex squeezed her a little tighter and quietly murmured, "Yeah, I guess so."

She continued, "So will you make me some dinner tonight and I want to drink some wine!"

He stared at her and replied with a little chuckle, "You think you can keep it down?"

She gave him a little punch in the ribs and laughed then said, "Probably not! You'll probably have to carry me to the toilet again and keep me from drowning."

As they continued to laugh, Alex said, "I'm sure you're right!"

Michaela added, "What do we have to fix tonight?"

"I've got some fish filets that I could bake and build a nice dinner around it with a good wine. How does that sound?"

She said, "Solid food, that sounds so good! And wine, oh, it's been a while. Go ahead, but we'll probably have to eat right here at the bed."

She was smiling, the thought of solid food made her happy. Then she hesitated, focused within her own train of thought, she looked at Alex and said in a subdued tone, "It'll be like my last meal."

At this, she bowed her head and Alex put his arm around her and held her tight. She simply laid her head on his shoulder.

They continued to talk and pray for the next couple of hours. It was some of the most difficult and agonizing conversations they've ever had. They were holding one another when there was a knock at the door.

Alex answered the knock, and it was Sheryl. He was taking her back to the bedroom just as Michaela called out, "Alex, who is it?"

"It's Sheryl."

Sheryl had not seen Michaela for several days so when she walked into the bedroom, she was almost aghast at who she saw. She stared at Michaela and could only feel sorrow, as this once most beautiful woman was looking very pale and gaunt. Sheryl walked over and sat on the side of the bed where they began to talk.

Alex spoke up, "Hey, I'm going to let you guys talk for a bit. I'll be back in a little while."

At that, Alex went for a walk as he needed to think and pray! He just couldn't believe this was happening. He felt that after all he had been through, he had finally met his soulmate, his intended, and now, he was going to lose her too. He wondered; *how can this be?!?*

While he was out, Sheryl and Michaela were having an emotional talk. Michaela told her that she would be going to hospice care tomorrow. Continuing in a low voice Michaela said, "Sheryl, you've been a great friend and I want to thank you for everything! Truthfully, it's said if a person has one true friend in their life, then that person is rich! Well, Sheryl, you make me rich!"

With a tear in her eye, Sheryl replied, "Thank you and I can say the same thing about you!"

Once again, there was a long silence when Michaela interrupted the quiet with, "Sheryl, I really want to thank you for introducing me to Alex! He's the best thing I've ever had in my life, and quite frankly, I don't know what I would've done without him! I guess I would have passed away several months ago for sure."

At that, Sheryl was feeling very sad as it began to hit her that Michaela was going to pass soon. This gave Sheryl a very heavy heart to the point that she really didn't know what to say.

Michaela recognized that Sheryl was feeling uncomfortable, so she spoke up. She started with, "Sheryl, you really have been a special friend."

Michaela was beginning to pause during her words to catch her breath. She could muster the energy to speak a sentence then have to pause a few moments to catch her breath again.

She continued, "Sheryl, you know I told you that I had to go into foster care when I was ten years old. But I remember what my mom and dad always told me. They would say to always want to go to school and get an education. Opportunities will open and close like a door so learn to recognize when a door opens so you will be ready to step through. You see, being bounced around through foster care was no fun and you don't feel loved or appreciated whatsoever. Then when I graduated from high school, I was basically kicked to the curb. Oh, it was so difficult! I was on my own, I had nothing but my clothes, and no support! The associate pastor at the church really helped to stabilize me. Helped me get a job and an apartment. I got into college and although I did receive some grant money, I still had to get some student loans. You know Sheryl, those years are a blur now! When I wasn't in class, I was working to make ends meet."

Michaela smirked and, with a chuckle, said, "You know, Sheryl, in college I never once had a boyfriend."

That admission got Sheryl's attention real fast as she replied, "I can't believe that! You mean, guys didn't ask you out? You're impossible to miss, statuesque, tall, absolutely gorgeous!"

Michaela replied, "Oh, I was hit on and asked out quite a bit. Yet I was not one to go out as I was generally working and would go home and rest or study. I did go out on three to four dates in college, but the guys mostly didn't show me any respect. Let's just say that their expectation level was way too high, if you know what I mean!" She laughed!

Sheryl laughed too as she retorted, "I can just imagine!"

Michaela continued, "That all seems so long ago. I liked the job I got after college, and moving to the north Atlanta area was nice."

Sheryl asked, "You did some modeling and had an opportunity to take that to a higher level and travel to New York and Europe, right?"

"Yeah, but that wasn't for me. All I wanted to do was clothing print ads and things like that. I was not going to go onto any runways and model some sheer top to show the world my breasts. Even with my print ad modeling, I would not do lingerie or bikinis. I do have morals and values and many in that business didn't understand that at all! I just wanted to make some extra money to pay off my student loans and to save some extra funds to get ahead. Know what I mean?"

Sheryl paused and asked, "Tell me about your husband?"

Michaela grimaced, "Those are bad memories. I had never had a boyfriend and he came off as charming and said all the right things, I guess. Even though I had some reservations about him, I figured well everyone has flaws so when he asked me to marry him, I agreed. Things seemed to be going along as I thought they should, but I began feeling something wasn't right. Then I got sick and caught him cheating and that was the last straw! In retrospect, he was probably cheating well before I caught him."

Sheryl was shaking her head then said, "Unbelievable!"

"What's unbelievable?"

"Your husband, I don't understand him. He is married to a gorgeous woman and he's cheating! Like I said, unbelievable! He had to have been one of the biggest scoundrels ever!"

Michaela quietly replied, "Well, you're pretty much on target with that assessment, but I also made the mistake of trusting and marrying him. So I also had to take responsibility for my actions too. Doesn't matter anyway, I have forgotten all about him. He's not worth the energy it takes to even give him a second thought."

Sheryl continued, "It's difficult for me to imagine how you went through all your chemotherapy and radiation treatments before all alone! I don't see how you did it!"

Michaela speaking slowly and softly whispered, "We can generally persevere through a lot in our lives as I can attest to that, and prayers don't hurt that's for sure. All I can say is, I just had to survive the best I could! And I truly believe that the good Lord helped as it surely wasn't my time yet."

As she completed that statement she was continuing to gasp for air and her voice became a high-pitched squeak as tears were running down her cheeks.

Michaela looked up at Sheryl who had tears running down her face as well.

She continued, "Sheryl, my life has been very difficult, but the best thing I ever did was to move here. Because I met you, who became my best friend! And you introduced me to a man I call my soulmate! God bless you!"

At that, her breathing continued to be very heavy and gasping.

Sheryl took hold of Michaela's hand and said, "You really love him, don't you?"

Michaela still trying to get her breath simply glanced up at Sheryl and nodded her head up and down. She finally got her breath back enough and said to Sheryl, "After I'm gone, I want you to do one thing for me."

"Sure, anything, just ask."

Michaela continued, "I am really worried for Alex, would you please look out for him once I'm gone? I know that his grief will simply be unbearable! He is such a good man and deserves nothing but good things for the rest of his life!" Her voice crackled as she said it.

"No worries, I know it'll be devastating for him, and I will help out any way I can, I promise!"

Michaela went on in a low voice, "Thank you, he does so much for me so effortlessly, and he's never grumbled or complained one time. Plus, he never looks tired, yet I don't know when he sleeps. He takes care of my needs during the day and his other work at night. In some ways, he's an enigma to me, but he has always put me first or served my needs first. Sheryl, because of his strength, he has given me my *strength*. He is just so calm and natural that it has helped me more than anyone can comprehend. He has allowed me to endure. He's so unselfish, just amazing! He's the only person ever that I felt like we were part of one another. So please, please look out for him!"

Sheryl hearing this had tears streaming down her face again replied, "I'll see to it! I'll make sure we talk things out. I think he should celebrate his memories of you. Plus, if I know him, he will jump right back into his work after a short grief period. Don't you worry about a thing!"

Again, Michaela couldn't respond as she was breathing deeply trying to catch her breath, so she simply nodded in approval.

After they had been talking for a while, they heard Alex return.

He joined them, and they all sat around talking for a few minutes when Alex excused himself and went to the kitchen to prepare their Last Supper!

Sheryl stuck around for a while longer while Alex got dinner ready. It was very difficult for Sheryl to say goodbye this night, as one might expect. She pretty much knew by then that this may well be the last time she would ever talk to her friend. Once Sheryl exited the apartment she began crying profusely as she could no longer hold it in, all those pent-up emotions were released. Her heart was breaking as it had finally hit her square-on that Michaela was going to lose her battle with the cancer.

Alex had fixed dinner and brought it to her on a serving tray. He poured her a glass of wine and they sat on the bed and enjoyed dinner. All during dinner Michaela kept wiping the tears from her cheeks as she knew that it was about over. He tried his best to be strong during dinner, but it was extremely difficult on him as well.

As they were finishing up dinner and their wine, Michaela asked, "Will you finish the novel tonight?"

"Absolutely!"

Alex quickly placed all their dinnerware and glasses into the kitchen as he thought he'll clean up the kitchen after she goes to sleep.

Alex began to read the *Count of Monte Cristo* right where he left off. Michaela got up late today, so she wasn't too tired yet, although, when she spoke, she did gasp for air. She was listening intently and enjoying the story. Her imagination wandered as she could see herself being part of the story itself. This made her feel relaxed and helped to tolerate the pain. Alex kept reading until he completed the book.

At this, Michaela looked at Alex and said, "That was really good, I liked that novel. What a great story!" She paused a moment longer then quietly whispered with a gasping voice, "Alex, thank you for reading all those books to me, they were great! I loved your selections and the way you kept changing the different types of storylines from one book to another. Again, thank you so much!"

Alex with a smile said, "My pleasure."

After a moment, he continued, "Michaela, you've now read quite a few and some of the best novels ever written! Actually, the more I think about it you've probably read more of the classic novels than most people."

Michaela, looking exhausted, said to Alex, "This day has wiped me out and I'm hurting quite a bit. I need some pain pills," which he got for her along with a glass of water.

"Oh, thank you so much for dinner it was great! It was nice to be able to drink a little wine too." She was breathing deeply and rapidly.

Alex just held her while she got her breathing under control.

Michaela said, "You know what I want?"

"No, tell me!"

She continued, "Get these pajamas off me. Get one of my sheer nighties out, would you? I know it'll be way too big for me due to my weight loss, but I don't care."

Alex helped her out of her pajamas and into the nightie. He thought she's still the most beautiful woman around and always will be.

Michaela further asked, "I'm going to hospice care tomorrow will you lay here with me and hold me tight?"

"Of course!"

*****

The next morning was a rainy day and Alex let Michaela sleep. He checked on her every few minutes and noticed as it was quite apparent that she was even more ashen looking this morning. Alex was certain that the day and evening had drained her of energy that she didn't really have to give.

Alex called hospice care and they were ready to accept her anytime that day. After arranging admission of Michaela to the hospice care facility, he called her doctor's office. When her doctor came to the phone, Alex said, "I wanted to let you know that I've called hospice, and I will be taking her to the facility later today."

The doctor said, "Thanks for calling. How does she look this morning?"

"Actually, she's still sleeping but I can say that she is looking even more ashen this morning."

The doctor asked, "How long do you think she has based upon your observations?"

"Not sure, but my guess is about three days," Alex responded with the saddest tone in his voice.

The doctor continued by saying, "Thank you for calling me today. Please do call me when she passes, okay."

"I will."

*****

Alex assisted Michaela with getting cleaned up and dressed. He packed her suitcase with items under her direction along with bathroom items. Alex packed a suitcase for himself as well. He was going to stay with her at the hospice facility. He threw into a bag, a couple of games, some playing cards, plus a couple of novels: *Romeo and Juliet* and *The Princess Bride*. He thought she would enjoy each of these works, if she got that opportunity.

They took their time getting everything together. Alex knew that Michaela was trying to soak everything in about her life as she would never be seeing this place again. To Alex, it was all so surreal as he thought this simply can't be happening! Alex still held out hope and prayers that the good Lord would intervene on Michaela's behalf and come through with a *miracle* for her.

They arrived at the facility with Alex wheeling her in with her wheelchair. A couple of the staff assisted them with getting settled into Michaela's room. While Michaela was being readied for bed, Alex unpacked all their items and put them away. The room itself was kind of drab and ordinary without much color. As Alex looked around the room his thoughts went into thinking this simply won't do. He thought he's got to brighten this room up if he can.

Alex excused himself from Michaela for a few minutes. He went and ordered several arrangements of flowers to be delivered to the facility. When they were delivered, they made Michaela's eyes light up!

She smiled so big as she said, "Look, Alex, these roses are so beautiful, and these tulips too! And these, aren't they lilies and this arrangement of iris are lovely. That big bouquet of hydrangeas is gorgeous as is this orchid."

At that, she knew that Alex had orchestrated the delivery of all these flowers, but she loved it! Michaela spoke up and took Alex by the hand, gazed into his eyes like she had done ever since they had met, and said, "Alex, I love all these! They really brighten this room up, don't they? Thank you... I love you!" Then she hugged him with such adulation.

Alex took a few minutes to sit down with a lead staff member. He provided her a list of people to contact if or when Michaela passes away. The list included, her attorney, her oncology doctor, the funeral home, Sheryl, and her boss. Michaela had been out on medical leave with pay for the past five months.

Michaela was looking exhausted, and she was, although she wouldn't admit it. She was lying in bed with Alex sitting at her side when Michaela asked, "Did you bring some books?"

"Yes," he answered.

"What did you bring, and would you read to me?"

Alex replied with a smile, "Of course, you know I will."

"So what did you bring?"

He answered with a kind smile. "I brought a couple of books, but I thought we could start with *The Princess Bride*. Before you ask it's full of adventure, comedy, fantasy, romance, and well, you know the usual stuff," he said with a grin.

Michaela kind of pinched him on the arm and said in a lightly spoken voice, "You know me too well."

Alex leaned in and gave her a quick kiss then replied, "That's not hard, you always want me to tell you the story before we even read it. Well, this time you're going to have to listen while I read." He smiled and tapped her on her nose with his finger.

Michaela leaned back on her pillow and, with a smile, said, "Okay, I'm ready, read!"

At that, Alex began reading *The Princess Bride*. He read for some time and well into the evening even through the visits from the staff. There were times when Alex thought Michaela had dozed off yet when he would stop reading, she would say, "Don't stop, it soothes me, and I like you reading to me!"

She eventually fell asleep as Alex sat next to her, gazing at her affectionately. He brushed the hair off her face as she slept this night. She was looking even more ashen and so gaunt. Alex was feeling so sad as he gazed at her, wondering why was this most beautiful of women having to endure such pain. Tears ran down Alex's cheeks as he held her hand next to his face.

While holding her hand against his face, he began to pray, and at the end, he said, "Lord, I hope you are listening as I beseech you to either take away her cancer or admit her into your arms in heaven and restore her great beauty that you had blessed her with, please, oh, Lord."

That first night, Alex pulled a chair up alongside the bed and held her hand. He laid his head down on the bed while sitting in the chair and fell asleep. At different times during the night, he heard Michaela gasping for air and moaning in her sleep. He knew she was hurting. At one point, he arose and talked to the staff about getting Michaela some pain pills. They brought them in, and Alex held her up while she swallowed them with some water. This helped her to sleep much more comfortably.

The next day, a staff member brought in a little humidifier looking device where she placed in some drops which made the room smell very nice. They also turned on some light music to play. Alex assisted Michaela in the bathroom to get cleaned-up. He was rubbing lotion all over her body when Alex said, "You know your hair has been growing faster than I would have thought since your last chemotherapy treatment. I was looking at your hair last night and actually brushed a few strands off your forehead."

As Michaela sat on a stool in the bathroom, Alex applied lotion, and she answered with, "Yeah, I've noticed it too."

She chuckled for a moment then blurted out, "It's probably all those protein shakes you made me drink!"

"Yeah, probably so!" They each broke out laughing.

He assisted her with getting into pajamas then carried her back to the bed. She was trying to show a strong face, but Alex could tell she was being drained of energy. While she laid in bed, they played some cards and would talk a bit. Then she would tire quickly and take a nap.

While Michaela slept during the day, Alex would get some work done. He would check email, analyze data, and build power point presentations. Anything to keep busy while she was resting. When she was awake, he would intermittently ask her about her pain level. Alex wanted her needs met and be comfortable in the process.

Later that day, she awoke. Michaela just couldn't hardly eat anything, and they increased her pain medication dosage as well. Alex was sitting on the side of the bed rubbing Michaela's stomach.

She was quiet, enjoying his touch, gazing at him thinking about what could have been! Tears began leaking from her eyes once again Alex reached up to wipe them from her face.

Alex gently kissed her on each cheek then on the lips so tenderly. As he pulled back, Michaela with a wry smile said, "Are you trying to get fresh with me?" She let out one of her patented giggles and laughed.

Alex, eyeballing Michaela with a little sideways look, said with a smile, "Now you know I don't kiss on the first date!"

Michaela grabbed him by the face, shook his head, and said, "Oh, you teaser you," as they each continued to laugh.

After a moment, Michaela with a more serious look on her face said, "Alex, when you said that on our first date, that's when you had me!"

"What do you mean?" he replied.

Looking at him affectionately, she answered, "That's when I think I fell in love with you!"

This took Alex by surprise as he wasn't sure what to say next. He remained quiet with a little grin on his face with a slight blush when Michaela asked, "When did you fall in love with me?"

Alex took her by the hand and quietly said, "You know, I think it was that first day we met in the lobby. To be honest, my insides were jumping all over the place and I was scared at meeting the most beautiful lady I had ever seen."

In a low voice, he continued with, "If it wasn't in the lobby, then it was for sure when you said that you like tuna salad and egg salad sandwiches! I could hardly believe that you just said that! All I could think was what a woman!"

Michaela chuckled, "Yeah, that caught me off guard as well. It really got me to paying more attention and then you hit me with that I don't kiss on the first date bit and what can I say, I was hooked!"

She went on, "Okay, that's enough about that stuff. You need to open that book and start reading."

"You got it!" he replied.

Alex opened their current book, *The Princess Bride*, and began reading. He read to her the rest of the afternoon and into the evening.

Alex would only pause to take a drink of water, go to the bathroom, or assist the staff in giving Michaela her medication. He could tell she was tiring, but she hung in there. She wanted to hear the end of the book as Alex was getting close.

Michaela would smile when Alex read a romantic section of the novel, and every so often, she would reach out and hold his arm or run her hand through his hair. It wasn't long until Alex got to the end of the book and read "The end!"

She smiled and whispered in a very tired tone, "That was good, I liked it too! I'm tired." Michaela rolled onto her side and went to sleep almost immediately right after Alex kissed her and whispered, "I love you!"

Alex sat on the side of the bed for a long time after turning out the lights. He stared at her, but couldn't help to notice prior to the lights going out that she was looking even more ashen tonight! His heart hurt so bad simply because he knew her time was running very short. He finally got up, walked over, and laid down on the couch. He tried to get some sleep but mostly laid there awake most of the night.

The next morning, Alex was up early and got cleaned up. He was catching up on work before Michaela awoke. When finally awake, she commented on how beautiful the flowers were and how great the room smelled.

Alex carried her to the bathroom as she couldn't walk at all. Alex looked at Michaela this morning and didn't say a word to her, but when he carried her by the mirror Michaela said, "Stop!"

He stopped as she asked, she peered at herself in the mirror as Alex was holding her. She kept silent for several seconds before letting out a little giggle and said, "Look at me, I look like a blue-eyed raccoon!"

At her comments, they began to laugh a little. Michaela appeared to be wearing dark makeup all around her eyes and face. Then in contrast with her brilliant and radiant crystal-blue, sparkling eyes, it really was something to behold. They would be funny looking if not for the fact it was so sad.

He was getting her cleaned up when Michaela asked, "Do you have another book?"

Alex answered, "Why, yes, I do! How does *Romeo and Juliet* by William Shakespeare sound?"

"Is it a long book?" she asked quietly.

"No, it's not very long at all."

Michaela, quietly nodding her head up and down, softly said, "Good, maybe we can get through it today!"

Alex didn't respond, but the way she said it, he understood what she meant or what she was thinking. Her tone told him that she felt her time was getting very short. He could also tell just by carrying her around that her weight must be down some more as she was looking so very gaunt. He could see that her energy level was nearly gone. Alex's heart was breaking, yet he was showing all the strength he could muster for Michaela.

By this time, it was late morning and the staff had brought her some liquid nourishment along with her pain medications. Alex had helped her into some fresh pajamas after he had rubbed lotion on her once again. Alex sat on the side of the bed for a while, and they talked privately and quietly as some of the staff and housekeeping were in and out. Once alone again Michaela said with a sheepish grin, "Okay, Shakespeare, start reading!"

Alex began reading *Romeo and Juliet*. As he read about the Montagues and Capulets, he kept a sharp eye on Michaela, who at times appeared that she would doze, but then she would open her eyes again.

He read the story just as he had with all the rest. He inserted emotions fitting for the dialogue. Even with intermittent interruptions from the staff the afternoon went by quickly, and it was evening before they knew it. However, Alex read the entire story of *Romeo and Juliet* this day and he smiled at Michaela when he said, "The end."

Michaela was looking particularly drained this evening, and she even refused her liquid dinner. All Alex could do was grimace and bear his heartache in silence. They talked for a while and told each other how much they loved one another. Michaela assured Alex to not worry about anything as all arrangements have been made.

Michaela, reaching for Alex, quietly said, "Hold me, please."

"Of course." He laid in the bed next to Michaela and held her tight. She snuggled up tightly against Alex and whispered to him, "Thank you for loving me!"

He didn't say a word, he simply kissed her! They fell asleep there in bed just as they lay.

The next morning, Alex was surprised when he awoke much later than usual, and that Michaela was already awake. He wiped his eyes and gave Michaela a kiss. He then said, "Wow, I can't remember the last time I slept like that, I was really out."

In a soft voice, he asked Michaela, "Is there anything I can do for you?" Alex was closely examining Michaela's face as she appeared to be so calm and serene. He thought it was almost uncanny, but for some reason, she looked almost radiant this morning, but he couldn't quite put his finger on it!

He continued to gaze at Michaela with great affection when she answered, "No, I'm actually okay!"

The way she said that began to peak Alex's curiosity.

His thoughts were interrupted when a nurse came into the room with her morning liquid nutrition and pain medications. Michaela whispered to the nurse, "Just set them on the side table, thank you."

The nurse replied, "Don't you need to take your pain meds?"

Michaela glanced at Alex first then back to the nurse and answered her with, "No, I have no more pain!"

This took the nurse by surprise while Alex was trying to assess her closely Michaela answered, "Really, I am pain-free!"

Michaela continued with, "Nurse, will you take this big envelope and give it to my attorney when he comes by?"

The nurse, peering at her and looking a little perplexed, simply said, "Yes, I will, and I'll leave your pain meds here in case you need them." The nurse turned and left the room with the envelope in hand.

Michaela had her fingers intertwined with Alex's and quietly told Alex, "Believe me, I am pain-free!"

Alex, unsure of quite how to answer as her admission, took him completely by surprise. He paused for a few moments then whispered in a crackly voice, "That's awesome!"

Alex asked, "Do you need to get up?"

Michaela quickly replied, "No, let's just lay here. Will you please hold me?"

They laid there for quite some time, and neither whispered a word. He was slowly caressing her hair with his fingers as she rested her head on his chest. After a bit longer, Michaela again whispered, "Alex, I love you so much! Have I told you that lately?"

Alex, with a whisper, replied, "I love you too!" He continued, "Are you still pain-free?"

"Yes, I am."

Alex asked, "When did you stop hurting?"

There was a long pause, then Michaela said, "I've been pain-free ever since the angels got here!"

Alex was momentarily taken aback and found himself dumbfounded for a second then rose and deeply looked into Michaela's eyes and asked, "Did you say angels?"

"Why, yes, I did." She said it in a very quiet, calm, and matter-of-fact voice.

Alex's brain suddenly went into overdrive. He knew that many times end-of-life patients on morphine would experience hallucinations. Then he thought, *Wait, she's not on morphine. She hasn't been on anything stronger than hydrocodone.* He continued to think, *She hasn't even taken her pain meds since yesterday afternoon.* He quickly concluded, there is no way she's hallucinating.

It was then that he smiled affectionately and sincerely asked, "Are they still here?"

Michaela with a serene smile on her face said, "Yes, they are."

Alex couldn't help himself as he quickly looked around the room and over each shoulder.

This made Michaela chuckle and say in a low voice, "You can't see them, silly!"

She continued, "They've been here for a few hours now. They took my pain away and we talked for a while. You know something else. They are really tall. They are at least three feet taller than you, Alex."

Alex was a bit stunned but tried to take it all in stride.

A few moments later, Michaela whispered, "Alex, my time is short." Her eyes gazing sadly at Alex said, "Listen, I don't have long now but just know that I'm going to be all right and they are here to escort me. Please understand, Alex, you saved me!"

She gasped for a few breaths then continued to whisper, "Knowing you these past months, you made my whole life worthwhile. I can't say it enough, I love you! I love you with all my heart and soul. Don't be sad, okay? Just know that we will be together again. My new friends here have told me that it will be many, many, many years for you, but only a moment in time for me. So I will be waiting for you in heaven. But anytime you need to talk, just gaze out at our stars and speak, I will hear you!"

While she was speaking, Alex began to weep as the reality of losing her hit him square in the heart!

They were sitting up in the bed, and Alex put his arms around her to hold her close. He said with a whimper in his voice, "Michaela, I love you!"

"Yes, that's the beauty of us. I know you do!" she answered, still gasping.

After a moment of silence he added, "I'm so sorry, I thought with your treatment, our faith, and our prayers a *miracle* would happen, but it didn't."

She replied in nearly an inaudible voice, "Don't you worry about that because a *miracle* did happen."

A few moments later, she looked up at Alex and said, "It's time! They are telling me it's time to go."

"Oh no, please, Lord," Alex blurted out.

Michaela said to Alex in a very low whisper, "It'll be okay. Do one last thing for me."

"What? I'll do anything."

"Please kiss me so that I will stay kissed until the next time we meet. I want to feel your full passion and love as I'm passing into the light."

At that request, Alex embraced her with all his passion and planted his most tender kiss! He held it even as he felt her spirit leaving her body. Then her body went limp in his arms. She was gone!

13

Her Miracle

Alex laid there in shock, holding her lifeless body; crying, he said, "Lord, I know she's with you now, please take her into your kingdom, heal her, and make her whole again, bless you, O Lord!"

He held her in silence for some time before a staff member entered the room and discovered that she had passed away. Multiple staff began to appear, and notifications were made. Alex was still holding her when the funeral home arrived. He assisted them with preparing and loading her while saying goodbye one last time. Alex stayed in her room and simply sat on the couch in a daze of disbelief.

After a while, the nurse in charge came into the room and sat down beside Alex. Alex was nearly oblivious to her presence. She began to speak and said, "Alex, I am very sorry for your loss, and I know it hurts beyond belief right now, so you take your time here. Also, I was able to make all the notifications. Obviously, the funeral home was just here. I talked to her oncology doctor personally, and he passed along his condolences as well and said that he would reach out to you in a few days. I let her attorney know, and I was able to connect with her boss as well. Everyone passed along their condolences, and all said the same thing that she was an incredible woman! Her attorney said that he would be reaching out to you soon as well." The very kind nurse gave Alex a little hug and again expressed how sorry she was for his loss.

Alex continued to be oblivious to his surroundings as all he could think about was Michaela. He hadn't even realized that the nurse had left and there was someone knocking at the door. She came over and sat next to Alex and put her arm around him then took hold of his hand. It was Sheryl. She leaned her head against his and was weeping as she whispered, "Alex, I am very sorry! I don't know what else to say but know that she would want you to grieve, move forward, and celebrate her life. Your time together was short, yet amazing! She told me it was by far and away the greatest time of her life!"

Sheryl continued, "I know right now it hurts dearly, just know that it will pass little by little. She truly loved you with all her heart and soul."

Sheryl paused for a few moments then broke the silence with, "Alex, I think it's time for us to go so they can clean the room. Let's walk out together." At that, Alex and Sheryl left her room.

*****

A couple days had passed, and Alex was struggling to sleep and dearly missed his beloved Michaela. He wasn't getting any work completed, and Sheryl had brought by to him lunch and dinner each day. He really appreciated Sheryl's efforts and told her so daily.

On this day, Alex had taken the time to call Michaela's doctor. They talked for quite some time. In addition, several of his staff added their condolences.

Her doctor told Alex, "I know you're hurting as she was a phenomenal woman, and you have my utmost sympathy! Be thankful that you had as much time together as you did as we all felt like she lasted much longer than what her cancer dictated so just be grateful."

The doctor continued, "That's not what you want to hear right now, but the hurt will subside. Bear in mind, even though the hurt will fade your memory of her will not!"

This did help to relax Alex's mind somewhat at least for a short while. Alex was silent when the doctor spoke again, he said, "I've spoken with the other doctors in New York and Houston. I informed them that she succumbed to her illness. We all agreed that she was truly an anomaly. None of us have ever had a patient who had that much cancer but still managed to survive. What was amazing was that she not only survived but had a fairly decent quality of life. In our eyes, she was an absolute miracle. She may have had some spiritual or heavenly support, who knows, but I believe a lot of it was you, Alex."

Alex was silent for a moment then replied, "Thank you, Doctor, that means a lot to me. I also want to thank you, and everybody involved with her care. Everyone was absolutely great! Can you let them all know?

"Yes, I can, and I will."

"Thank you, Doctor," Alex replied.

*****

Alex received a call from Michaela's attorney and he said, "Alex, she wanted me to let you know about her final details."

He was thinking where do I begin when he said, "First, let me say that it was her desire to be cremated, and she gave me specific instructions as to where to scatter her ashes. I will take care of that myself in a couple of days."

As he paused, Alex was thinking back remembering the time that Michaela told him that when she passed that she wanted to be cremated and not buried. He kind of smiled when he thought, *Yep, that is definitely Michaela! She liked her anonymity!*

Her attorney continued, "She put me in charge of gathering all her assets and executing her last wishes."

Alex briefly interrupted by saying, "I have collected all her jewelry, and I have her car keys as well. What I can do is leave them at the complex office with the manager Sheryl for you or one of your staff to pick up."

"That sounds good."

He continued, "She wanted me to fill you in on some things. Per her will's instructions, I have started the process to combine all her financial assets, bank accounts, 401(k), and life insurance, into a single account. I'm to pay off any debt, but as you probably know, she was almost debt-free. The balance after all debts is paid will be divided and donated to a couple of charities that she has chosen. That only leaves her wardrobe and a couple pieces of furniture. She would like for you to do with those items as you please."

The attorney finished up with, "Well, that pretty much covers it. Let me say that I am so sorry for your loss as she was a beautiful person and she told me that she loved you very much!"

Alex replied, "Yes, I loved her as well and thank you for letting me know her specific last wishes, it helps."

*****

Alex and Michaela were each very private people indeed. This made it a little more difficult for Alex to talk with others to discuss how he was feeling. Yes, he had Sheryl and she was an absolute gem. However, he felt he needed some additional counsel. Thus, he made an appointment with an associate pastor from their church who knew them pretty well.

The pastor and Alex sat down to talk a couple of times over several days. They prayed, and he really helped Alex to talk about her passing. He greatly assisted Alex to deal with her death. The pastor had met Michaela many times, so he was able to talk about her with firsthand knowledge.

He noted, "Most people recognized her as a beautiful statuesque woman on the exterior, but those few who knew her more in-depth knew she was an exceptionally fine person. She had strong values and convictions to go with her great faith."

He continued by recommending to Alex, "I feel that Michaela would want you to celebrate her life within the confines of your personal relationship. You guys were great together! You made each other better. Michaela was passionate about her love and loyalty to you. I know it hurts, and I'm not going to try and tell you that it will pass quickly because I know it won't. Alex, you have a strength about you to focus when required. So allow yourself to grieve and pour out your feelings even if to no one else but yourself. Honor her, be grateful for her, and be thankful for your time together! Lastly, always enjoy the fact that Michaela absolutely adored you!"

The pastor advised that Alex continue to pray, and he also stated, "Remember Matthew 5:4, 'Blessed are they that mourn: for they shall be comforted.'"[3]

*****

A few days after her passing, Alex was still wondering if God had abandoned them as they had prayed every single day for her cancer to be healed. His *faith* was being shaken to the core when suddenly something was telling him in his heart to read her letter.

An envelope had arrived a couple of days after Michaela's passing. It was from Michaela, but Alex couldn't bring himself to read it at that time. Now, something was speaking to him to read the letter.

A voice inside Alex said, *Open the envelope and read the letter!*

So Alex did!

Her letter began with "My dearest Alex," and he couldn't help himself as just thinking about her made his heart hurt and his eyes began to tear up. Alex managed to collect his emotions and hold them in check for a few moments as he proceeded to read Michaela's letter:

My dearest Alex,

It is very early. You are asleep with your head resting against my shoulder. I want you to know that an angel is here and will be with me until I pass in the morning. The angel tells me that Jesus is waiting for me. My heart feels at ease as I now know that I'm going to a far better place. Please don't be too sad, just know that we will be together again in heaven.

The angel has taken away all my pain!

Yes, I am writing this pain-free and with no medication. And no, I am not hallucinating.

I'm lying here feeling your heartbeats while watching you rest in peace. I've been thinking about the first time I realized that I loved you. I always figured it was on our fourth date, remember the picnic dinner? We were stargazing. But now, I think it was that first date.

Alex, you had my heart from that first night!

Everything you did and said was so genuine, honest, and you were so courteous. You had such a respect for people, the way you interacted and treated others, one could tell that you had the knack to quietly lead. I was literally in awe all night. In addition, it was adorable how you asked me out in midsentence for a second date. I loved your grin when I said yes with a smile. Truth be told on the inside, I was screaming, "Hell yes!" Admittedly, I didn't sleep a wink that first night!

I know I actually didn't tell you that I love you until we were walking in Bryant Park in New York City. We had just seen *Phantom,* and it was a nice evening. You know I felt like you were getting ready to tell me that you loved me, but I wanted to say it first! Primarily because you are so special! No one had ever treated me like you do in my whole life! I feel like I'm a whole person not just some beauty object when I'm with you.

I want you to know that all this time we had been praying for a miracle of healing.

Well, I received my miracle…it's you!

Meeting and falling totally in love with you is my miracle.

I got to experience something so very special. Few people get that chance! I should have died before Christmas, but God granted me four extra months to enjoy my miracle...you!

You made that time extra special. All the little things you did like picnics at the babbling brook, stargazing, making mealtime fun, putting pictures in the shower, stringing the blinking lights on the ceiling, reading all those classics, and so much more! Yes, you are my miracle!

At times, I know you would be exhausted, but you never once showed it or complained. You simply were serving the one you loved...me!

I just adore you!

I would wake up sometimes at two, three, four in the morning and stare at the stars on the ceiling. I would hear you in the other room typing and working away. You never seemed to sleep, yet you always were refreshed, ready to meet my needs, always with a smile. Yes, I indeed did get my miracle...it was you, Alex!

In the morning, I will be leaving with the angel going bravely into the light. I only say bravely because my angel has explained to me that heaven is glorious!

When we talk in the morning, I am pain-free. I will be speaking in whispers as my body shuts down.

Please understand that I appreciate the way you kept our relationship anonymous and private. After all, our relationship is our story!

I was so looking forward to meeting all your family especially since I didn't have any myself. But as we know now, God had other plans for me.

Alex, I know the next few days, weeks, and months will be difficult and you will be grief-stricken. Rest assured, you will be fine. You have great strength and sense of purpose, so I want you to celebrate our time as it was so precious.

Please know, whenever you want to talk, just speak, I'll be listening. Know that I will always be with you!

The angel has been talking to me, comforting me, and telling me about the glory that I'm about to experience in heaven.

I told the angel that I was worried about you. I requested that they help you with your grief.

The angel quickly replied to me, "Do not worry about Alex...his faith and strength will help him bear his grief. Eventually his grief will fade. But what won't fade away is his never-ending love for you." The angel reassured me that we will be together again one day!

Alex, the angel informed me of several experiences that will occur in your life. All I'm allowed to say is that life has its ups and downs, but you will persevere, so always have faith.

Lastly, not sure if I'm allowed to say, but you know how we discussed adopting a child one day. And you said you always wanted a daughter. Well, guess what, it is still several years away, but you will have the joy of adopting a daughter. It makes my heart smile with such great joy in the thought that you will be the father of a daughter. I know you will be a very special dad!

Listen to me, I want you to move forward with your life. Get busy doing what you do best...that is to serve others.

I can't say it enough: I love you, I love you, I love you!

Alex, I will be waiting for you in heaven where we will once again be able to enjoy all His stars. It will be many, many, many years for you but only a moment for me!

Alex, I adore you! You are my miracle! God bless you…

Love,
Michaela

Every word was griping and heartfelt. Afterward Alex sat there and cried simply unable to control his grief. His heartfelt pain was literally numbing. He now understood her *miracle* but was painfully brokenhearted. Alex prayed for help!

Sitting there crying, he kept having this inward feeling or voice saying, Psalm 34:18.

He paid no attention, but the voice repeated, "Turn to Psalm 34:18."

Finally, Alex said out loud, "Psalm 34:18, what is Psalm 34:18?"

He opened his Bible to Psalm 34:18 and read, "The Lord is close to the brokenhearted and saves those who are crushed in spirit."

This verse was exactly what he needed. Alex continued to think about the verse and then quietly prayed. It helped to bring a level of calmness to Alex.

14

Moving Forward in Life

Although Alex had always had the innate ability to focus, he was struggling. Over the next few weeks, he began to slowly get back into the swing of his everyday life, yet it was not without great effort.

A friend of his was a clinical psychologist in the air force so discussions with him were invaluable. He stressed, "With a love as heart-warming and strongly connected as yours, it will never fade nor be forgotten."

Well, his friend was correct; here it is, some twenty-plus years later, and the love Alex felt for her is still as powerful today as it was at that time. Nothing has ever faded from his heart.

His friend noted, "The best thing you could do to honor Michaela was to not try to understand the *why* but simply to leap back into life full bore. That is exactly what she would want you to do! Celebrate your time together, that is how you honor her!"

When he said that, it reminded Alex of a proverb that was drilled into him growing up. He remembered, whatever happens in your life always keep in mind Proverbs 3:5–6. The verse states, "Trust in the Lord with all your heart and lean not on your own understanding; in all your ways submit to him, and he will make your paths straight."

His air force psychologist friend wanted Alex to focus on the positive side of their relationship. He asked, "Hey, Alex, you remember last fall when you brought Michaela to our dining-out ball?"

Alex thinking back answered, "Yes."

"Let me tell you that night you guys were the talk of the evening and well beyond. You two looked absolutely incredible together, but for sure Michaela was an absolute goddess! We were all in our air force mess dress uniforms, looking all debonaire. However, that gown Michaela was wearing was stunning by itself then by adding her, it made her appear even more exquisite!" In addition, "I'm sure you noticed how everyone kept coming up to you two to pretend to get introduced!" I kept hearing or being asked, "Is that the colonel's girlfriend? In reality, everyone wanted to meet and stand close to Michaela!"

Laughing, he continued, "Well, except several of the wives, they were not going to linger too close to her for long. Can you say jealousy?" He continued chuckling! "Bottom line was that you two looked great, just incredible but more importantly she had a very relaxing and entertaining evening. She had fun!"

Alex, with a gigantic smile, said, "Yes, she did!"

He paused then said, "Those are the times I want you to remember!"

Alex, nodding with a smile, replied, "Thank you!"

*****

Alex's life was beginning to return to normal. He stayed engaged with several clients on multiple projects, which helped him focus. His interactions with Sheryl, their associate pastor, and his air force psychologist friend all helped lay the groundwork for Alex to move forward. He even began performing some Air Force Reserve duties which kept him busy as well.

Because he was always so private as was Michaela, he didn't let most of his family, friends, or colleagues know what was going on. After all, family and friends were close to meeting Michaela if not for the cancer. She valued her anonymity and he honored her for that!

Alex had reached out to Tim, he let him know that he was grateful for the opportunity to work in headquarters and accepted the secondment. Tim noted, "I will let them know you accept."

Tim continued, "So how is your personal problem coming along if I'm not prying?"

Alex succinctly said, "All is not great, and I'm dealing with a lot emotionally, but let me just say the problem has come to a conclusion. For now, I'll leave it at that!"

"May I ask now what it was?" Tim replied.

"You may ask, but I'm not at a point to discuss it quite yet. Maybe in time."

"I understand! I know you well enough to understand you are a very private person. So whatever it was I know that it must be something which is extremely hurtful! I will leave it alone and maybe you'll fill me in one day."

"It truly is and thank you!" Alex replied in a soft, crackly voice.

At that, Tim let it go and they discussed his upcoming secondment in New York headquarters.

*****

It had been almost two weeks since Michaela's passing, so Sheryl asked Alex to come over for dinner. Much of the immediate hurt was beginning to wane, which enabled them to talk more freely without going all to pieces. They engaged in swapping stories about each other's time together with Michaela.

Sheryl reminisced about Michaela's first time walking into the office lobby to ask to look at an apartment. Michaela told her that she had been driving back and forth from Atlanta for the past four to five months, and in her words, it was getting old. However, it did allow her to get to know her clients and the area better. She said she liked this complex because it was gated.

Sheryl said, "Alex, that first time when she walked through those doors and walked across the lobby, my first thought was, *Oh my gosh, who is this?* Let me tell you, as she strolled toward me, I thought this woman is stunning, simply gorgeous!"

After a short pause and smile, she continued, "It was then that we started talking and it was like we had always been friends. I showed her the apartment she rented but then she stayed, and we talked for a couple more hours. It was during this first conversation that I found out she was divorced. Let me tell you, my first thought was, what kind of an idiot would divorce her? She was a very quiet, smart, seemed to be confident, naturally gorgeous lady. Of course, overtime time I did get the whole story about her marriage, and all I can still say is, what an idiot!"

At that, they each busted up laughing as Alex knew the whole story as well.

Alex interjected, "Well, I'm glad he was an idiot!"

"Why is that?"

"Well, obviously if he hadn't been an idiot, then Michaela would not have moved here, and we would have never met! Interesting how life's twists and turns leads to other doors to open," Alex replied.

Sheryl, smiling simply, said, "I guess you're right!"

They continued to talk and laugh about different events and reminisce about all their times together while they sipped on some wine.

After a bit, Alex asked Sheryl, "Do you know why she stopped modeling? Did she ever tell you that story?"

Sheryl, pondering for a moment, said, "Yes, she didn't want to go be a runway model because with her morals and values, she was not going to model any sheer clothes to show her breasts to the world or worse! She was quite modest that way!"

Alex smirked while peering at Sheryl finally replied, "Well, that's why she didn't want to go make modeling a career as her agency boss tried to push her toward. Yes, she definitely stuck to her morals and values partly for the reasons she told you. Yet that is not why she just up and quit modeling one day."

Sheryl, looking at Alex quizzically, asked, "So why did she quit?"

He answered, "She told me that one day she was on a photo shoot. She was changing into and out of many outfits as the pictures were for some print ads. Near the end of the shoot, everyone had left except the photographer. He took the pictures of the last outfit and then he started to try and get her to take some shots with far less clothing, if you know what I mean. She said he turned into a creep! He ended up putting his hands on her, and she said she kneed him in the groin. She grabbed her bag and clothes and left without even changing out of that last outfit. Basically, she got away from him as soon as possible. She immediately called her agency boss and gave her notice that she was done modeling. She told me that by this time the modeling gig had allowed her to pay off all her student loans, and she had saved another $150K, which most of that went into the home that she and her husband had bought. However, with the divorce she ended up losing about half of her original amount because of their equity split."

Sheryl stared at Alex then replied, "I never knew that was what happened."

"That's what she told me. She actually said that she had been thinking about quitting the modeling job anyway, so the creep just helped her to make up her mind!"

Sheryl said, "I didn't know that but, I can see her clearly doing that!"

"Yeah, me too!"

Sheryl thought back for a moment before saying with a smile, "Did you know that she told me what you said on your first date about not kissing on the first date?"

Alex, biting his lower lip with a slight grin, replied, "She told you that?"

Sheryl said, "Oh, don't worry, she thought that was adorable! She told me that you guys were getting along great at dinner on that first date. She added that you two so easily engaged in conversation. Then you said that about not kissing on the first date, it absolutely disarmed her from what she told me. Then she added that you took the lead and slyly noted that you guys had another date. She was hooked!"

Sheryl continued, "I asked her one night after you had been dating for a couple of months, so what was it that attracted you to Alex?"

Alex, being curious, said, "So what was it?"

Sheryl smiled and said, "Of course she started by answering that she liked you, your presence, your manners, your demeanor, but then she added that you emanated loyalty, trust, and commitment.

She said that she could see values in you that she had literally never experienced before from a guy. Also, very importantly she felt that you were genuine with her. You were not putting on an act just for a date. That was very important to her as well. She adored you!"

Alex smiled and finally responded to Sheryl with, "Thank you for sharing. You know me I try to simply be who I am, take it or leave it."

Sheryl was grinning. "That's exactly what she liked!"

Each were quiet as Alex was reminiscing in his mind about times together with Michaela when Sheryl broke the silence with, "She thought you were a great guy and loved you dearly, but she didn't necessarily love you because she thought you were the best guy, but because of your focus and genuineness to her you made her a better person!"

Alex was staring at Sheryl, not knowing how to respond to what she said, when Sheryl added, "Don't worry, she thought you were the best guy too!"

This made Alex's heart smile.

Sheryl continued, "You know what you did for her birthday was something that she never expected, yet she cherished that time in Costa Rica like nothing else. She would occasionally mention little pieces of that trip from time to time when we were together. You could see and hear in her voice that she treasured that time!"

They were each sipping on their wine, continuing to think about Michaela when Sheryl spoke up, "Oh, I almost forgot about something, I'll be right back."

Sheryl came back a minute later with a little notebook.

Alex asked, "What's that?"

Sheryl with a little wry smile said, "Did you know Michaela was kind of philosophical?"

Alex replied, "Yes, I did, and she was!"

Sheryl continued, "A few times, she would begin spewing some ideas that I thought were very good, so I began writing some of them down in this notebook. And no, she didn't mind. Would you like to hear about some of her philosophical thoughts?"

"Yes, I would," Alex replied.

Sheryl continued by saying, "Sometimes I would sit in amazement when she would talk about different things. Her level of understanding, her practicality, her sense of purpose, and the way she didn't allow her emotions or feelings to rule her life. Yes, she was truly different than most people. She definitely had emotions, strong emotions at times and feelings of course, but she didn't allow them to govern what she thought or decision-making. That trait alone I thought separated her from the crowd, if you know what I mean."

Alex, listening intently, replied, "I know exactly what you mean and yes you nailed her exactly. We would have long discussions around many topics, but we would try and keep our emotions in check if something required a decision."

Sheryl, agreeing, said, "As you know, she was always reading different books to try and make herself a better person. Let me read you some of my notes from a couple of the talks which Michaela and I had."

Pausing for a moment to thumb through a few pages in her notebook, Sheryl said, "Here we go. One thing that Michaela used to say to me was that life was a journey, but it was love that makes our journey through life worthwhile."

Alex simply sat there, nodding in agreement as he thought, *That's her.*

Sheryl continued, "Alex, she loved you so very much and thought you were an incredibly terrific person. She used to say that you have so many great qualities it was easy to fall in love with Alex. But she would tell me that love was a choice. She would make sure I understood that love is a choice, and it represents a commitment. Michaela would stress that it's a choice in a couple of ways. One way was that we make the choice to love with our actions. This is by far the most preferred way. The second way was that we make the choice to love with feeling. This way is recognized, but it's not very good. Our emotions can be unstable at times. Feelings can change quickly. Therefore, reasonable people know that one should never make decisions based upon their emotions or feelings. She would say that we can choose the way we see our loved one and put away the critical, judgmental thoughts that cloud our view. Choose to remember and focus on the good qualities that attracted us to our loved one in the first place. Although love varies, it also deepens. This is how she thought about love, and I must admit that I always thought she was correct. These are only a few of the comments from her that I wrote down. But she said so much more."

Alex, merely smiling, said, "Yep, you are so right. This has her fingerprints all over those thoughts. She would say, *Love is a commitment, not a feeling.*"

Sheryl replied, "That is a reason Michaela would say that we should love unconditionally. Even in the most difficult moments of a relationship, you need to choose love above all else. She would say that every couple experience challenges, but so what! There is no such thing as a perfect relationship. She would say all that matters is growth then quote. *'Love... keeps no record of wrongs' from 1 Corinthians 13:5.* She was a pretty sharp lady!"[4]

Sheryl said, "Alex, you know there were certain things that she was always working on to either improve or do better with you. She told me that you had natural strengths that made you, you! You sparked her to try and improve as well. One thing was she always wanted to show you gratitude, that was important to her. She wanted to improve her personal communication skills. She would say that you were doing a good job working on those yourself. She would usually blush a little when she said that you two had great physical touching and how important that was to her from a trust standpoint. She liked how you accepted her for who she is, and she thought she was accepting of you as well. Sometimes you wouldn't always agree, but that was okay. The other thing that Michaela would tell me is that you guys would have almost no arguments, yes, disagreements, but not really arguments as you always kept it adult and civil. Plus, she said that you would each make sure that you would forgive quickly as being flawed is part of being human. Well, that's about all the notes I have in my journal. Bottom line was, she was an incredible woman, who loved you and you loved her each unconditionally. Every day you worked to serve one another, and in the end, you grew together."

Alex leaned back, sipped on his wine, taking in all that Sheryl had said. He was absorbing all her words and was replaying them back in his own mind. His memories of Michaela were deep in his thoughts and everything she had just read was indeed Michaela through and through.

Sheryl could see that Alex was reminiscing about Michaela in his mind just by seeing the smile on his face, so she didn't interrupt his thoughts. She waited a while then Sheryl exclaimed, "She was an incredible person!"

Alex quietly and sadly said, "Yes, she was!"

*****

Alex went to New York City and enjoyed his secondment. During his eight-week stay, he researched and worked with several headquarters' teams. One of his primary projects was to help write a whole new set of job descriptions for a potential new medical team. Alex's presentation of his findings, recommendations, and target clients with projected return on investment seemed to go over well with senior management. A couple of months later, a new national client focused medical team was approved.

Alex was added to the team with a singular focus to develop stronger medical relationships with the company's largest clients. This position was right up Alex's alley and management knew it, so he was the first colleague on this new team! Headquarters management wanted Alex to move to the Chicago area, which he did a year after her passing. The move kind of acted as a fresh start for Alex.

*****

Through the course of the rest of the year, Alex remained exceedingly busy with client projects and evaluations. By year's end, he had indeed surpassed his accomplishments from the previous year. In the year prior, he had two journal publications to go with his twenty-two poster presentations. Fourteen of those presentations were at that one national meeting last December.

However, this year, Alex had completed and presented a total of thirty-one poster presentations across five national medical meetings.

At that one end-of-year meeting where he had fourteen last year, this year he managed to complete and get accepted eighteen posters. In addition, he collaborated with clients to publish three manuscripts in medical journals. So indeed he did take Michaela's advice to get back to work and to do what he does best, which is to serve others.

*****

Here it is, some twenty-plus years later, and Alex still thinks of Michaela. To him, her love and his love for her have never faded and certainly has not been forgotten.

In Michaela's letter, she predicted that Alex would adopt a daughter one day. Well, she was right. Alex adopted a beautiful baby girl about seven years ago. She was also correct that he is a great father, and his daughter simply adores her daddy!

Although Michaela could not specify other predictions within her letter, she did note that Alex would go through a number of significant ups and downs in his life. Well, to date, she was quite right about that as well.

Yet in the twenty-plus years since Michaela's passing, Alex has continued to grow and is not only older but much wiser. Alex is in terrific physical condition, and it appears that indeed it will still be many, many, many more years before he sees his Michaela again. But for now, he has a daughter to raise!

At times, Alex will sit alone, view the stars, sip on some wine, and talk with Michaela. He can still feel her in his heart where she has always been and will never leave. Alex enjoys celebrating all the wonderful times he had with Michaela versus worrying about all the time they didn't get to share. When thinking about Michaela, he feels that they endured, they shared, they compromised, and they loved, although they only had a moment in life.

Alex still bears grief all these years later and understands his own pain. He could always wipe the tears in his eyes, but he could *not* wipe the pain in his heart. Although life moves on, Alex feels that there's not anything he wouldn't give to hear her voice or see her shining eyes or see her smile or hold her hand and gently kiss her just one more time!

Her letter so eloquently described her *miracle*, but she also laid out for Alex his own path forward. She ended the letter by saying, "I will be waiting for you here in heaven where we will once again be able to view all His stars. It will be many, many, many years for You, but only a moment for Me. Alex, I love you!"

The End

Notes

1. Zondervan, *New International Version (NIV)*, 2011. Psalm 34:18, p 892.
2. Zondervan, *New International Version (NIV)*, 2011. Proverbs 3:5–6, p 1034.
3. Zondervan, *New International Version (NIV)*, 2011. Matthew 5:4, p 1599.
4. Zondervan, *New International Version (NIV)*, 2011. 1 Corinthians 13:5, p 1941.

About the Author

Allan "A. D." Stowers was born and raised in the beautiful hills of eastern Oklahoma. Allan is a retired Air Force colonel. After the Air Force he went to work for Pfizer Inc. within their medical affairs group from which he retired in 2019. Allan has a vast array of experiences and has personally been to over one hundred countries. Allan considers his faith and family most important to him. When not serving others, he is trying to keep his golf ball down the middle. *Michaela's Miracle*, with romance and heartache, is his first book.